MANCHESTER:IT NEVER RAINS...

A CITY PRIMED FOR PUNK ROCK

Gareth Ashton

First published in 2019

This book is copyright under the Berne Convention. All rights are reserved. Apart from any fair dealing for the purpose of private study, research, criticism or review, as permitted under the Copyright Act, 1956, no part of this publication may be reproduced, stored in a retrieval system, or transmitted, in any form or by any means, electronic, electrical, chemical, mechanical, optical, photocopying, recording or otherwise, without the prior permission of the copyright owner. Enquiries should be sent to the publishers at the undermentioned address:

EMPIRE PUBLICATIONS
1 Newton Street, Manchester M1 1HW
© Gareth Ashton 2019

ISBN: 9781909360662

Printed in Great Britain.

chapters

disclaimer

"We do not know the past in chronological sequence. It may be convenient to lay it out anaesthetised on the table with dates pasted on here and there, but what we know, we know by ripples and spirals eddying out from us and from our own time." –

Ezra Pound.

The thing about memory is that it self-curates. We're not dealing with facts here. The brain sieves out certain moments in time, compartmentalises events, perhaps it unconsciously preserves a 'best bits' compilation. Some people have 'photographic' memories whilst other's recollections are muddied and muddled. During the time spent interviewing the people for this book, I have encountered a number of contradictions to the same events and places, along with varying degrees of lucidity. Those contradictions aren't through some personal act of self-promotion or ego, or a chance to embellish their own part in the birth of punk in Manchester. I believe that they were genuine recollections, remembered fondly or otherwise, but always honestly, which is why I have left them in. After all it was a long time ago; Manchester in the 1970's was a very different city, in a completely different world.

Also, this book isn't anti-London, anti-Liverpool, anti-Sheffield, or anti any other city or town which played it's part in the growth of punk rock in the UK, I just wanted to celebrate the role that Manchester and it's people played in punk's infancy; The Sex Pistols' first television appearance happened in Manchester; the Spiral Scratch EP by Buzzcocks, the first truly independent D.I.Y. Punk record, was recorded and released in Manchester; Pips pre-dates Blitz Club by 7 years; The Electric Circus pre-dates The Roxy by a couple of months. Also, the standard torch bearer of popular music Top Of The Pops, was first aired in the city. But just as important to punk's impact were the people who embraced it, braving the 'beer boys' and the knuckle-draggers who couldn't handle anyone who was different to the norm. Manchester's situation was by no means unique, some of these accounts could have been told by people from all over the United Kingdom, albeit perhaps at a later date, so may I suggest that someone takes up the mantle to celebrate their own environment. Some of the subject matter here will be familiar from other books that have been written over the years, but it would be churlish not to include them on that basis, although I feel that I've managed to find a different slant on them. This is primarily a tale told by the people who were there; punters, band members, and promoters. I want to thank everyone who gave up their time to let a complete stranger into their lives, and in some cases into their homes. Some of my requests for interviews or a contribution to the book were politely turned down or never acted upon, so in their absence I hope that I've done justice to their memories.

biographical notes - interviewees

Una Baines	Original keyboard player with The Fall. Interview; 29th August 2017. Location; Manchester Vegan Cafe. Oldham St. Manchester.
Andy Blade	Founding member and guitarist with Eater. Interview: 3rd May 2018 via email.
Dawn Bradbury	Attended the first Sex Pistols Lesser Free Trade Hall gig. Interview: October 2nd 2016. Location: Gullivers Pub, Oldham St, Manchester.
June Buchan	Former Production Assistant at Granada TV. Interview; 15th July 2017. Location: Cafe Nero, Piccadilly Approach, Manchester.
Fred Carr	Bowie fan, in and around the early Manchester scene. Interview; 19th January 2017. Location: The Waldorf Pub, Gore St. Manchester.
Mickey Carr	Younger brother of Fred. Football punk, and early 'Ranch-ite'. Interview: 16th October 2016. Location: Lymm Services, M6.
Gail Egan	Friend of Paul Morley, and former girlfriend of Pete Shelley. Interview: 23rd November 2017. Location: The Blacksmith's Arms, Henbury.
Ian Fawkes	Attended the second Pistols gig as well as The Electric Circus. Interview: 9th September 2016. Location: Buxton Conservative Club.
Brian Grantham	'Mad Muffett'; Original drummer with Slaughter and the Dogs. Interviews: 27th Nov & 30th Dec 2016. Locations: Unit 26 Recording Studio, Trafford Park and The Sawyers Arms, Deansgate, Manchester.
Chris Hewitt	Promoter of Deeply Vale Festival, P.A. Provider for Electric Circus.

	Interview: 13th February 2018. Location: At his home in Cheshire.
Brian Johnson	Pips/Ranch Bar attendee. American Bowie fanatic relocated to Bolton. Interview: 9th October 2018 via email.
Alan Keogh	In and around the very early Manchester punk scene. Interview: 23rd October 2016. Location: Gullivers Pub, Oldham St. Manchester.
Mike Keogh	Frequent attendee of The Ranch Bar 1976-1977. Interview: 1st December 2016. Location: Macclesfield.
Chris Lambert	Lead singer with Physical Wrecks. Interview: 22nd October 2016. Location: Gullivers Pub, Oldham St. Manchester.
Steve McGarry	Designed SATD logo plus sleeves for Rabid Records. Interview: 18th January 2018 via FaceTime.
Sarah Mee	Bowie fan, early Ranch attendee. Interview; 15th November 2016 via email.
Geoff Moore	Producer of So It Goes 2nd Series. Interview; 17th September 2017 Location: Stretton, Cheshire.
Ian Moss	Attended the first Sex Pistols gig at The Lesser Free Trade Hall. Interview: 5th January 2017. Location: Mossley
Steve Nuttall	Member of the gay community in 1970's Manchester. Interview: 27th November 2017 via email.
Ian Hodges 'Odgie'	'Drummer' with The Worst. Interview: 19th January 2017. Location: Odgie's workshop in Leyland, Lancashire.
Carol O'Donnell	Early on the scene. Lived with Pete Shelley. Interview: 8th April 2017 Location: Dry Bar, Oldham St. Manchester.
Daniel O'Sullivan	DJ at Rafters, early on the scene. Interview: 17th November 2016 Location: Jam Street Cafe, Whalley Range.

INTERVIEWEES

Ken Park	Guitarist with Physical Wrecks. Interview: 22nd October 2016 Location: Gullivers pub, Oldham St. Manchester.
Stephen Perrin	Founder member and guitarist of The Distractions Interview: 23rd April 2018 via email.
Martin Ryan	Produced Manchester fanzine 'Ghast Up!' Interview; Location: Rams Head, Disley.
Denise Shaw	Manchester punk icon, much photographed. Interviews: 2nd Oct 2016 & 2nd Nov 2017 Locations: Gullivers Pub, Oldham St. Manchester & Denise's house, Rochdale.
Steve Shy	Produced 'Shy Talk'. Manchester Punk fanzine. Interview: 27th November 2016 Location: Unit 26 recording studio, Trafford Park.
Terry Slater	Worked in The Ranch Bar. Interview; 21st November 2016 Location: Terry and Joanne's house in Heaton Norris, Stockport.
Fran Taylor	Early gig goer, worked for Buzzcocks as a roadie/Drum Tech. Interview: 4th February 2017 Location: The Glasshouse Stores, Brewer St. London.
Michael Tait	Early on the scene, Vocalist for Nervous Breakdown Interview: 2nd November 2016 Location: Michael's house in Urmston.
Andy T	Went to The Electric Circus, The Oaks. Early on the scene. Interview: 20th July 2017 Location: Andy's house in Todmorden, Lancashire.
Stanley Vegas	Bass player with V2. Early on the scene via Slaughter And The Dogs. Interview; 12th April 2018 via FaceTime.
Peter Walker	So It Goes Director when Sex Pistols made their TV debut. Interview; 15th July 2017 Location: Cafè Nero, Piccadilly Approach, Manchester.

Juliette Williams	Bass player in The Shock, Manchester's first all female punk band Interview: 29th August 2017 Location: Manchester Vegan Cafe. Oldham St. Manchester.
Steve Cundall	Bass player with The Drones Interviews: 27th Nov and 30th Dec 2016 Locations: Unit 26 Recording Studio, Trafford Park & The Sawyers Arms, Deansgate, Manchester.
Deb Zee	Early on the scene at a young age, went to The Electric Circus. Interviews: 22nd Oct 2016 and 8th April 2017 Locations: Gullivers Pub & Dry Bar, Oldham St. Manchester.

This book is dedicated to the memories of Pete, Mark, and Joan.

introduction

The UK Punk scene started in London, that's not under dispute. The embryonic scene was limited to a few like-minded souls, it was a movement formed around art and design, Situationist theory and fashion. It lasted in its purest form for just over 12 months, when it self-combusted into the national consciousness via a short tea time television interview with an inebriated television presenter goading for a fight. But before the implosion was the explosion, and the fallout of the blast was felt strongest some 200 miles further north, with life-changing consequences. The adolescents of Manchester were already primed for punk through David Bowie, Marc Bolan, Roxy Music, Iggy Pop, and Lou Reed - Punk was just a natural progression for them, there was no fanfare needed, and no hysterical headlines heeded. Whilst some of the boys and girls had been colourising their monochrome worlds with clothes and music via the nightclubs in the city, others were instigating a private revolution in their heads and homes through their ever-growing, eclectic record collections. They were looking for a musical epiphany that they could call their own, one which would take them on that next step to independence and individuality.

This is a story of how Manchester became such a critical city in the development of Punk, as told through the eyes of those early protagonists, the foot soldiers if you like, the ones who had the courage to confront conformity not with violence but with an attitude, as well as a healthy helping of curiosity; although sometimes the only option was to fight back physically, because there were no shrinking violets here. This was Manchester.

1. urban damnation

"Study the past if you would divine the future" – Confucius

Manchester was at the heart of the Industrial Revolution, gaining its position predominantly through the textile industries, creating an unprecedented, unplanned urbanisation, which led to cramped, lugubrious living conditions. Coal smoke and cloth dyes from the factories polluted the air and water, and the life expectancy of the inhabitants of the slum dwellings was low. The medieval squalor continued on into the 20th century, and it took a global human catastrophe to start the process of alleviating the problem. But it would take years to improve things, and the situation is still unresolved to this day, as the recent Grenfell Tower tragedy has proved.

Social housing problems in Britain had been escalating since the end of the First World War when the then Prime Minister, David Lloyd George, pledged to give soldiers returning from the battlefields 'homes fit for heroes'. This promise eventually led to the Housing Act of 1919. Seventy-five years earlier, before any policies on housing conditions existed, Friedrich Engels concluded in his book 'The Condition Of The Working Class in England 1844', that the notorious, and inaptly named area of Manchester, Angel Meadow was a 'Hell upon Earth'. In 1931, just over a decade after The Housing Act was introduced, and approaching a century after Engel's damning verdict, the Angel Meadow district on the Northern edge of the city was once again being described by the Manchester and Salford Better Housing Council as "unfit for habitation". Its report went on to state that "all the houses suffered from dampness, leaking roofs, crumbling plaster work, badly fitted doors and another army of rats and beetles". In another area of the city, the New Cross district of Ancoats received a similar incriminating indictment which recounted that "almost all of the houses were worn out completely". The acute lack of basic human necessities such as water and food storage were highlighted and the area was depicted as being "without a vestige of beauty", and "with little beauty and constant noise". Nothing had changed since Engel's report but Manchester was merely a microcosm of the wider social deprivation in Britain as a whole. This time there was no north/south divide.

Following the Second World War local councils were left with cities that had endured bombing raids and as a consequence, huge urban areas had been turned into rubble. The 1942 Housing Committee Report concluded that over 76,000 houses would need to be built to satisfy the need of the slum clearances, as well as meeting the long term increase in demand. This meant looking further afield, beyond city boundary lines. 'Overspill' estates were built but the projects were met with hostile resistance from the relevant local authorities, who were opposed to the prospect of having thousands of inner city slum families being dumped on their doorstep. The families who moved were stigmatised by their social environment and became associated with crime and grime and it was generally agreed that they would drag respectable areas down. In Bredbury near Stockport, local residents even went as far as to build a 6ft 'iron curtain' between themselves and the council houses. But in reality many of those moving from the slum clearances were proud people and took great pride in making their houses into homes. Una Baines, a founder member and keyboard player with The Fall, recalls the pride they took "they used to call them 'little palaces', they kept their houses really beautiful."

Although the council provided affordable, subsidised housing to a certain extent, they couldn't transcend the class divide due to the mismanagement of their 'housing regeneration' project. In 1954 the council drew up a five-year slum clearance plan but although approximately 70,000 homes were identified as being unfit for human habitation, the clearance plan had earmarked only 7.500 homes to be demolished. At the end of those five years, in 1962, with completion rates nowhere near high enough, the council hatched another more radical plan to get things back on track by projecting to build 4,000 houses per year. This ambitious plan only resulted in the same low quality housing inhabited by the same low income tenants, which, when added to the national economic situation, meant that the skilled workforce and ambitious locals moved out of the area. Essentially all they had done was to provide houses for the people who had been left behind, or the ones who had stayed because nobody wanted them in their neighbourhood.

In some areas of the city relocating was at first quite exciting, with the prospect of a better standard of living and an enhanced environment.

Una Baines: "You got a choice of three places… a lot of people went out to Wythenshawe. They called it the slum clearance. Me and my mum watched our house get knocked down. I grew up in Collyhurst, all my childhood was in Collyhurst, and then [we went to] Monsall estate, where we had baths and under floor heating. We were a big family; there was my mum and dad and five kids. We moved into a house, literally they knocked down the house and moved us 200 yards onto the new estate. It was wonderful at first, I had my own bedroom, we had a bath, two toilets; one upstairs and one downstairs, under floor heating so you could put your feet under the carpet in the winter and toast your feet. My dad, when we first moved there, said, 'it's wonderful now, but it will be a slum in 2 years'."

The under floor heating was indeed a luxurious highlight of the new houses, but it was expensive to run, and winters in Manchester could last from November until March. The community didn't need luxuries; neither had they asked for them, they just needed a home fit to live in, with the basic essentials to allow some self respect.

Una Baines: "That community in Collyhurst, was tight knit and it seems like a lost world now. Consumerism is massive now, whereas back then it wasn't... people didn't have anything. But we had a brilliant childhood, all the games we played outside. You'd go out after your breakfast and you'd come back at teatime, and you had to come back then because if you missed it you'd be in trouble. The older ones always watched out for the younger ones, it was the natural thing to do, that's what human beings do when they're left to be real, human beings."

The principle of elevating people from their decaying houses, which possessed outside toilets but no indoor bathrooms, was a well intentioned one but there were logistical barriers. By the mid 60's the architects and town planners in Manchester began to voice opinions on a different style of housing scheme; tower blocks and 'deck access' systems. There were a lot of people keen to move but a lack of ground space meant that the new flats and homes would have to be built upwards, although they stopped short of building 'high rise' towers, preferring the design of the 'deck access' developments. The architect's vision of a Utopia in the sky was acutely short sighted, their bombastic rhetoric dazzled and mesmerised the councillors into believing that the future was literally looking up. The slum clearance programme was meant to solve the housing problems, building nice new flats all over the city, but still nothing had been learned from previous decades, or indeed since Engel's report over a century earlier.

Design flaws in the deck access system were there from the start; flat roofs in a rainy city; the Bison concrete structures, designed in a Lego style that would begin to erode, corrode, and eventually breakaway little more than a decade after they had been erected. But the biggest failing was afforded to the inhabitants, who, after being used to living side by side, now found themselves living on top of each other. Tower blocks began to blight the already gloomy landscape in Beswick, Ardwick, Harpurhey, and Hulme, where the jewel in the council's crown would be built – the Crescents.

The Hulme Crescents was a £20 million redevelopment described as "unique" and "a fascinating concept that should make not only the planners but the citizens proud". The final cost was estimated at £4 million and the final topping out ceremony took place on 14th January 1971. Inspired by Georgian buildings in London and Bath, the council claimed they would "bring a touch of eighteenth century grace and dignity" to the area. It didn't take too long for residents to realise that there was nothing dignified nor graceful or indeed Utopian about the place. To add insult to irony the four crescents were named after the architects of the structures on which they were modelled; Charles Barry, John Nash, Robert Adam, and William Kent. The plan to replicate the community spirit from the terraces backfired and as the sheen of the contemporary design soon began to fade, the cosmetics were soon in need of a makeover. The buildings may have been new but the social problems remained the same. Social segregation was compounded by the architectural follies of the new buildings, isolating the residents even further. The planners thought that planting a few trees would help but human beings also need roots to grow, and the younger generation growing up in these monolithic Soviet style fortresses wanted something better. One of those youngsters was Fred Carr, and this environment in which he was living would have a profound effect on his adolescent life. A self confessed low level mischief maker, Fred would find escapism through music and clothes, whilst developing a fierce political attitude to his, and many other's situation.

Fred Carr: "They ethnically cleansed us. They took the old 2 up 2 down terraces, the old culture, and wiped it out and what they put up in its place were these fucking estates. I can tell you what was on them as well; a load of houses all facing different ways, our kitchen was facing a block of flats which was ten yards away, all you could see was a brick wall. At the back there was another brick wall with a two foot garden. They brought people in from all over the place, you never knew who anybody was. They were all mustard coloured brick, they've all got a square with a hairdressers, a bookies, a post office and a pub. Every estate was the same: Fort Beswick, Fort Ardwick. We had one in Harpurhey which was knocked down after two years, the rest got knocked down after 5 to 10 years and people made a lot of money out of it. From that estate… a lot of people didn't come out the other side."

These new estates were usually on the outskirts of the city centre, one of which, Fort Ardwick, was finished in 1972 and consisted of 500 available 'homes' for the slum clearance evacuees.

Mickey Tait: "I grew up on Coverdale Crescent which is Fort Ardwick, a big block of flats about a mile outside the city centre."

Mickey was another one of the kids who would eventually find an outlet in punk with the band Nervous Breakdown. He would be the youngest of his peers when the group formed and had the nous and the demeanour that was needed to fit in with the older crowd. That confidence would have been fostered from his time spent on Fort Ardwick.

Fort Ardwick was built in the deck access style, also using the Bison concrete material. Only a few years after they were completed, the council had to bring in a team of consultants to make emergency repairs at a cost of £60,000. This included the re-bolting of concrete panels, as well as addressing the design fault of the leaking roofs. The late Gerald Kaufman was the constituency MP for the area at the time and said this of Fort Ardwick in the House of Commons in 1974,

"The scale of the buildings is often daunting. I have in mind Fort Beswick and Fort Ardwick in my own constituency. The design is frequently all too forbidding. That is why the two estates are called "Forts". "I am on the Fort", constituents tell me. Such developments are often unsightly. The approaches are not attractively landscaped and are often strewn with litter and debris. Refuse disposal is too often haphazard and infrequent, and this can lead to the proliferation of insects and vermin which are already fostered by design defects. A few weeks ago, on one of my visits to see the estate, I had a long discussion with a number of the residents. One of them said to me, "If Labour wins the election, it ought to do two things: abolish the House of Lords, and demolish Fort Ardwick."

But it wasn't just the physical structures that were crumbling, the economic climate of the country was also eroding people's quality of life. The progressiveness of the 1960's was, like the trains and the factories, slowing to a halt by the beginning of the new decade. On the outskirts of the city, a few miles south along the A6 was Stockport, where Paul Morley worked for a time at a book shop on Great Underbank which would also sell a small selection of records, which included Spiral Scratch, and early punk fanzines. Stockport was also home to Stephen Perrin, co founder and guitarist with The Distractions, a band who, like so many of the Manchester bands that formed around 1975-1977, ploughed their own individual furrow, and found an allegiance with the punk crowd.

Stephen Perrin: "It is difficult to convey to anybody who has only experienced Manchester during the 21st century exactly how grey it was in the 1970s. By the time myself and my peers came of age, we had gone through the Gulf crisis of 1973. There were power cuts, the three-day week, raging inflation and the beginnings of mass unemployment. I had three O levels and a clerical job with Stockport council where, some of the time, I was working by candle light due to the power cuts. It felt like history had punched me in the stomach."

The ripples of austerity, exacerbating the potential breeding ground for violence, fanned out to reach communities just beyond the inner city and further out into Greater Manchester. North, south, east and west, the circumference of Manchester riddled with people on a mini migration to a supposedly better life. The community that had been built between the families and their children was disrupted and not everyone wanted to move.

Fran Taylor: "They moved us out to Brindle Heath which was a right fucking shit hole. We got compulsory purchased out. All my neighbours got moved out to Ordsall in Salford, which is down near the docks towards town, but my dad wouldn't go. It wasn't until years later when I realised why..."

Fran's role in the story of punk in Manchester was significant due to his involvement with Buzzcocks. He was first and foremost an avid fan, after attending the early gigs in the city he then progressed to working for the band. Further afield to the east of the city in Tameside, future musician and non-conformist Kevin Stanfield was having to grow up pretty quickly.

Kevin Stanfield: "I was from a completely working class background, secondary school education, no qualifications, dragged through school and fell out the other side and went carrying the hod on building sites. I was born in Mossley, and my father was a traveller so we moved all over, I could write a book about my father. I did my Secondary school education in Ashton-Under-Lyne. People used to say that if arseholes could fly then Ashton would have its own airport. You could go into any pub and buy the shittiest drugs in the world, or you could get shot, one or the other."

The satellite towns which lay just north of the city limits, which were once the heartbeat of the Industrial Revolution, providing the world with the finest cotton and textiles, were now littered with the decaying husks of the once noisy, throbbing mills. Poet Andy Thorley, whose eclectic musical tastes saw punk as the next logical step, remembers the landscape he grew up in.

Andy T.: "Rochdale had its fair share of deprivation. They knocked a load of houses down and moved everybody into blocks of flats. We ended up living on the tenth floor of a block of flats, after having a nice house with a garden and fields all around. Our playground growing up in the 60's was derelict houses and bomb sites. You'd find guns and all sorts under the floorboards. It was a dirty, horrible time."

Una Baines: "We were playing in abandoned buildings, climbing about. We moved into Monsall estate when it was only half built, so we'd be playing on the scaffolding."

As a result of being raised in such abject conditions, the youth on these estates grew up very quickly and they were as sharp as needles. The antagonistic attitude that came a few years later, with punk initially manifesting itself with kids looking like the casualties of the grim surroundings that enveloped them, actually took root in completely the opposite direction. Some of them may not have had much pride or respect for where they lived, but they could at least colourise their world with clothes and culture, not only as a fashion statement, but also as a statement of intent.

Fred Carr: "I'm a political animal. You don't grow up where we grew up and not become political. If you had any sense about you, you'd have to have asked 'What's going on?' Growing up it was grey, monochrome. You couldn't wear anything that wasn't brown or black, you had to have a white shirt or a blue shirt, you had to have grey trousers or black trousers, there was nothing else. The estate was just fucking deadly. The telly's on all the time and it's the same old shit so you've got to get out, you've got to go out, you can't sit in front of that. You're on The Croft, your mates are on The Croft, and you're up to no good. It's just mind numbingly, exceedingly fucking boring."

Mickey Tait: "Where I grew up (Fort Ardwick) it was pretty mixed, and it was pretty cool. I had a lot of black friends. You see the trendy punks wouldn't have been in that sort of environment, whereas we were from the inner city, and a few of the black kids we used to mess about with were punks as well. We were walking around, pre-punk, in drainpipes when the majority of people had flares."

But it wasn't just the inner city kids who were inquisitive and looking for something more. A short journey out of the city, in any direction, would take you to a disparate landscape of clean air and wide open spaces; to the south-east the reservoirs and idyllic splendour of the Peak District National Park; to the north-east you find the bleak, expansive moors of Saddleworth, which would forever be tainted by the heinous depravity of Myra Hindley and Ian Brady; northwards, westwards, and beyond lie the Pennines; 'the backbone of Britain'. Growing up out here the kids were close enough to feel part of the city, but far enough away to escape its menacing undertones and a different kind of boredom. Juliette Williams was one of a small group of women who would defy her parents and dismiss the sexist attitudes to how girls were expected to dress and act. She would also go on to form the only all female Manchester punk band.

Juliette J. Williams: "My childhood was completely different, I grew up on the north side of Bolton, in what was then, I suppose, the countryside. From my bedroom window I could see nothing but fields and cows. It was quite idyllic really, looking back I have to say that my childhood was one of the happiest times of my life. So compared to an inner city childhood, mine was completely the opposite. We used to make 'dens' and we'd have our own adventure playground in our big garden. Just down the road was Moss Bank Park, which was literally 5 minutes walk with no roads to cross, plus we also had Barrow Bridge, a local beauty spot, with waterfalls. It was quite pastoral really. We weren't well off. My dad was a junior manager at Burton's the tailors, which is actually where he met my mum. I had a best friend who lived in a grand house that would have belonged to the landowners, with a summer house. They kept chickens and I'd call for her sometimes and she'd be having piano lessons."

Stephen Perrin: "My parents were working class Labour voters but they were extremely socially conservative. They had grown up knowing war and economic hardship and they didn't want any more trouble. Nor did they want their kids making a show of themselves in front of the neighbours."

Despite the prodigious contrast in circumstances, and growing up in individual communities, there was a common thread that would stitch together these disaffected youths who felt disenfranchised, or just restless within their respective communities. That thread was music, which in turn for some led to clothes and fashion as a means of self-expression. Whether it was used as a therapeutic antidote to acute shyness, an escape from the hum drum, the inspiration to build up the courage to stand up and defy whatever other people's preconceptions of them were, or simply as just an excuse to dress up - music would give them their own identity as well as the voice to say, "Fuck you, this is me!"

2. i just want to be myself

"Life isn't about finding yourself. Life is about creating yourself"
George Bernard Shaw

Part of growing up is finding your own identity. The most obvious ways of gaining individuality was through music and clothes, and the two have been inextricably linked since the 'Teddy Boys' of the 50's. Given the dramatic title of being 'Juvenile Delinquents' they were the original menacing and moral threat to decent society and the antidote to the 'Crooners' of the time, propagating the first 'generation gap' between youths and their parents. They were the first to really benefit from the new found freedom of peacetime and the beginning of consumerism. They had money in their pocket for music, fashion and going out. The young upstarts were starting to find their voice and as the 60's began the splinter groups of Mods, Rockers, and Beatniks all came under one banner - Teenagers.

Ian Moss, along with his younger brother Neil devoured music, nothing was off limits, from McCartney to The Stooges to King Crimson and Reggae, they consumed everything that suited their pallets. But the main criteria was honesty, as long as the artist 'meant it', it was absorbed into their musical consciousness. It was no accident that Ian would be one of the small number (delete as applicable) of inquisitive minds at the Sex Pistol's infamous Lesser Free Trade Hall gig.

Ian Moss: "I remember being in Manchester, along Oxford Road on a Saturday afternoon, and The Beatles were playing at night, and there were these gangs of people - teenagers - that were like aliens. When you're 6 or 7 you know? Looking at these people with their skinny jeans; they're not people that I'd seen before, this was amazing. If you remember back, a bit later on all your teachers wore flares and had collar length hair and everybody up to the age of 70 seemed to be in this uniform."

Stephen Perrin: "I subscribe to the view that what has come to be known as the 1960s in the UK was basically about two hundred people in London having a pretty amazing time. My generation only witnessed this via black and white TV but these people appeared to be living their lives in colour and gave us something to aspire to rather than emulating our parents. I was sent to an extremely dull technical school to be groomed to be a BT engineer or minor civil servant. The experience was mind numbing but that was okay as I was clearly going to escape to London where I would hang out with Paul McCartney and David Bailey and probably marry Twiggy."

It's hard to believe in these times of the iPod, Smart Phone, and the World Wide Web that in the late 1960's just having access to the most basic item of home entertainment equipment would be regarded as a hard-earned luxury and something to be cherished. The television set would be, more often than not, on loan from the local Radio Rentals or Rumbelows shop and even access to a record player became a precious commodity which took more than a little effort to achieve, so when the opportunity arose it was gratefully accepted.

Una Baines: "We had a borrowed record player. It was an elderly lady's who was in hospital and we gave it back to her when she came out of hospital. It was someone my mother was looking after. One of the local shops used to sell records and the first record that I can remember buying was 'Love Grows Where My Rosemary Goes' by Edison Lighthouse. We used to listen to the radio quite a lot; Radio 1 mainly but there was also Radio Luxembourg."

Juliette J. Williams: "We had a radiogram and my mum and dad were into the 'big bands' as well as the crooners like Bing Crosby and people like that."

Stephen Perrin: "My mum used to have the radio on all the time and like most kids my age I was crazy about The Beatles and The Rolling Stones. I mithered my dad into taking me to see 'A Hard Day's Night' and girls were screaming at the screen. That and The Monkees TV show pretty much convinced me that I'd better get a guitar and start practicing."

Once the music bug bites you, there's no going back. The pursuit for new sounds required a lot of time and concerted effort, the frequent pilgrimages to record shops, which were goldmines full of undiscovered musical gems waiting to be plundered, places which held more treasures than could ever have been afforded, meant that monetary constraints added to the dilemma of making a cognisant choice but it was all worth it. Or as Tony Wilson once pronounced, "Manchester kids have the best record collections".

Andy T.: "I had three or four paper rounds when I was a kid, and I'd take pop bottles back to shops just to buy records. I used to go through boxes of singles on Tib Street. I got into Marc Bolan, and I started collecting his singles on his T Rex/EMI label, and because he was also on Fly Records I'd collect Fly stuff. They were about 10p a time."

You could also buy to the Top 75 singles from a variety of outlets in the city, not only from the local record shops. Places such as the Post Office, Kendall's department store, Woolworths, and Boots the chemist would also stock singles and albums. Many small towns all over the country would have a multitude of record shops, some specialising in certain genres including Jazz, Blues, and Classical. Picture sleeves weren't issued in great numbers due to the record companies wanting to reduce the costs in production, so the 7 inch single would be housed in sleeves depicting the relevant, iconic record company logos that would soon become instantly recognisable to the discerning listener. This meant that certain labels could be quickly visually counted or discounted; Silver Bell, Purple Pye, Blue Decca, Green Harvest, RAK rocket, Polydor Red, plus the concentric circles of Vertigo and the Mad Hatter of Charisma. For instance RCA usually meant Elvis or Bowie, Bell could be Gary Glitter, and T Rex had their own logo on the EMI label. Every weekend and school holidays would be spent building up a collection. The all consuming obsession to collect as many releases by whoever was your artist of choice is an addiction which carries on throughout the rest of your life.

Ian Moss: "It just built up and I suppose I was probably 12 or 13 before a record player appeared in the house, which would have been 1970. I immediately started buying stuff. The first record I ever bought was either 'Another Day' by Paul McCartney or 'My Sweet Lord' by George Harrison, I can't remember which came first. They were within a month of one another."

Another source of musical enlightenment, whether it would be positive or negative, would come from a sibling or a friend.

Carol O'Donnell was another maverick woman. A young girl coasting along with the mainstream chart acts of the time until she was enlightened by a boyfriend of a friend and she would go on to be a main player in the early Manchester punk scene. She lived with Pete Shelley for a short time and was a fleeting member of the The Negatives, a semi fictitious band whose line up included Paul Morley, Kevin Cummins, Richard Boon, and Steve Shy.

Carol O'Donnell: "In our house my mum was into the Bee Gees, my brother was into The Beatles and Melanie, and my sister was into Motown. For my sins my first album was 'A Portrait of Donny' when I was 12. The first 'proper' album I got was 'Hunky Dory'. I lived in Stretford and my friend was going out with Steve Morrissey and we used to go round to his house and it was him that got me into Bowie and

Marc Bolan. After that 'A Portrait of Donny' went out of the window! This would have been about 1972/73. I remember he played 'Five Years', and I was like, wow, and that was it you know? So I ended up begging him to play some more. One of my really good mates was heavily into Gary Glitter, she absolutely adored him. He used to make my skin crawl, way before what we know about him now. She was also into the Bay City Rollers. All I can say is thank God for Stephen Morrissey because otherwise I might have ended up going down the same route myself. He changed my life basically."

Parents also play a major influence in the musical development of their offspring.

Fred Carr: "My Mum was a singer, she used to sing the ballads and that gave me a love of music."

Mike Keogh, who would go on to be a regular at The Ranch Bar, was good friends with Gail Egan along with Terry Slater, who worked behind the bar there.

Mike Keogh: "The best time for me was Slade, Glam Rock, and prior to that my parents were into Sinatra stuff. My dad was Irish so was into all the Irish Celtic music and my mum was into Sinatra, the crooners you know, from that generation. My dad's influence was the Irish tunes; rebel music. My mum left when I was 10. My dad was my hero; he brought me, my brother and sister up by himself."

There were also those who knew what they liked from an early age, and tried to impress it onto their friends. Deb Zee was another feisty young girl who knew her own mind very early on. She was younger than many of the other women when punk broke in the city. This didn't stop her from being a force to be reckoned with.

Deb Zee: "Some of my friends were into David Cassidy and some were into Donny Osmond, but they had to listen to Alice Cooper, David Bowie… they knew Diamond Dogs all the way through by the end anyway!"

Further down the A6, past the environs of Stockport was Hazel Grove, the home of Gail Egan. Gail's profession as a hairdresser was her route into the inner city circle, visiting The Ranch and other places, meeting and mixing with the people who were at the forefront of the new scene. She also went out with Pete Shelley for a while.

Gail Egan: "I bought 'Ziggy Stardust' when I was about 13. When I was at school everyone was into Michael Jackson, Jackson 5, but I was into Alice Cooper, David Bowie and Roxy Music of course."

It also helped to have family members who were in a position to encourage and financially facilitate any musical interest shown at an early age.

Juliette J. Williams: "My mum and my nan took me to Liverpool one day and I came back with four records; two singles and two albums; 'Baby Love' by Diana Ross and The Supremes; 'My Boy Lollipop' by Millie; 'With The Beatles', and 'A Hard Day's Night'. I would have been about 5 at the time. The first single I bought with my own money was 'Honky Tonk Woman'. I just loved that guitar sound, I didn't know who the guitarist was. My first musical influence came from my eldest cousin, John. He had 'Sticky Fingers' with the real zip on the front. He also had the Tyrannosaurus Rex album, and he'd let me borrow them. Marc Bolan was my pathway into glam, which was my pathway into punk. People site Bolan as being the first glam influence. I liked Heavy Rock. I loved Alice Cooper. I bought 'School's Out' when it came out and I painted on it with Black nail polish and Silver glitter, 'Alice is ace!' But I was only about 11 at the time. But again it was the guitar. The b-side was fantastic… the intro is just amazing. The defining moment for me with David Bowie was Mick Ronson's guitar. Again I didn't know who played it… it was always about the guitar for me."

Una Baines: "Suzy Quatro! I thought she was ace, the leathers and the bass. That was cool."

Ken Park: "My first album was Sticky Fingers by The Rolling Stones and then I got into Iggy and Bowie, and New York Dolls, so when the Pistols came out I thought; this is it, this is what it all means. So we wanted to do that."

The resulting musical outlet for Ken was Physical Wrecks, who played sporadic gigs around the area in 1977, most notably the Deeply Vale Festival, one of the first punk bands to do so.

Another band, whose notoriety will be covered in greater detail later, was The Worst, a duo of pre White Stripes/Royal Blood style guitar and drums. Ian Hodges and Allan Deaves were two mechanics from the Preston area who briefly swapped motorcycle tuning for musical detuned cacophony. Ian is now known only by his nickname; Odgie.

Odgie: "I bought 'The Rolling Stones' in 1963. I always liked the Stones rather than The Beatles, because they had that raw edge to them. I liked The Who for the same reason even though they were a Mod band and we were Rockers; messing about with motorbikes and that. Originally I was into Hendrix and the Stones because that was my era. I can still remember; it was summer, I was outside and my parents came out and announced that they'd found a new radio station; Radio Caroline. So I can remember that being a big thing because it would play popular music unlike the BBC. For me in about 1969, music stopped and I know everyone says that now but that's what happened for me. It had lost that earthiness really. Then my mate 'Deavesy' got me into stuff like the New York Dolls and The Tubes, stuff that I didn't know about. I thought, these guys are alright you know, a bit wacky."

Ian Moss: "I was pretty obsessive about music, probably because as a pre-teen we were pretty much starved of music in our house; there was no record player or anything like that. From a very early age, things tend to lodge. I remember hearing 'Help!' visiting an Auntie in Hyde, so all the music that I picked up on, it was just snippets here and there you know, like visiting someone's house, and that sort of thing. Not because we were denied it, it wasn't as austere as that, it just wasn't there, but we'd still watch Top of the Pops."

Another avid viewer of Top Of The Pops was Mark Windsor. Mark formed the band V2, and was heavily influenced by Bowie and Bolan after seeing them on the programme.

Mark Windsor: "When we were young there was one hour of music a week on the telly. You had Top of the Pops and The Old Grey Whistle Test, so everyone was watching the same thing. It was like a communal type of thing which you can't get now because you've got about 500 channels."

Another first for Manchester, Top of the Pops was originally transmitted live from a disused Wesleyan chapel on Dickenson Road in Rusholme, in the south of the city. It was New Year's Day 1964 when Jimmy Savile hosted the first episode which featured The Beatles, Rolling Stones, Dusty Springfield and local lads The Hollies. It would remain in Manchester for the next two years before relocating to London. Savile was also one of the regular DJs at the 'Belle Vue Sunday Top Ten Club', along with Dave Eager. It was a members-only discotheque held on Sunday evenings between 7-11pm which throughout its tenure featured live acts such as Little Stevie Wonder, Jimi Hendrix, Small Faces, The Supremes, and The Rolling Stones. But Top Of The Pops was where the world of music and fashion came crashing into millions of living rooms, opening up a cornucopia of styles and sounds which inspired and informed in equal measure. From that visual information, mixed together with the aural experience, the initiation of individual musical taste would inevitably follow.

Denise Lloyd (Shaw) was one of the first punks on the Manchester scene. She is also the most photographed, her striking appearance has been featured on the covers of books, posters, and record sleeves, along with being the subject of the BBC documentary on punk, 'Brass Tacks'.

Denise Shaw: "I started seeing things on Top Of The Pops and I was blown away by Roxy Music. As soon as I saw them I had to go out and buy whatever they had out."

Another essential contributor to the enhancement of what was happening musically and culturally were the music papers; filled with interviews and articles of the major artists of the time, they also covered the up and coming bands and singers and featured gig guides and reviews of singles and albums as they were released. Although they didn't cater for all tastes.

Andy T.: "We used to buy the *NME* and stuff like that religiously, but there was so little written about bands we liked such as New York Dolls."

Being able to afford what you wanted to buy was a major frustration, prioritising and diversifying became quickly acquired life skills.

Ian Moss: "As your tastes start broadening, and because there were still economic constraints, there were the 'Tighten Up' albums, Reggae stuff, which was cheaper. A 'Motown Chartbuster' was £2.50; a 'Tighten Up' was 17s and 6d, you know what I mean? So when you're a kid that meant a lot, and it was still all this great music. So Reggae in the very early 70's was really big in our house. Because of economics, not because I was some kind of soothsayer, it was more by default than design. Come '73/74 as the move into Roots and Dub and stuff like that, I was getting interested in that."

It's all about taste; but what is good taste, and what is bad taste? It doesn't matter, it's how it affects your senses, a song can transform a bad day into a good night, a state of mind in the shape of a 7" or 12" plate of vinyl. Sometimes it's not always as straightforward as a catchy tune, it's not just the melody of a song that resonates. The beauty lies in the ear of the listener. Although sometimes, it doesn't matter how open the mind wants to be, certain things don't penetrate it.

Una Baines: "I tried to get into Prog Rock because all my posh friends from school listened to Pink Floyd, Yes and ELP and all that. I tried to tune in to them, and get onto their wavelength but I'd just switch off. But it made me think about what I *did* like about music. I remember Silver Machine by Hawkwind, I was obsessed with the way the drums came in. I just wanted to listen to it over and over again, but I can't explain why it made me feel like that."

A natural progression was beginning to take shape, a musical family tree began branching out, planting new seeds into inquisitive minds.

Andy T.: "Through Bolan you found Bowie, and through Bowie you found Iggy and the Velvets, because Bowie would be doing 'White Light…' and 'Waiting For The Man' on the radio and you'd be thinking 'where's that from?'"

Chart music was easily accessible, but anything outside the jurisdiction of the 'popular' chart music would take more effort to track down, and was usually only be available on import and therefore more expensive, but consequently more expansive. There were exceptions to the rule of music and fashion being inextricably linked, some people had no adherence to follow any particular musical tribe, so the most unassuming person could surprise and educate in equal amounts. Artists like The Velvet Underground, MC5 and The Stooges were obvious reference points to what was to come a few years later. The American 'punks' were raw and slightly off kilter, an amalgamation of garage and glam rock, which was slowly gaining an audience in the U.K.

Ian Moss: "My brother, even though he was younger than me, he'd be ten, he had a very old mind, and even at that age he could organise his pocket money and he had very advanced tastes musically. I remember our Neil getting The Modern Lovers album, about 1974, so all this proto-punk… but we loved all the obvious stuff too. We liked Alice Cooper, John Cale, Lou Reed, Bowie - a real mish-mash. I liked the storytelling. My brother bought a Velvets album when he was 11. Between us we had a real taste of esoteric stuff, I mean 'Pearls Before Swine' we loved. King Crimson's first album… fuckin' hell you know? Wow, what's all this about? It was all this excitement and discovery."

Financial constraints were critical in what the pre-work kids could listen to, and the outlets could spring from the most unsuspecting places. Alan Keogh was an adopted Mancunian, having been born in Glasgow, his tough exterior belied a love of art, poetry and music, but when things got physical, he could handle himself when the occasion arose. Although it was the friends he made that shaped his teenage life.

Alan Keogh: "There was this guy called Fudge. He was like a real geeky, wimpy kind of guy, but he was obsessed with David Bowie, Lou Reed and Roxy Music. He had money, and we didn't have money, so he used to get albums straight away. He had this bootleg of Iggy and Bowie live at Santa Monica. So between Ian, Adge, and Fudge, they introduced me to Iggy and the Stooges, MC5 and other bands."

Denise Shaw: "When I was sixteen four of us girls went down to Torquay for a holiday, it was the first time we'd been allowed to go on holiday on our own. One day we went down to the beach and there were these four lads from London, proper cockneys they were. One of them had really bright red dyed hair, all spikey, and he fascinated me. I was like Mrs. Normal compared to this guy. They had a cassette player and all of a sudden 'Walk On The Wild Side' came on, and I just said, 'Oh my God who is that?' He said, 'It's Lou Reed, have you never heard it before?', and I went 'No'. My friends are all going 'What, you like that?' And I was like 'Yeah I really, really like it'. So we became good friends for the week that we were there, and he was telling me about Bowie and this, that and the other. So when I got home I started going out and buying Bowie records and Lou Reed records, in fact I've still got the single 'Walk On The Wild Side'."

Sometimes music can provide the experience of a profound intervention - a simple act of fate that can change a life forever.

Fred Carr: "When I was about 14, me and our Mike and about 8 or 9 of us went to town on the bus, causing a bit of mayhem, and we went into Lewis's. We were just running around causing mayhem and Mike nicked some toffees, the store detective grabbed hold of him and tried to pull him away from us but we got hold of him and ran away and got on a bus. Just up the road from us on Moston Lane there was a shop that sold what in them days you'd call 'fashionable' trousers called 'Electric Blues', so I wanted to go and see if we could 'lift' some of these trousers. Next door was like a little record shop. So as we walked in the door, the owner was still in the back, and by the time he came back out I'd lifted 'Hunky Dory' on cassette tape. I'd seen Bowie on the telly. Anyway he came out and he must have seen the gap but he couldn't say that I'd nicked it because he didn't see me. So I took it home and asked my mum if she could get us a cassette player. So she got one and I used to listen to it until I fell asleep, I listened to it all the time and it sort of changed my life. We were just getting to the stage of nicking cars and things were escalating. I used to write all the lyrics on my schoolbooks and Hunky Dory was like a pivotal album really. From that moment on I was mad on David Bowie, so I dyed my hair Red. I wanted to be him and so I dressed like him. But I was fair haired and the colour faded so it came out a bit Pinkish. I was the only guy who dyed his hair in our school and there were about 1400 other lads".

In those early days of the 1970's David Bowie was the catalyst for a diverse cross section of society; the disenfranchised, the curious and the fashionistas, all evolving at a time when just having long hair made people question your sexual orientation. You didn't have to be gay to think that he was beautiful. He was a figure of empowerment, pushing boundaries in attitudes to gender, fashion and music which, when you live in an environment that is antagonistic to difference, can mark you out as a target for abuse. But appearances could be deceiving.

Fred Carr: "There were quite a lot of people into Bowie or Roxy, it was basically those two really. So you had these other Bowie guys, and I remember we went down into town one night and ended up going for a meal. We ordered the meal, ate the meal, and then fucked off. Ha! Ha! Ha! We were running over the tops of cars... we were pretty outrageous anyway, and sometimes there'd be a bit of friction you know? Because we looked effeminate, not the norm, so there'd be a bit of tension, a bit of a punch up."

The idea of sex in the '70's was a combination of the sexist smut of the 'Confessions...' series of films, or the double entendre laden sitcoms and seaside postcard humour of the 'Carry On' films. The television programmes were no better. 'Are You Being Served' for instance, gave us the double entendre of Mrs Slocombe's pussy, as well as a busty young female assistant continually being letched at by another member of staff, and an as acutely stereotypical male homosexual as you are ever likely to witness, all in half an hour on prime time TV. Despite its future legacy of being tainted by association with sexual deviants, Top of the Pops on the other hand would occasionally serve up some era defining sexual moments. Once you got past Dad's favourites, Pan's People of course. One performance in particular has been the subject of forest destroying eulogies - 'Starman'.

Fred Carr: "The thing with Bowie... it was fucking sexy. That song 'Starman' is so sexy and in them days there was a partition of the sexes, you weren't allowed to be together, you had to go into separate doors at school. There was a male entrance and a female entrance in school, if you look at a lot of old schools you'll see a male entrance and a female entrance. They went to these schools until they were 14 and then straight into work. If you so much as talked to a member of the opposite sex you were practically married! Death was on everyone's tongue and sex wasn't. Now sex is on everyone's tongue and death isn't. Even David Bowie said that you wondered what was going on behind the curtains, because it was never spoken about. Those were the times and it's difficult to put into words what it was like."

Whilst Bowie and Roxy epitomised all that was sexy, glamorous and androgynous, some of the white working class kids were planting their pre-punk roots in the more down to earth genres of American Black music.

Una Baines: "In Collyhurst where I lived, Tamla Motown was a really big deal, and Soul music. There was a guy who had every record that Motown produced. I remember people like Joe Tex, Otis Redding, and James Brown were the iconic heroes in the poorest part of Manchester."

As with the majority of youth cultures, Northern Soul combined a fervent attention to detail, a non-verbal etiquette, and a religious devotion to 'The Faith'. Even those who weren't as militant in their approach to the scene took little snippets of it to mix in with their own tastes.

Kevin Stanfield: "Wigan Casino was the big thing at the time ('73-74) everybody was into Northern Soul and I drifted in and out of that because I've always liked Blues and Soul which is why I play Saxophone now."

Deb Zee: "In our house, my brother and sister used to play Motown and Northern Soul, and my brother used to go to The Twisted Wheel. I went to Wigan Casino with a friend from school and I taped it, and I've still got the tape somewhere!"

Soul music had everything; the tunes, the passion, and a healthy slice of realism, everything that punk would later encapsulate. Martin Ryan, was the co-creator of Manchester punk fanzine *Ghast Up!* along with Mick Middles. He also cut his musical teeth on the genre.

Martin Ryan: "The first music that I was into was Motown. I suppose they were the first records I bought. Although the first single I bought was 'The Liquidator' by Harry J. All Stars and Motown Chartbusters Volume 3 was out then. They were really good because there were loads of various artists: Stevie Wonder, Marvin Gaye and all them you know? Plus over three quarters of them were pretty big hits weren't they, and obviously it was dance stuff so you'd hear them in the clubs."

Juliette J. Williams: "A lot of the kids, definitely at my school were into Soul and Disco and Tamla Motown, you know? You were very much the odd one out if you weren't part of that crowd really. I had a brief foray into Disco and Soul but it wasn't my cup of tea."

For some though, just listening to records at home wasn't enough, they immersed themselves into the whole lifestyle, from perfecting the iconic dancing, to the forensic detail of the music, which took record collecting to a whole different level.

Alan Keogh: "I started by getting obsessed by Northern Soul when I was about 12. I was going to Wigan Casino when I was 13, Blackpool Mecca at 14 to 15 and there was Samantha's in Sheffield. The Northern Soul scene was like a real awakening for me. I was buying and selling records by the time I was 14. I'd go to Sheffield and exchange and sell records, so I used to spend my summer holidays going around the markets in Manchester or Mazel's on London Road looking for singles or Hyde Market looking for stuff which I knew were worth trading."

As a side note Mazel's was the shop where Peter Hook bought his first bass guitar.

Fran Taylor: "I was very much into soul music, especially Motown, not so much Northern Soul. I knew kids at school who were fucking monstrous about Northern Soul and who had huge record collections which they'd paid fortunes to get certain records on certain labels."

There were also definite similarities between Northern Soul and when punk broke a few years later. A theory not lost on Chris Lambert, who became the lead vocalist with the aforementioned Physical Wrecks.

Chris Lambert: "I came from Northern Soul, it seemed like a natural progression to punk. They were both Amphetamine cultures for a start. I had really good access to amphetamines, it was like tablets in them days, so you knew it hadn't been cut, not powders, so I did become, not really by choice, a supplier to my mates. When I was going to Wigan in '73/74 the chemists were a lot easier to screw. I remember going to Blackpool Mecca, my mates organised a lift. So there's six of us in this Mini, and it pulls up near Bolton, two lads dive out, then you hear this alarm go off, then they come back in with these canisters; 'you can have one of them, keep your mouth shut.'"

Alan Keogh: "I actually think that there's a real connection between Northern Soul and Punk Rock. It's partly about the drugs, it's partly about the hours that you were out you know because Wigan Casino, infamous as it was for drugs, I mean there was no licence, you couldn't get a drink's licence for all night, you just couldn't get it in those days, which didn't matter because everyone was using speed. Personally and just for the record, and this is the truth, I only ever dabbled a little bit with drugs, because I was more enthused by the music and especially the dancing. I danced all night."

Ian Moss: "I knew quite a lot of lads, and girls, who came off the Northern Soul scene and they were the people that I gravitated to. Of course the drug of choice was the same."

One other connection was that feeling of being apart from the 'straights' and 'longhairs'. The energy and passion of the music brought out a different breed of peacock. There wasn't the preening and posing of the Glam and Bowie/Roxy set, instead the Soul Boys attracted attention, and admiration, through their dancing. But they weren't primarily competing against other dancers, they were totally engrossed in the tune; the music was everything. The all nighters and specialised club nights brought together people from all over the north of the country to Manchester, Wigan, Blackpool, and Stoke, and then there were the standard disco nights in and around Manchester where a greater cross-section of youngsters would go.

Alan Keogh: "Talking about the early days and that transition between Northern soul and punk, for me was the Concord disco in Droylsden, which was an under 18's disco. Without sounding too big headed, I was a really good Northern soul dancer and so in an ordinary club people used to crowd around me so I'd be doing my back flips and showing off really. I suffered for it; I got two black eyes and a bloodied nose. So I'd go home and my Ma's furious and she's like 'what's happened to your eyes? What's happened to your nose?' I'd be like 'it's just for dancing Mum'. So I was already beginning to avoid mainstream culture, because people hated others trying to be original or just being yourself. Coming from soul and into punk, at the time seemed weird but now it makes perfect sense because they're both outsider cultures, even though one type of music is much more palatable, much nicer, but actually there's a raw energy in there because the guys who were making that soul music were impoverished outsiders. The only difference was that they were black."

Mickey Tait: "Alan was a good dancer. I remember him dancing to a few tunes. Alan was from Levenshulme which was a couple of miles up the road from us, so we used to knock about a bit."

While the Northern Soul scene was all about sweaty, amphetamine induced nights of endurance, with an understated dress code, there was a more ostentatious, brightly coloured collection of the fey and the cool, where appearance was the ultimate statement.

3: oh! you pretty things.

"We see people, brand new people. They're something to see."

'Nightclubbing' - Iggy Pop.

Long before club culture became a Sunday supplement lifestyle choice, there were Discotheques, Cabaret bars with chicken-in-a-basket style cuisine and dance halls which would also cater for 'old time' and ballroom dancing. Which meant that if your tastes weren't mainstream it could be quite a difficult task trying to find somewhere that catered for your alternative predilections in the mid seventies. The carefully chosen sounds that had been curated in bedrooms all over the city hadn't fully transcended to the outside world.

Una Baines: "There was a Great Depression in Manchester at the time. There was nowhere... there weren't many places where you could go and listen to music that you liked. I mean yeah I liked Bowie, but we also liked The Kinks, Velvet Underground, you know? I used to bribe DJs with a pint of Guinness to play one track because all the clubs would play was Prog Rock, which I never liked. Although I did like very early Genesis."

Fred Carr: "We used to go to the Polytechnic and University on Oxford Road, they weren't playing Disco, it was just '70's music, things like 'Alright Now' and stuff that you could dance to. That's what it was all about then, just having a drink and a dance."

Deb Zee: "When I was young I used to go to The Anchor in Urmston which was like a rockers/youth club type of place. So I got into Alice Cooper, then into Bowie and the Alex Harvey Band, stuff like that. Then I dyed my hair Red, spiked it up and got into punk."

The odd club in town that did have an 'alternative' music policy were often challenging places to frequent, where the lure of hearing decent music was traded in for a distinct lack of a pleasant customer experience.

Fran Taylor: "There was one particular club we used to go to called 'Waves'. It was on Dantzic Street in the backstreets of Manchester where pretty much all the weird clubs were, around the Shudehill area of the city. 'Waves' was this shit hole of a place, I mean it really was a dump. The gents toilet was just a piece of plastic drainpipe on coat hanger wires, and it just went out through a hole in the wall and into the car park. But it was full of really heavy bikers and 'greasers' and played really heavy music."

Una Baines: "What they did was that they let all the young people in and paint it, and they painted it Black and it had The Velvet Underground painted on the wall. We used to go there and take Tenuate Dospan and Coca Cola, so we'd be sat there speeding away, and they played records that we really liked, we didn't have to bribe the DJ to play anything. It was 30p or 35p to be a lifetime member, and it was really cheap to get in. But it wasn't a sustainable thing and it was great at the beginning but then all these bikers started coming, and you'd get young girls jacking up in the toilets, 14 and 15 years old. When you went to the bathroom you'd have go through this crowd of blokes. It was vile."

Martin Ryan: "I went there once. It was downstairs and it was a dark and dingy place. But to be fair all rock venues were then, at that time in the 70's if you went to a place that put bands on, that's how they were. The film 'That'll Be The Day' with David Essex, while not great acting I think it's really good how you see these bands coming through all playing these really shabby dives. And that's right because we loved the music but the places you had to go to see them were just complete dumps."

Denise Shaw: "There were a lot more bar type places that were open late, like 'The Great American Disaster', 'Springfields'. These were really just meeting places."

A lot of the places that would be conducive to good music were where the gay community would frequent. They'd also be more accepting of anyone who dressed differently from the norm. Stanley Vegas, bass player with V2 and friends with members of Slaughter And The Dogs was one of those who would prefer to socialise in that environment.

Stanley Vegas: "There was this gay club called 'The XJ6' which was on Whitworth Street I think. They used to have the front end of an XJ6 Jag which was the DJ booth, and you had to go down a load of stairs to get in there, a right seedy little place you know?"

What Manchester needed was a club that wasn't seedy or edgy. Somewhere that was as safe as it possibly could be in the '70's, where most people's musical tastes could be accounted for. It was also a place where you could be different and dance to your favourite tunes. For the small group of Bowie/Roxy obsessives it was a lifeline to escape the drudgery of the litter strewn streets and derelict buildings of the city.

They wore homemade outfits to look glamorous and beguiling, before punk would take them to the next logical step. Sarah Mee and her sister Linda epitomised that individuality, and in some cases bravery, of the women who dared to be different. Because although they had found a place of night-time sanctuary, there was always an edge to a night out.

Sarah Mee:"Then there was Pips, in the heart of Manchester, which again had us in the back corner having to run the gauntlet of abuse from the Soul Boys."

In 1972 a club opened its doors for the first time, a decade before The Hacienda and 6 years before 'Billy's' in London, the embryonic New Romantic club that grew up to influence the 'Blitz Club' a year later. The DNA of punk in Manchester can be traced back to 55 Fennel Street, as it was home to an eclectic range of music, which meant that it attracted a varied clientele. Its layout was unique too, with multiple rooms which could disorientate you before a drink had been taken, so much so that it was rumoured that the first influx of punters were initially given a map to find their way around. This was a meeting place in the city centre where the peacocks could strut, dressed up in all their flamboyant finery; a night time refuge for the stylish and the chic, who didn't fit in with the 'straights' and 'longhairs', plus they had their own dance-floor. It was somewhere which added colour to a black and white landscape. It was "Behind the Cathedral".

The club's DJs over the years included Tony Barry, Dave Lee, Mike Shaft, Dave Booth and Jimmy Barry.

Jimmy Barry:"I was a DJ at Pips in 1974 aged just 18. I worked in the main room on Saturday nights and sometimes midweek when artists appeared. Some acts I introduced on stage included Hot Chocolate and Marmalade. Also working at the same time was Mike Shaft who is now on BBC Radio Manchester, I did work the Roxy room just the one night to cover the regular DJ who was late but it wasn't really my thing at the time, I much preferred to play all the latest soul and disco. The DJ in the soul cellar, which was a smaller room downstairs, was Tony Barry (no relation) and a guy called Dave Lee took over from me, I used to get £5 a night back then which was okay but I used my own records. The owner at the time was Jerry Summers".

Another of the club's members were Win Norris, and Karen Jackson, to whom the place left a lasting impression, as it did to many others who would spend many happy nights there.

Win Norris:"I started going in '74, I was really into soul/northern soul to begin with and we used to go into the Roxy room to gawp! But I loved the whole vibe and was soon converted!! I lived for my nights in the Roxy room... I was never into punk but liked some stuff. I had a mate at the time who was going out with John Cooper Clarke and much later on she would get us free tickets to the Factory in Hulme and we saw some great bands: Siouxsie, Slaughter, Chelsea, Buzzcocks - to name a few. I also worked in the cloakroom at Pips and saw different genres come and go but I don't remember DJ's names etc. From 17 to early 20's Pips was my life and very influential; you could be who you wanted to be."

Karen Jackson: "I started going as I got free tickets from the owner's daughter, this was pre-punk. At the time I was into Bowie/Roxy but just went for the disco at the start, but I was soon converted. I was into Roxy in a big way so dressed 1940s all the time. You had to take your own records for the DJ to play, I remember buying New Rose and asking for it to be played, but you had to remember at the end of the night to collect it! Rambo the Manchester tattooist was a regular with the Teddy Boys."

Denise Shaw: "I remember being in the fifth form at school and you could take your own records in to play on the school record player. There was one lad who was one of the rugby boys and he got hold of my records and said 'What's this crap?' and threw them across the room. I went ballistic and so I drifted away from my school friends, and when I did leave school I kept thinking, there must be somewhere that plays this sort of music. So I started getting the music mags and that, and then I saw this advert for Pips, I went down on my own and after 2 or 3 months I met Joan who became my best friend. We met in the girl's toilet, just chatting and we became really good friends. Pips became our life."

Pips was many things to many people and Janine Hewitt was a regular.

Janine Hewitt: "Before punk came along I used to listen to mainstream music and wear the fashions everybody else wore. I was influenced by what was on Top of the Pops and Radio 1; Glam Rock, Disco and Soul music. Later on I became interested in David Bowie and Roxy Music. I used to wear a narrow skirt with a White shirt and tie like the dancers with Bryan Ferry. I used to go to a couple of clubs in Sale; The Blue Rooms and the converted cinema next door. It was only because I was into David Bowie that I heard about Pips where they had Bowie/Roxy room. They would play punk later on. It had seven dance floors each playing a different style of music - Pop, Soul, Reggae, and Rock 'n 'Roll (a small room downstairs). You had to walk through the Pop room to get to the Bowie room. Pips was the most upmarket of the clubs and had a smart/casual dress code. Woody from The Worst couldn't get in one night due to his appearance. One room had long oblong mirrors on the walls. I have a picture of me taken in here for the *Manchester Evening News* wearing a tail coat, short Black hair and Dave Vanian style make up. You had a membership card, which I no longer have, with your name on it and a photo. People were very friendly and I never saw any trouble in there, it was all about the style and posing."

Odgie: "We were going to a place called Pips in Manchester which was dead, dead posy. You'd wear a Black suit, or a White jacket and a bow tie, whichever was the album or tour at the time. It was kid's stuff really but good fun."

Daniel Sullivan would go on to work there and was an early convert to punk, hanging around in The Ranch and The Electric Circus.

Daniel O'Sullivan: "It was a much nicer evening in Pips. Sometimes it was a hassle getting in, but once they got to know you, and that you weren't going to cause trouble, it was okay."

Andy T.: "Half of Manchester went to Pips. It was one of the few places that played 'current' music. I went there a few times before punk, not often, but you got to know the 'lookers' and the 'dresser uppers'. They became the likes of V2 and some of the faces from the Circus; people like Denise, and there was a coloured lad who used to bleach his hair. I can't remember his name"

That lad was Paul Doyle, who would go on to feature on the Brass Tacks BBC television documentary.

The world was a very large place in the mid 70's. Family holidays were usually taken in August in the school holidays with many people having no choice but to take them during the two week shut down of the factories where they worked. Not many could afford to go on holiday abroad, and the destination for those that could push the boat out would invariably be the Costa Brava in Spain. Coming into contact with foreigners was quite rare for a lot of young people, so when any encounter came about it was something of a cultural awakening.

When Brian Johnson made the 3,000 mile trip from America to the northwest of England, he never envisaged the life that awaited him, a life of acceptance and friendship.

Brian Johnson: "When I was 15, I lived in Northern New Jersey in the US. My school days were miserable. I was slightly androgynous, through no fault of my own, and the kids at school pretended not to know if I was a "boy or a girl"; shades of things to come. Cruel, daily bullying was the norm. In early 1976 my parents told me that we were moving to England. I couldn't believe it! The mysterious land of Bowie! So in March we were off. So eventually, weeks later, we ended up in Bolton, and I started school. I was the only American kid they had ever met! It was like instant celebrity. It was the total opposite of my experiences in New Jersey."

But it wasn't just the new kid on the block who was intrigued and mesmerised by the unique surroundings of this slice of debonair decadence in the heart of an uncompromising industrial landscape. It was literally a life changing moment.

Mark Windsor: "Dave (Bentley) first took me to Pips in 1975 and I remember the impact it had on me… walking through the 'normal' bit with the disco and into the Roxy room. Fucking hell! The thing I remember most was that all the women were beautiful, in that they dressed like film stars, while in the other rooms it was all cheese cloth shirts and lank hair. Then there were the Bryan Ferry type blokes swanning about on casters."

Dressing to excess was part of the fun, although the lengths that some people would go to would be sometimes extremely impractical.

Denise Shaw: "My mum made me a dress, which was pale blue, a proper 'Roxy' dress, dead tight right down to my ankles with a feather boa around it. I got to the bus stop, the 17 bus stop, and the bus pulled up, but it was that tight that I couldn't lift my leg high enough to step onto the bus! In the end I had to toddle back home and get my dad to take me. It (Pips) was great for dressing up and being totally different and it opened up a world to loads of people that didn't exist before. Plus gay people had a place to go when they wanted to express themselves and be different. I don't remember any problems there at all."

The main reason for the magnetic attraction to Pips was the music. Not just for the Bowie crowd - the more niche the better for them, it was the fact that the place catered for nearly everyone's tastes.

Gail Egan: "Pips was great because they didn't play that sort of music everywhere."

Brian Johnson: "Steve Lowe and I had hunted down Pips from an address someone gave us. I had a car, and we parked on some dark street until we saw the entry to Pips. It was advertised as "Behind the Cathedral" and there we were! To say we were nervous was an understatement! We were under 18, and had no idea if they'd even let us in but we decided to try. My mother had gone to Manchester to find some clothes for me to wear. She found this shop called Roxy, and it had the hippest clothes at the time. She had to go to a haberdasher to find a black Fedora, as I was really into the Thin White Duke and the Man Who Fell To Earth look. Black pants, waistcoat, and white shirt were all that I could think to wear. My friend Steve had made some of his own clothes, as his hair looked more like Ziggy Stardust, Oh, the Henna experience! Mine was definitely the Thin White Duke. He took clothes and cut them up to look more like something Ziggy would wear! It was actually clever and pretty amazing. We walked to the door, the bouncers let us by, we paid 75p or something like that to get in, and we were in. I think we had to ask someone where the Bowie room was and we were corrected that it was the Bowie/Roxy room. Then they pointed straight ahead.

"It was an interesting concept - attracting as many people of different types as you could into one place. Heavy Metal, Northern Soul... we put our heads down and rushed towards the back past this small bar on the right we heard David Bowie blasting from the other side, and in we went into what looked like a cave! There were Thin White Dukes, Ziggy Stardusts, Diamond Dogs, Young Americans, and Bryan Ferry's everywhere! It was surreal. It was like a dream come to life! Guys danced alone or with other guys, girls danced with other girls, handbags tossed on the floor in the middle. We studied everyone and how they stood, sat, danced, etc., so we could fit in. It wasn't long that we sat down in one of the cave alcoves and began talking to some other Bowie guys. It was super easy and smooth to talk with them, they were all so friendly. As we were relaxing a bit, I noticed the girls in the club. Their hair was styled *avante garde*, their clothes were dresses that looked like something out of a 1930s film (I found out later, they made a lot of them), and some of the make up was so glamorous, it was hard to believe they were around my age."

Despite the camaraderie of those early days, the potential for trouble was omnipresent because of the diversity of the music on offer, and the clientele it attracted. Plus, as word spread and the club's popularity increased, it became the place to go to, with people travelling long distances to experience what was one of the biggest Discos in the country. Unfortunately the culture shock was too much for some.

Brian Johnson: "Not every night went smoothly, though. Some nights we would meet in a pub, then walk to Pips after an hour or two. One night, about six or eight of us were walking to Pips, when we heard some racket behind us. Here were some stereotypical football fans, apparently very drunk, chasing after us, throwing pint pots, yes, it's true, and we just took off. I don't know how the girls ran so fast in their heels, but we barely made it to the front of Pips before dashing in! That was one of the scariest times!"

Mark Windsor: "I got kicked up the arse one night in Pips! You'd walk around the corner and there'd be a couple of coaches parked up, and we'd be like, 'Fuckin' hell a coach party!' They'd come from wherever to this big disco in Manchester and they'd go in the Roxy room, and of course they'd never seen anything like it, men wearing make-up and glamorous women, so it would all kick off. As soon as you saw the coaches, you just knew something was going to happen."

Stanley Vegas: "I seem to remember that we got barred from Pips, because there was a bit of a bust up with some Rod Stewart fans, Ha! Ha! So we started to go to The Ranch, I mean we all used to wear make up and stuff, so we'd go to the gay bars because they were the only places that'd let us in"

Brian Johnson: "Another incident that sticks out in my mind is the scandalous 'no make-up policy' Pips instated. I was so pissed off! Not that I wanted to run around with make-up on all the time, I actually didn't, but Bowie did it, so we did. Basically, we were mostly banned from going in, and it was really the principle of the thing that bugged me the most. So much so that when I explained this to my mom, she got pissed off too, and called them and told them off! She said something like "if you have a David Bowie night, and he is famous, and he wears make-up. Then you have no right to ban boys from imitating their idol at the club. It's hypocrisy!" And then I think she threatened them some more somehow, until they relented! Mind you, we were all mostly still underage, but boy were they nice to us when we showed our faces the next time."

Pips was also a breeding ground for up and coming DJs, some of whom went onto be successful in future years. The music was getting more eclectic, mirroring what was happening in the industry. Debra Madden remembers some of the Pips alumni who plied their there.

Debra Madden: "I started going late 1977, in the Roxy room mainly. One of our DJs was John Richmond who is now a leading Fashion designer. Also Dave Booth, (just over 20 years later Dave was the DJ at The Stone Roses' legendary Spike Island gig), Hewan Clarke, who became a Hacienda DJ, plus Gary Davies who was on 261 Piccadilly Radio before he joined Radio 1, and Alan Mansell amongst others. Pips played the Doors, Iggy, the Joe 90 theme, and Bowie of course as punk was emerging."

There are conflicting memories of actually how many rooms there were.

Ken Park: "Were there 5 rooms?"

Chris Lambert: "Yeah I think there were 5 rooms. I think that there was a Soul room."

Alan Keogh: "Maybe even more you know?...There was the rock room? It was a really successful idea, and it was a good idea. In most clubs you go to, you can only hear what those D.J's play in one place. I used to wander in and out of the rooms out of curiosity you know? What are disco people like? How are they dressing?"

Denise Shaw: "We stayed in the Bowie/Roxy room. I still remember the stairs going up to the ladies toilet, and I also remember going in and going down the steps, and we had to walk through the 'Disco' room to get to the Bowie room at the end."

Deb Zee: "Pips was brilliant with all the different rooms. You'd have your Bowie and Roxy room at the back, there was the big Disco room wasn't there? There was a room that led up to... the toilets were at the top. I fell down there after too many drinks....backwards. Didn't feel anything, I just got up and carried on. Ha Ha! Concrete steps...not sure what was in that little room, but that's where I saw Warsaw, it was on a Wednesday night. I think that there were only about 5 people there and it was like 50p or something, and it was about 20p for a double Rum and Blackcurrant. I remember when you walked into one of the rooms at Pips and they're all dancing to disco and they'd be like... you had to be careful going in there, but we used to do it... go on the dance floor just to wind 'em up you know, with our Blue hair and that."

In 1977 the club had caught the attention of the television media.

Brian Johnson: "One night, I was just dancing at Pips as usual, and a man and woman approached me. They said, "excuse me, we are from the BBC, and we were wondering if you would like to be part of our special on the dance scene in Manchester." This was spring, 1977. I was extremely wary. But they persisted and gave me their card. They told me to call them. I took it home, and after talking with my parents, said yes."

The scenes that were filmed at Pips were featured on the Omnibus documentary series, which at that time was the flagship arts based programme of the BBC and ran from 1967-2003. A couple of years earlier in 1975, Omnibus had made a David Bowie special, 'Cracked Actor', recorded at the time of Bowie's cocaine habit emanating into his 'Thin White Duke' period. Now it was the time for his avid disciples to share some of the limelight. Once again, as with any musical/fashion devotee, the attention to detail was paramount. It's difficult to comprehend the backlash from the viewing public in these more enlightened times, but even though men had worn make up for hundreds of years previously, people didn't want it in their living rooms.

Brian Johnson: "The "story" was me and this girl were going shopping for clothes at The Last Picture Show, getting ready to go out, including the famous, normal boy puts on make-up scene that is still shown today, and was even in the Spandau Ballet movie! Then off to Pips, which had posted big Pips signs on all of the posts! The songs we actually danced to were swapped out for different ones because of copyright, I guess, but the result was awesome, I thought. We had a little fantasy dance sequence, including me dancing in the shower? There is one quick scene where my friend Mark gives me a kiss on the face! He has since told me that he did that because he was jealous they chose me instead of him, and he wanted to get in there! The BBC told me they had calls about that and the make-up scene, and that they didn't get calls very often. My friend Steve says part of the clip was used just recently in another show about music!"

As punk began to gather momentum and bands started to get deals and release singles, there was a growing demand to hear them in the club, but there was some reticence at first.

Daniel O'Sullivan: "The Bowie room was right at the back so you'd have to make your way through the 'squares'! We went in the Bowie/Roxy room but if you mithered the DJ he'd probably put something a bit more punk on. Once you had your overload of Bowie and Lou Reed."

One night one of the DJs was handed a copy of the first single by Warsaw/Joy Division 'An Ideal For Living' by Peter Hook to see what it sounded like through a big speaker system. The result wasn't great to say the least. Soon in the middle of '77 Pips started to put punk bands on in the week, although the attendances weren't great. Plus there'd be the venues trying to cash in on the latest trend.

Stanley Vegas: "Around about that time (early '77), all the clubs were playing... well, trying to get into the punk thing, seeing where it led them because it was a new thing wasn't it? Even the pubs, if they could see a penny to be made... So there was a lot of places that would open for a couple of weeks and the guys who owned it would be like 'Oh no this is too much for me', so they'd switch back to their original style. So a lot of clubs came and went really."

Pips was always a forward thinking establishment so the burgeoning punk scene was embraced, and gradually siphoned into the weekday nights that would normally be quiet customer wise.

Chris Lambert: "I saw The Drones there one night."

Mark Windsor: "I think it was the night that Bowie played keyboards for Iggy Pop at the Apollo we went and there were leaflets everywhere advertising The Drones' gig at Pips, so we went there afterwards."

For the bands it was a learning curve, as the target audience was very small and not easy to hit, so a few concessions were made. One such band was The Drones, a pop/rock band who had turned to punk as the next step in their music career. Bass player Steve 'Wispa' Cundall remembers having to mix in some songs that people would recognise.

Wispa: "Pips was a Roxy-cum-Bowie club at the time and people didn't know how to take us. The clubs we used to frequent were Pips and The Ranch Bar. Everyone was dressed like Bryan Ferry or David Bowie you know? We were doing a few covers like 'Search and Destroy' and 'My Generation' and that, plus a few of our own stuff. We started to get a following and it just stemmed from there."

Although the doors were open for the punk bands to walk through, it never really had the impact or kudos of The Electric Circus or even Rafters. But the club would go on to outlive the first wave of punk and as mentioned earlier, it was a few years ahead of the London 'New Romantic' clubs of the late '70's and early '80's. It closed in August 1982 leaving a wealth of sublime memories for those who ventured through its doors, to the extent that over 35 years later there are still well attended reunion nights. The important role that Pips played in Manchester's music history cannot be denied or overstated. But it was also the stepping stone for the early punks who moved on to a new home.

Fran Taylor: "There weren't many gigs at Pips on Fennel St. The Drones did a gig there, Joy Division (Warsaw) did a gig there, but it was a club. When it started it used to have five dance floors all playing different kinds of music, but basically it was a place where kids got dressed up. You had all the Bowie/Roxy fans who'd go to the Bowie/Roxy floor and they'd all be dressed up to the nines and all that. Now that's where part of the clientele for The Ranch Bar came from."

Brian Johnson: "I can't remember the order of how this happened. I believe we found out about Pips and the Ranch Bar right around the same time."

Ian Moss: "A lot of people basically came from the Pips scene and straight into the punk scene."

MAY - JUNE - JULY 1979

WEDNESDAYS ADMIT HOLDER Valid until 10.30 pm	30p
THURSDAYS ADMIT HOLDER Valid until 10.30 pm	40p
FRIDAYS ADMIT HOLDER Valid until 10.30 pm	50p
SATURDAYS ADMIT HOLDER Valid until 10.00 pm	£1

WEDNESDAYS FREE DATES	THURSDAYS FREE DATES
16-5-79 13-6-79 18-7-79 ADMIT TWO	10-5-79 21-6-79 12-7-79 ADMIT TWO

PIPS No. 1 in Europe

Janine Hewitt: "It was in Pips that someone told me about The Ranch."

Stephen Perrin: "There was no shortage of good music around at the time but there was a shortage of small venues which meant there was nowhere for new bands to play. The clubs in which the beat groups of the 1960s had thrived had mostly become discos. Most of these either played chart music or soul but Pips had the 'Roxy Room' which catered to the glam crowd, many of whom made the transition to the early punk scene. I remember seeing Mark and Dave, who formed V2, in there and also Denise Shaw and her mates but I can't remember if we spoke at that stage. Whatever, there would have been a shared sense of solidarity as to get to the Roxy Room you had to shove your way through a hostile crowd in the main room who didn't take too kindly to men wearing makeup, or to their extravagantly dressed female companions, come to that. In fact, this hostility, and the fact that Pips' door policy could only accommodate a certain level of eccentric garb, drove a number of people away and towards the gay clubs, one of which was the Ranch."

4: rum and coca-cola

"PVC pants and zips were always on show down at Pips, a woman dressed like Jerry and a look-a-like Bryan Ferry, at least five David Bowie clones; we could be heroes. A punk band called The Drones inhabited this cellar, some monochrome Weller, fans of The Jam; the mods. We are the mods, we are the mods, we are, we are, we are the mods. It was a meeting of odds and sods, a rag tag and bobtail collective with no clear directive apart from to dress and enjoy what we could of the mess that was; Great Britannia. At that time for escape we had Vodka and Lime, and Pernod, Cider and Black, drunken funk and Monkeys on our tender young backs. Across town at The Ranch bar things often went too far with the sex and the violence and the drinking. We called it Bohemian thinking yah, when I was 16."

Alan Keogh.

The Ranch Bar was situated in the basement of Foo Foo's Palace on Dale Street in the city centre, near to Piccadilly train station. Its important contribution to Manchester's punk history has been criminally overlooked, with only fleeting mentions in a few books about the city's musical heritage. The Ranch didn't actually turn into a punk club; some people stuck with the Bowie/Roxy look, and some turned onto punk, but whatever the personal predilection, it gave the small core of these strange new breeds another safe haven to escape the Neanderthals, for a short while at least.

It was also a place of casual employment for a time to Steve Nuttall, a gay man who'd been forced to leave his family home in Hazel Grove because his parents wouldn't accept his homosexuality.

Steve Nuttall: "Frank 'Foo Foo' Lamarr owned Foo Foo's Palace and the Ranch Bar, he also owned a gay sauna somewhere near Pips, if I remember rightly it was called 'Unit One Sauna'. He preferred the Bowie crowd but he didn't really have a problem with anyone as long as they didn't cause any trouble. He was after any young boy he could get his hands on! In those days the age of consent for gays was 21; no one was 21 at the time, most were still in their late teens. I worked in Foo Foo's Palace as a waiter serving chicken and chips in a basket. An elderly guy called Arthur ran the kitchen and he is who we actually worked for, and when I had to leave home for being gay, he gave me my own bedroom in his house. There was him, his boyfriend Geoff, and me and a guy called Jono and we had a bedroom each. Working in Foo Foo's for one night paid our rent, and we could keep our dole money at the time which was about £7 a week. Frank used to come into the club as a man, then he was in drag doing his act, then he would come back on stage as a man at the end. He used to give a lot of blow jobs to supposedly 'straight' guys in his dressing room."

Sarah Mee: "We shared it (The Ranch Bar) with Foo Foo Lamaar and it felt like we had a kindred spirit in this drag Queen who didn't judge us on our difference. This was the tail end of the Bowie/Roxy/Glam era and the beginning of punk which led us to have our very own club, without the aggravation of having to run through the corridors of abuse."

Joanne Slater: "It's strange how things work out because my dad grew up with Frank Lamaar, well Frank Pearson as he was then, he went to school with him; Quality Street Gang and everything, I've got photographs of him playing tennis in a tennis dress with my Uncle Alfie. My Uncle Alfie was gay and he was shunned by the family at first. It's surprising how years ago everybody knew each other, you know? And they all grew up in very poor areas. I remember my dad telling me about Frank's first gig, which was at a pub in Ancoats, and his dad got told that his son was singing. But what he didn't know was that he was wearing a frock and sprawled across a piano. He chucked a bottle of beer at him and said to him 'You're no son of mine'."

Joanne was the girlfriend of Terry Slater at the time and they would go on to get married. Terry worked behind the bar at the height of The Ranch's popularity.

Terry Slater: "He used to make me laugh, Frank. When it was my turn to bottle up, I had to go there an hour and a half early. So I'd knock on his dressing room door, 'Is it about sex?' he'd say, 'No Frank can I just have the key please?' He was a character. Sometimes I had to go through... when we were running out of spirits in the bar, I had to go through to where he was on stage. I'd be walking through and he'd stop the show; 'Here he is, the fuckin' window cleaner. What you robbing me of now' you know? I'd be going bright Red."

Homosexuality had only been legal for less than a decade in 1976, and the prejudices that gay men and women had to endure were still deeply entrenched in society. Sons and daughters were shunned by their parents, and 'queer bashing' was an occasional 'sport' for the ignorant and the thugs. The protection that was given to the citizens of the city, and indeed the whole country, by the Police wasn't always afforded to those in society who didn't fit into its 'decent' category. In the mid 70's one of the popular, albeit stereotypical, professions of the gay man would be as a hairdresser.

Gail Egan: "A guy that I went to school with called Steve Nuttall had come out as being gay, so he'd gone into Manchester to get involved in the gay scene there, because there certainly wasn't one in Hazel Grove. He was friends with Cath West, so Cath, knowing that I was the biggest Bowie fan ever, took me to The Ranch. Also the people that I worked with as a hairdresser went as a crowd to The Ranch as a gay club, and because they played music I liked they took me, and Cath took me. Steve was there and his parents had kicked him out of the house because he was gay."

Stephen Perrin: "If you were working class and had artistic leanings, one of the few jobs you could go into where you could have some form of self-expression was hairdressing. Hairdressing was also a safe haven for gays and a lot of straight girls who went into the profession found that not only did the gay boys know how to have a good time but that they could go along to the clubs and not get hassled by men. They could go out with their mates, have a few drinks, a dance and a laugh and feel much more relaxed and safer than they would in a straight club."

There is conjecture over whether or not The Ranch was officially a gay club, or just a place where open minded people went for an after hours drink.

Fran Taylor: "What I didn't realise at first about The Ranch was that it was a gay club. As far as I was concerned at the time it wasn't, because there were women there, so how could it be a gay club?"

Steve Nuttall: "I'm not sure when The Ranch opened, but it wasn't a gay club as such, most of the clientele in there were either bisexual, or straight people who didn't care what other people did. The straight guys were mostly wearing make-up and clothes which were often bought from girl's shops. It was hard to tell who was straight and who was gay. I wasn't really into the punk scene I was more Bowie, Lou Reed and Roxy Music. Although I did share a basement room in a large Victorian house with Pete Shelley from Buzzcocks in Lower Broughton, Salford for about a year until we got evicted. I think the rent was £5 a week. Howard Devoto lived next door but one with his girlfriend Linder, she designed the record sleeve for Orgasm Addict for Buzzcocks. She spelt here name Linder and not Linda cos she didn't want to get caught out as she was signing on."

Gail Egan: "We used to go in the Thompson's Arms before going to The Ranch. It was near the bus station and that was a gay pub. It was a bit of a tour, we'd meet in there and then we'd go to Tommy Duck's, which is sadly no longer there, then we'd go to The Brunswick before ending up at The Ranch. We always used to sit round a corner of the (Brunswick) pub before going to The Ranch, and it was the most bizarre place, because a fight would break out and there'd be tables and chairs getting smashed while we were sat around the corner, which was the safest place as you'd be less likely to have a missile thrown at you! We all used to drink 'Blue Tulips', which was a cocktail; it used to get you pissed from the feet upwards! So you'd be sat chatting away and get up and... Occasionally we'd go to The Ritz with the bouncy dance floor. There was a place in Offerton called 'Gladrags'? I think it was called 'Gladrags', and they had a Roxy room so I could go there and it was quite local. It was okay to be straight and go into a gay club, I used to go into Sims and Dickens as well. I was lucky to get into Sims because they didn't really like 'Fish' as they say, going in."

Steve Nuttall: "The gay clubs in Manchester at the time were Dicken's on Oldham Street, Napoleon's on Sackville Street, which Frank had something to do with, The Picador on Shudehill, a lesbian club which was jointly owned by Frank Lamarr and a guy called John Foster. I worked in the snack bar of The Picador, next to the bar downstairs. There was also, I think it was called The Long Bar on Oxford Road. In the 70's there was very little hassle from 'straights' or anyone, the police were the ones who had a problem with it. The only community I knew was the people that went in the Ranch. The pubs we went in were The Thompsons and the Rembrandt on Sackville Street, the New York on Bloom Street and the Union on Canal Street/Whitworth Street. The Rembrandt was run by two elderly guys who were deaf and dumb and the customers were a mixture of young and old, the New York had a mixture of ages. Now the Union was the best place to go, it was run by an elderly couple, I can't remember their names, the customers ranged from prostitutes, rent boys, drag queens, transvestites, camp boys, old queens and lesbians, I think that was the only place that I never saw any trouble. Another place was on Oldham Street and that was Yates's Wine Lodge, a really old place, we used to go there cos it was cheap and we could have a couple of large Blobs or All Ins, they were Australian white wine, sugar, lemon and hot water three large ones and you was on your way to getting pissed."

Fred Carr: "I don't know how The Ranch came up but we ended up going there. They were really good nights, they really were; lots of drinking, lots of dancing. The blacks had their own culture and their own scene, and there was also a gay scene as well. I think The Ranch Bar... that was owned by Foo Foo Lamarr wasn't it? One night the bogs must have been fucked so I had to walk through his club. He spotted me from the stage and he says, 'Look at him, he's got eyes like piss holes in the snow!'"

Steve Nuttall: "He never swore on stage because his mother was there every night. Instead of 'fuck' or 'fucking' he would say 'ucking', for instance if there was a 'larger' lady in the audience he'd say 'ucking hell love, I bet you've flattened some grass in your time!' Foo Foo was never offensive and the club was packed every night, it was always busy. Sometimes he used to go and have a look in The Ranch while he was still in drag, just to see what was going on.

Dawn Bradbury: "Foo Foo would have a wander through from The Palace next door... well it was all one place really... and in between was the cloakroom for both where they used to make chip barms and what have you."

Someone who had first hand experience of Frank's personality traits was Steve McGarry. Steve was a close friend of future Warsaw/Joy Division manager and Slaughter and the Dogs fan Rob Gretton, and a very talented artist.

Steve McGarry: "I designed the sleeve for his album 'My Life At The Palace' and we went to see him about what he wanted it to be like. I'm leant against this filing cabinet, leather jacket, tight trousers on and baseball boots. All the while that we were talking he's not paying attention to what's been said to him, his attention is firmly on my crotch. In the end he came out with, 'Look at the cock on her!'

There was an obvious connection between the gay community and the androgynous boys and emancipated girls of the Bowie and punk persuasion. Both were on the outside of the conformist society; atypical and audacious, sympathetic of each other's indifference to convention.

Mark Windsor: "The gay scene was important, we used to go to gay clubs before and during punk."

Fred Carr: "So there would be gay clubs where you could go after hours and not get fucking hassled. I think there was a bit of drifting into those clubs, as somewhere where they had their own culture and they weren't about to put a fucking bottle over our head."

Stanley Vegas: "All the outsiders kind of banded together really. That's the one thing you could say about punk, not just up north, it was totally non-judgmental, so there was no homophobia, or racism from us, there was none of that shit you know? Any 'weirdo' could join the gang."

People were introduced to The Ranch in many different ways. But once inside, the impact was profound and stimulating.

Alan Keogh: "I was DJ'ing around the youth clubs playing soul music…I had a great record collection even at the age of 15. So I'd go down to this youth club in Levenshulme - Zion youth club on Clare Road on a Sunday night. I never said a word unless somebody asked me to wish someone happy birthday, but I was playing some classic Northern soul in there. I played a record called 'Landslide' by Tony Clarke and I actually got up and danced to my own record. Ian Dalglish said 'Fuckin' hell, you're really into this aren't you? What do you like about it?' so I just said, the energy… it's got great energy. So he said 'I'm in a band, do you want to join?' So I ended up going to his house and he played me Iggy and The Stooges and MC5 and he got me into all that. Then a couple of weeks later he said that he was going to this club called The Ranch and did I want to come. So I said okay, I'll come down with you one night. That very first night that I walked into The Ranch… I was with Keith Tiller and Ian Dalglish who were a year older than me. We went in early because I was only 15 and we thought that we'd probably not get in later, and I saw these two guys snogging at the bar. There's a woman over there who looks like a bloke… where the fuck am I? I can remember being in awe, fascinated by what I was seeing. It was a bit of a shock, a culture shock. The music was fantastic. It would have been late '75 maybe early '76.

"I wasn't a drinker, I ran for Sale Harriers and I was super fucking fit… no drugs, no cigarettes, nothing, absolutely nothing… and then I started going out to The Ranch… then it all changed. It was more dangerous… more dark… it was darker… Pips was quite safe."

It wasn't the most salubrious of places but that didn't matter. Once inside, if you were lucky enough to negotiate the terms of actually gaining entrance, you'd go down the stairs into an intimate room which resembled an odd mixture of Nashville crudity with brothel type decor. Amongst the faux Americana, country style fixtures and fittings, (Cow horns and Horse saddles used as seats), you were brought back to north-west England via the ubiquitous neon sign at the bar advertising 'Hot Pies'.

Janine Hewitt: "It was very small with the bar taking up the length of the longest wall. Upturned beer barrels were used as tables and it had floor to ceiling pillars and a wooden floor. It was very dark and smoky. The doorman used to look through a slot in the entrance and let you in if you looked okay. They didn't have a dress code so you could go in anything you wanted, no matter how extreme, and you all knew each other. It was too loud for conversations though."

Kevin Stanfield: "I'd been painting the flat one day and I wandered down in my overalls to The Ranch, because I knew that I could get in with my overalls on. I supposed that it looked fashionable! You could basically wear what you wanted. I can't recollect in all the time I was in there, and I went nearly every weekend, it was part of my tour around Manchester, I never saw a fight either inside or outside. It was just wild, but it wasn't threatening, that was the great thing about it. I never ever saw any fights in there although my memory isn't too great."

Denise Shaw: "Me and Joan started to go to The Ranch and at first Joan thought that it was a bit of a dump, but when our friends from Pips started to come down we kept going."

Kevin Stanfield: "Talk about dark satanic mills, it was in the back streets off Piccadilly."

Ken Park: "Like most places then, they wouldn't have passed any of the new Health and Safety regulations"

Deb Zee: "It might not have been glamorous but I didn't see it like that, it was just a really comfortable place and we used to have a good time. It had a really good vibe."

It was a culture shock to anyone on their first visit, it wasn't even a case of 'expect the unexpected'. There was no benchmark for The Ranch virgins to compare it to.

Mike Keogh: "I started hanging around a bit more with Terry (Slater) and we started going… I can't remember how we picked up on The Ranch, I think he started going there first. I think one night he said, 'come down to The Ranch, I'll get you in'. What I didn't know then was that you used to get free tickets every now and then, Thursday night free entry if you knew someone. When we started off the night, we'd go to 'The Great American Disaster' which was a restaurant-cum-bar. It was down the backside of the Arndale off Exchange Street. Then over to The Ranch. It was a typical underground place, the only people who go in through that door are people who are allowed in, so of course the door isn't open, you have to knock on the door. A little shutter comes across, and I'm like, shit where are you taking me Terry? There was no signs, it was just a doorway right? There was a guy behind the door just looking at you, big bristly whiskers, slicked back greasy hair. So I went down these stairs, and it got darker and darker, louder and louder, until eventually I walked in. My jaw hit the floor, oh my God! Bearing in mind I was only 17/18 at the time, it was like, look at all these weird people in here.

"There were these 2 girls, who were I think sisters but I can't remember their names. One of them had her hair pink; basin cut one side, straight down the other, they had white make-up on, black eyes. Then there were guys walking past us with make-up on and I'm like… Terry had to keep nudging me… 'behave! Stop staring! You'll get smacked you daft twat!' It was my introduction into what I would class as the adult world. I wasn't old enough to drink. That would have been '76"

Terry Slater: "I thought that it was a friend of Mike's who found The Ranch. It was completely different, they were playing all kinds of new music – David Bowie, Roxy Music, Deaf School and stuff like that. Jerry and Alf, they were both on the door, and Mary who did Frank's bit. They could be a bit funny you know? 'I don't feel like letting you in tonight, go away', that sort of thing. That was in the early days; 'Oh you're not dressed right'. But there was no dress code. Anything went. When we walked in I thought wow, this place is cool. It really was, like 'Cracked Actor' was being blasted out… my mouth hit the floor and straight away I thought, I love this place. This would have been late '76.' Basically all the other discos were like, dancing around their handbags, all the women."

Brian Johnson: "Some of the people we were talking to told us about a place called The Ranch Bar. They said it was smaller than Pips, but very cool and played the same kind of music. We got general directions into the middle of Manchester, and one night, Steve and I tried to find it. We drove up and down the street we were told it was on, but couldn't find the entrance. Finally we saw some Bowie looking guys wandering down the street to this door."

Mickey Carr was Fred Carr's younger brother, and like Fred his life was turned around by music and took him out of a negative environment into a positive one.

Mickey Carr: "Frank's brother used to work on the door… big Geordie on the door, he was gay as well. He didn't sound or look like it, he was just your archetypal bruiser; big sideburns and a big booming voice. We got to know them, the guys on the door, after a few visits so… once you'd been in a few times you were okay."

Chris Lambert:"One of our mates got knocked back for being too old. He was younger than me!"

Daniel O'Sullivan: "There was a guy on the door who always made life… he was a kind of biker character called Alf. From what I remember it was Alf. Anyway, he kind of scared the shit out of me. He would decide whether you were in or out… if he liked you, you were alright, you know? He was gay and was a huge, big fella… and I think he liked the idea of these androgynous boys coming in, so he'd grope you on the fucking way in which was a pain in the arse! So no it wasn't the most pleasant place to be. I watched as new people arrived on the scene and had to go through this… it was almost like a rite of passage."

Dawn Bradbury: "Jerry was on the door at The Ranch, he was always a bit of a character. He'd open the little sliding hatch and whether you got in or not depended on if Jerry knew you, liked you, or fancied you. Those were the three criteria and as long as you ticked one of those boxes, you got in. No matter how much people said, 'I'm friends with such and such…' He was like, I don't care you're not coming in. You knew you were safe in there because there was no way he was going to let anybody in who was going to give you any grief."

Brian Johnson: "It was straight out of a dime store detective speakeasy: a door with a small rectangular closed window on it. We looked at each other and knocked. The window slid open and someone looked out. The window closed, and the door opened! We walked down some stairs, paid admission, and walked into a small one-room dance floor/bar that had a western theme. There were people we knew from Pips, and other glamorous people we didn't know, but wanted to! The music was similar to Pips, but once in a while some other music, very odd and different music, came on. I walked up to the DJ and asked what he was playing, and he showed me an album that said The Rocky Horror Picture Show on it. I stored that in my brain, as we were treated to many songs off of it during that night 'Time Warp', 'Sweet Transvestite' etc"

The Ranch was about to be introduced to someone who would become one of the prime non musician protagonists in the story of punk in Manchester, Steve Shy. Steve's lack of musicianship meant that he put his ideas into the first specifically Manchester punk fanzine *Shy Talk*. He was also a work colleague of Wayne Barrett, a pairing that led him to the second Lesser Free Trade Hall gig by Sex Pistols. But the seeds of the future were sewn in The Ranch.

Steve Shy:"It was May '76 and United had just lost to Southampton in the cup final. But they still did an open top bus tour around town, and I met this lad, Don, who I used to go to school with and there were these two girls with him. I mean I was into Funk at the time, but these two girls were like Roxy chicks, they were doing like somersaults in the fucking bus station in Piccadilly. They had like stockings and suspenders on, tight skirts, lifting them up so you could see… we had a belting day and he said come to The Ranch. I wasn't into Bowie or Roxy, I liked sort of Alex Harvey, Mott The Hoople. I could take Bowie but I didn't like Roxy Music, I preferred Gary Glitter. The first night I went down there… I used to knock about at the gay clubs and all that, I'm straight, but when I went that night I had a vest on which, I don't know where it went but it disappeared - I was toned back then. I had combats on and a pair of women's 'Scholl' shoes on, that's what I was wearing in them days. That first night, I was tripping. All of a sudden you'd been going to all these clubs, and everywhere's sort of dark and dingy, and now I'm just seeing all these bright colours – people with dyed hair and all that, fuckin' hell. It was great so I started going there."

Mickey Carr: "In the Summer of '76 a lot of my pals from the estate where we lived, they all started going to the pubs and the clubs in town. Well I completely cut that out and I started to, under the influence of my brother Fred, go to this bar I'd heard a lot about called The Ranch Bar. It was a bit scary really… whether or not you were going to get in you know? So the Bowie thing… we were already that way inclined, and it was easier to be alternative, it really was then. It's not like the fashion now, kind of all the same, then it was easier to be different. It was only a small dingy place and my first impressions… I sat down, I'd got a lager and lime, and I was just looking at all these people, strange people; boys with make up on and gay people being completely open about it. It wasn't a gay club as such but because it was quite open-minded in the way that people dressed, that was its niche really. There were a lot of people who were quite regular there, a lot of Bowie impersonators. I had a pal from school who also started going in there. We left school and went our separate ways and then almost immediately bumped into each other. That was Alan Keogh."

Alan Keogh: "Eric (Random) was a good friend of mine. There was me, Eric Ramsden as he used to be known from Wythenshawe, his cousin Beano, Mickey Tait who would end up in a band called Nervous Breakdown, Dominic, Joey Tyrrell and we all used to meet at Granada Bowls, the Belle Vue Ten pin bowling place before we went to The Ranch."

Mickey Tait: "So I was 14 when I first went to The Ranch, I was probably a few years younger than a lot of the others as well. That would have been early '76. Looking back it was a very, very enjoyable time and I remember going into The Ranch with Eric Random. We grew up in Heywood House, which was in Bennet Street in Ardwick. I couldn't believe it when I walked in there. It was very camp, full of beautiful women who were dressed as 20's to 40's film stars. We were really into it, bands like Deaf School, Lou Reed, Bowie, Roxy Music. I remember getting on the 210 bus with Eric and he had a full dinner jacket on with his hair all Bryan Ferry... his fringe. You can imagine, people who would be listening to the mid 70's music... I dunno, say The Eagles, calling us 'fuckin' puffs'. I went to the Opera House in Manchester - Bryan Ferry was on. I remember being dressed as a Priest. Pre-punk was, you know, you were still dressing very fashionably for the times, and you were getting a lot of shit for it. From school as well my hair bleached white you know and a bird turned up outside the school gates with stockings and a short skirt on".

Carol O'Donnell: "We went to the Saturday Tea Discos, and the Village Hard Rock used to have an under 18's night. Then we started going to the Piccadilly Club, we went there 2 or 3 times and then we found out about this place around the corner, so me and two friends Teresa and Debbie started going there and that's where we met everyone. I was sixteen when I started going to The Ranch, and my friend had only just turned fifteen. We'd pay two pence on the bus to get there, I can't remember how much it was to get in, then two bottles of Special Brew which we drunk through a straw. At the end of the night we'd hitch it home. After a while when we got to know Jerry on the door we didn't have to pay... we blagged our way in. The music was just like... we didn't know a lot of it. I was never into Disco or anything like that, but this was a game changer for me and I never looked back. I was on the dole at the time, I'd just left school, and I got £7.20 a week and I used to give my dad £5 of that so I had £2.20 a week to live on, and that got me 3 or 4 nights out!"

As well as the allure of good music and hassle free vibes there were other more basic justifications to go there.

Fran Taylor: "The thing was, back then the pubs shut at 11 o'clock, you were out on the streets and we couldn't get into clubs because we were 'hairies'. So one night after the pub, Jon (The Postman) says 'I know a place where we might just get in late, let's go and have a look'. So he drags me round into Back Piccadilly into Dale Street and we knock on this door, a slide goes back; 'What do you want?', 'Can we come in?' He looks at us and says 'Yeah alright, come in'. It was 50p. That was The Ranch. So we get in there and there's all these people that I'd seen at the gigs, although we're not talking to them at this stage, we're just keeping ourselves to ourselves."

Odgie: We knew Hookie and Bernard and they got us to go to The Ranch Bar, and of course the gays have all the best tunes. You'd get the oddball tunes and stuff from Rocky Horror, and you could turn up there wearing what you liked. It was a good underground place and I'm kind of thinking that we were there before punk really broke. There was just me and Deavesy up here (in Preston). He used to nick his wife's 'Chalkys', slimming pills. We were messing about with old American cars and shit like that, and we had a yard. We used to jump in a Morris van and fuck off to Manchester to go to The Ranch Bar. So we knew when you go somewhere regularly enough you get to know the people there, you know? My recollection of is going there, dancing a bit, speaking to a few people and coming away again, because I'm not a sociable person but I'm guessing that's where we must have met Denise and Joan, it was already becoming a focal point early on."

Denise Shaw: "The first time I met them two (Alan and Odgie) was when they turned up at The Ranch and funnily enough I was surprised that they got let in because they were dead normal, I mean super normal. They were stood at the bar, and you could see that there weren't that many people in, and I just went up and started talking to them. They were saying to me how much they liked the music and that they wanted to come down to Manchester because they thought that was the 'in' place. They came the week after, and I took a picture of them because I couldn't believe the transformation from the week before. Ian had put all this cochineal stuff in his hair and this dirty old raincoat."

As with Pips, it was a place that possessed all the criteria that the unconventional and the non-conformists required to congregate with other people who had similar tastes. Plus there were other benefits.

Chris Lambert: "It was a placed where you got served. The centre of Manchester was quite a heavy place, you know? Especially if you looked mildly out of place, never mind slashed shirts, safety pins and make up. At The Ranch you just felt safe because it was all like-minded individuals. There was a group of us who'd meet after work and go to gigs and that. We used to hire mini buses and go to The Ranch, basically because it would normally kick off on the last bus. We started going to Sheffield later on."

Stephen Perrin: "The thing about the Ranch was that the crowd was very accepting. They didn't mind how you dressed, what you drank or who you slept with as long as you didn't bother anybody else."

Joanne Slater: "If you weren't drinking, you were dancing. It was a case of 'anything goes'. We thought we were being good if we stayed in on a Tuesday night."

Terry Slater: "There was one girl who used to come into The Ranch Bar, and she used to come in quite a lot with two other girls. I served her, and this bloke said to me, 'Do you know how old she is?' and I said I thought she was 19. 'No she's 14'. I had to tell someone about her though and she got chucked out, along with her mates. Sometimes you couldn't move, it was chocka... everyone trying to get served. It was just crazy... fabulous nights. It was always busy, even on a Sunday."

Kevin Stanfield: "Basically Sunday night was the main night. I used to go to the Wine Lodge, get three parts pissed on cheap White wine and find myself in either the Electric Circus or The Ranch. I was 18 in 1977 when I first went in. I used to drink Cider out of a bottle with a straw in it. I thought that you got pissed quicker that way."

Mark Windsor: "The last 6 months that I was in the Air Force in South Wales, I used to hitch home every weekend. I'd go to Pips on the Friday and Saturday and then I'd go to The Ranch on Sunday until midnight. I'd have to get six trains to be back to where I needed to be and I'd have to hitch the last 30 miles of the journey. Mental, I couldn't imagine it now. It was near the station, so at about five to midnight I'd be running to catch the train. I hated that bit, leaving there, it was horrible."

Before there were any punk records to play the music that was played was an eclectic mix and a direct alternative to what was being played in the 'normal' clubs.

Steve Nuttall: "Andrea True Connection's 'More More More' was always played in The Ranch."

Mike Keogh: "The Ranch was a mixture of different styles."

Fran Taylor: "The music, because there was no punk to play at that time, was largely Bowie, but there were a couple of floor-fillers which were really strange, one of which was 'Rum And Coca-Cola' by The Andrews Sisters. Every time that came on, the dance floor would be full of these strange looking women with weird make up on. You had to sacrifice your musical taste to get a late drink until The Ranch came along. Suddenly you had a place where not only could you get a late drink, not only felt a bit safe, but it had the music as well as it came filtering through.

As the first few punk records were released they would be added to the DJ's playlist.

Fran Taylor: "When they got their first copy of New Rose at The Ranch, the place just went off the fucking rails, yeah. And when the Buzzcocks record came out and they played that... the floor would just fill up and then empty. Gradually you broke the ice, there was a guy behind the bar called Steve (Shy) and it transpires that he was writing a fanzine (*Shy Talk*), which didn't come out until '77."

Gail Egan: "I lived in Hazel Grove and me and my friends, Catherine West and Julie Constable were going to The Ranch before it was a 'punk' club, because we were into Bowie and Roxy Music so that's where we went. Everyone got dressed up, Rocky Horror and all that...I can remember they put on 'Time Warp' and everybody jumped on the dance floor. You wouldn't have got that in most other places. I can remember one night we went in, and the DJ, a guy called Martin J. West, and he put New Rose on by The Damned, and it was like, 'this is incredible'."

Fred Carr: " My girlfriend at the time, Wendy, initially went to Liverpool to study art, she was a really good artist. She was quite far out, very arty, and quite radical in the way she dressed and the way she looked. She ended up going to Chelsea Art College where the Pistols played one of their first gigs if I remember rightly. So she was in on the scene straight away, she knew 'em all and she was part of that scene. She came back up to Manchester and she was the first person who showed us how to pogo, and that was in The Ranch Bar."

Mickey Carr: "I kind of went there with my brother and my sister... my younger sister... she was inclined the same way music wise. We liked the music and while we were there we got introduced to other music that we got to like. Stuff like the New York Dolls, even things like Deaf School and that. Even songs from, it might have been the forties or fifties I'm not sure, they just had a mix of music, but in the main it was Bowie/Roxy. That pressed all the right buttons for us."

Terry Slater: "You had 'straight' lads coming in, when I say straight I mean that they weren't dressed like punks, just flares and that, they just wanted to come and have a look. Half of them were alright but the odd ones used to take the piss out of people. There was two girls, we called them 'sidehead' and 'spike'. I'd see them coming down the stairs and they'd both have Carlsberg Special Brew and they used to put a straw in it. So they'd come in and the drinks would be there for them because I saw them coming down the stairs."

Despite its allure to the burgeoning punk cognoscenti, there were some dissenting voices, who took exception to what they perceived as nothing more than an elitist 'club' mentality. There was a small but influential group starting to appear.

Ian Moss: "I only went to The Ranch twice and I loathed it. I found it safe, conformist, like a load of fucking sheep, I really hated it. Me and my mates would go to 'normal' discos. We'd go to Heavy Metal rock bars and things like that, because to us that was more punk because there was confrontation. Very few times would it turn into outright violence, but there was always the potential for that, there were always arguments."

Daniel O'Sullivan: "The first time that I went in The Ranch, and I remember it very distinctly, because I was terribly embarrassed, because you got the impression that when you walked in, that this was a well knit crew. There were all these characters in there and they were quite heavy you know, and I went in with a girl the first time, and I'd had me haircut and I'd got a normal shirt on and tucked the collar down, and Dennis Edwards came over to me and went, 'fucking toy punk'."

Andy T.: "I only went in The Ranch a few times, I went to one gig in there but I can't remember who it was. It was more of a hangout, cliquey place really, and it was like a late night drinking thing as well. Because we came from Rochdale, we tended to go to the gigs rather than just go out in Manchester drinking. It wasn't really our crowd that, a lot of it was the Circus crowd and they'd gravitated towards that (The Ranch) and it'd become a bit more cliquey. It did get a bit, you know, 'Who are you?' not to me because they knew me, 'Who's this coming in? Who've you brought with you? You're not one of us, you weren't here last year' that sort of thing."

Alan Keogh: "Anyone who was anyone in Manchester at the time would be in there. I bought my copy of Spiral Scratch from Pete Shelley on the day of printing in The Ranch. He came in with a box so I bought it at the bar. Steve Shy, he's working on the bar, I'm buying it at the bar. Pete Shelley was in there quite a lot and Steve Diggle was in there quite a lot. In fact there's a famous photo of him being carried out by Eric Random. But if you look at the records of that scene up to now, I'm not going to appear. They will both appear, Denise will appear she was standing next to me when I bought it you know? All the people who are famous from The Ranch but I'm not one of them."

Ian Moss: "I was aware of hierarchies and what happens in these things because I'd been to the football, and you see that at the football so you're well aware of it, and I distrusted all that and disliked all that. I just wasn't fucking interested in any of that. I was really arrogant as well and a bit dysfunctional in that way. If I'd have lightened up over it I might have had a better time out of it."

Martin Ryan: "I only went in a couple of times, I wasn't a regular. I mean it was alright, but I preferred watching bands if anything."

Mike Keogh: "It was literally a closed club. The only people who got in were those invited or because it was attached to Foo Foo Lamarr's, you could get in through the back door behind the stage in Foo Foo's if you wanted to go and see all the weirdos in Manchester pogoing and dancing you know?"

Mark Windsor: "There was a little clump of us who knew each other, but most people knew each other, it wasn't big. This was before punk, it wasn't a big scene, I would have said about 40 people."

Denise Shaw: "There weren't that many. One of them in the core was Paul Morley, although he'd never admit to it. We used to get a lot of info off him you know, because he wrote for the *NME*, who was playing where etc. He used to slum it in the back of vans with us, he didn't act like the prima donna like he does now. Kevin Cummins was there to take photographs, but he wasn't really part of our group. There was me, Dawn, Dave Bell, The Drones, any of Buzzcocks, Ian and Alan were always with us. Lyn and Sarah Mee stayed quite 'Roxy' for a bit, then Lyn dressed the punk look, but Sarah never did, she was always the Bowie/Roxy girl. Lyn did come down to The Roxy with us, I remember her being in the van. They went to live in London."

Sarah Mee: "This was the happiest of times club-wise in Manchester, with the likes of Buzzcocks with Pete Shelley as regular clubbers and performers."

Terry Slater: "As for Devoto, I only saw him in there once or maybe twice."

Denise Shaw: "Howard was very quiet, he very rarely went to any parties or anything, it was mostly Pete. Pete was a nutter back then. I remember once, we ended up round at Dave Bentley's house, and Pete was absolutely pissed and he had his cigarette and he set the curtains on fire. We were all flapping, trying to throw drinks on it and all sorts and Pete's just sat there laughing his head while Dave's going bloody mental!"

Terry Slater: "Yeah Pete was in there quite a lot. He had a girlfriend at the time called Gail (Egan), and when the place shut there was a café around the corner where we all used to go in. We'd have cups of coffee, burgers, stuff like that."

Carol O'Donnell: "I met Pete (Shelley) at The Ranch and we got engaged with a White plastic ring. I was with Pete for about four years and lived with him for about two years; that was in Gorton. Before that we stopped at Fran Taylor's house. His dad was abroad for a while so he had his flat, which was in Salford Heights. We stayed there for about a month and there was me, Fran, Pete and Francis, then Pete leased this house in Gorton. I saw the Buzzcocks about 60 odd times altogether all over the country."

Una Baines: "I remember Pete Shelley wearing a cardboard badge with 'I like boys' on it, and I really admired him. I thought he was so cool."

Gail Egan: "There used to be a cafe around the corner from The Ranch called 'Chris's Cafe', I think it was open all night. So you had to walk past a normal club and hope that you didn't get your head kicked in, and I remember Glen Matlock being there. It might have been when he was in Rich Kids because we went to see them at Band On The Wall, because John Cooper Clarke was on."

Terry Slater: "Mike got on alright with Pete, I was sort of like…he was okay. He used to drink half a Lager and Lime and I remember when they signed for United Artists, I said 'you having a drink Pete?' and he said 'yeah Bacardi and Coke'. So I said 'No, you don't change your ways like that with me. It's Lager and Lime or nothing',"

Mickey Carr: "Paul Morley was always in there, acting the goat. I didn't know at the time that he was Paul Morley, I just recognised him later on. I'd see him occasionally coming down from Piccadilly station. I'd be like, 'there's that guy who used to fuck about in The Ranch with his mates'. Was it 'Egyptian Reggae'? Anyway, that song... him and his mates fucking about to that."

Terry Slater: "I remember Paul Morley, I used to cut his hair when I worked in Heaton Moor. There was one guy who was in there selling his own records. I can't think of the name of the band. The Panik, that was it! Steve Diggle could never tune his guitar. After virtually every other tune Pete would tune his guitar, but I mean they were young weren't they, they were just getting together and people couldn't play their instruments - 2 or 3 chords that was it you know?"

A fair amount of decadence and debauchery went on in The Ranch, the 'free love' of the mid 60's was still prevalent in the mid 70's and was a symbol of the changing attitudes to sex and marriage.

Pete Shelley: "Sex was something that you did with people, as normal as having a drink. It was an escape from the boy meets girl, gets married, settles down."

Mickey Tait: "They used to play things like the Andrews Sisters in The Ranch." The music was fantastic, but it was all about the women for me you know? At that age…that early scene was just fantastic. We used to mix, at that time there was loads of fantastic, middle class women who were a bit more… smoking Gitanes or Gaulloises. This was in '76 and so the punk thing was right up my street, short skirts, fishnets. I mean I was just bloody wild then, grew up in a home with no dad … I was the oldest kid. I was still at school then as well."

Steve Shy: "It was one of them places where there would be a party at somebody's every week, and you'd go and you'd just get in bed and someone would get in bed with you. It was all inter mingled, it didn't matter that you'd be shagging one bird you could go in another bedroom and shag another bird in the same night."

Kevin Stanfield: "I remember taking a girl home from The Ranch one night. I gave her a 'Donkey ride' all the home from the centre of Manchester to fucking Sedgely Park. She looked beautiful, she had Blonde hair and she was wearing long gloves and what have you, and I was in love you know? I'd had plenty of beer inside me. So I took her back to my bedsit and of course she stayed the night, and when I looked at her the next day, she'd had Talcum Powder in her hair - that was a big thing in them days – and her long gloves were hiding her Indian ink tattoos. She was about one and a half stone piss wet through, and that was with her money in her pocket. Rough as fuck like but she looked beautiful to me on the night. So I'd carried this punk rock chick all the way down Bury New Road."

Juliette J. Williams: "I'll always remember that Ian and Alan would always try to rip girl's bin liner dresses off. That would be on the way to ask the DJ to play a record, or on the way to the loo, that's when they'd grab you! I always took a clear plastic shopping bag with a change of clothes with me, just in case they did it to me."

That decadence was part and parcel of the freedom of expression that these adolescents were beginning to experience, which, along with the music they were listening to and the clothes that they wearing, meant that everything was coming together (no pun intended) just at the right time. But just as the rumblings of punk were beginning to get louder in 1976, there was another local alternative scene, which had been quietly infiltrating conventional society for some time, and it was about to up the ante.

5. year zero?

In reality punk people are usually the gentlest, kindest folks you'll ever know. They're like hippies, only they wear way more black.

Kate Rockland.

There was a large hippy following in and around Manchester throughout the seventies and it was still strong right up until punk started to penetrate the city. They were part of a successful counter-culture in and around the Greater Manchester area, particularly in the Rochdale and Heywood area. They were reading alternative magazines and fanzines, as opposed to the mainstream music press, and they tended to follow their own rules. *The Underground Press* and publications such as *International Times*, *Oz*, *Mole Express*, and *Grass Eye*, could all be found on the shelves in On The Eighth Day in Manchester or the 'head-shop' in Rochdale which was run by Barry Fitton. Bands like MC5 would be featured in some of these magazines, and they were a pre-cursor to the punk fanzines that would emerge a few years later. As well as running the shop, Fitton also published one of Rochdale's own alternative magazines, *Axis*. Some of those hippies were embracing an anarchic rhetoric and weren't averse to practising their own style of 'do it yourself' ethics, well before punk took over/stole that mantle. In fact if you look at the early footage of the audience of the very earliest of punk gig goers, there were still plenty of the longhairs and flared brigade in attendance, even right through to mid 1977.

Andy T.: "In Rochdale we had a hippie record shop called 'The Black Sedan', there were 3 or 4 record shops in Rochdale actually. Basically there was the 'freak' scene and there was an alternative paper called *RAP* (Rochdale Alternative Paper) plus a hippie book shop. There was the hippie thing, with bands kicking about like The Pink Fairies, who had come to Rochdale along with the Hawkwind/Deviants thing. That was my pre-cursor to punk I suppose, and it just seemed that the essence of, 'yeah you can do it yourself' was already there for us; Punk wasn't quite the shock... There was Kevin Coyne and Kevin Ayers; there was also the Virgin stuff, because there was a Virgin records in Manchester; the Faust album that they sold for 50p with the Bridget Riley cover. That led you onto German stuff as well. Virgin would do samplers that had a load of stuff on, and of course we'd be listening to John Peel playing all this left field stuff. So the thing that there was nothing out there is just nonsense. There was loads of it. I think that came from someone like Bernie Rhodes or McLaren, or one of the journalists like Caroline Coon. Someone wanted to make this 'year zero' thing come crashing through the doors."

Chris Hewitt: "The whole thing that it all started at the Lesser Free Trade Hall Sex Pistols gig is such bollocks, most people were already doing things. I mean Stackwaddy were the most punkish band in Manchester. They mostly played in London and around the country, they only did the odd gig in Manchester. They used to get their guitars back from the pawn shop and go and do a gig but they'd only have three strings on them, they'd just jam and make an awful noise, but people loved them. That would have been 1969/70."

Chris Hewitt was at the forefront of the music scene in and around Manchester predominantly through his PA business. Hewitt's PA system was a collection of equipment built up over the years, accumulated directly through the patronage of John Peel's Dandelion record company. He'd signed the Rochdale band Tractor to the label and Chris provided equipment as well as a recording studio for the band. Peel's affinity to Rochdale stemmed from his employment at Townhead Mill in the town in 1959. Peel's father was a wealthy cotton broker who wanted his son to follow in his footsteps, so he was sent out to work on the mill's shop floor to gain some experience. History tells us that John's father's wishes remained unfulfilled.

Despite all of the paraphernalia and reading material that was associated with the counter culture in Rochdale and its surrounds, there was one aspect of the hippie lifestyle that was missing from their repertoire - a festival. The inspiration that led them to put on their own emanated from another event that was held four years earlier.

In May 1972 the Bickershaw festival was the first major free festival in the north-west and was held over three days and included camping facilities. The site, three miles south-east of Wigan played host to an impressive and eclectic line-up which included Captain Beefheart, The Grateful Dead, The Kinks, Hawkwind, Donovan and many others. Inspired by the Isle Of Wight and Woodstock events, free music festivals of a much smaller, more domestic scale, started to be put on by local music lovers all over the country. But it was the Bickershaw festival in particular that was the catalyst for a group of people to put on their own event a few years later. David Smith, along with Andy Sharrocks, Dave Edwards, Andy Burgoyne and Chris Hewitt among others got together to organise their own free musical festival event at Deeply Vale. The venture's journey into fruition was not without some bumps in the road. The land that had been earmarked for the festival site was owned by local farmer Frank Turner who, despite his 'farmer' status had no farm buildings of which to speak, and actually lived in a council flat. The initial enquiry made by David Smith to Frank about hiring the valley was based on subterfuge, as the agreed understanding was that it was for ten campers only. The festival was given the green light and went ahead and it welcomed its first non-paying customers on 17th September 1976. Chris Hewitt's involvement was perfectly timed.

Chris Hewitt: "Someone came to see me and asked me if I would do the PA for the first Deeply Vale Festival. I think that I'd got my shop and PA system up and running for only a fortnight when that happened and it just spiralled from there really."

That first year attracted between 200 and over 300 people, depending on which article you read, and compared to today's corporate events, facilities were third world at best. According to the Festival Welfare Service's field worker, *'The toilet facilities consisted of 2 x 20 gallon oil drums sunk into the earth, and the bushes and hedges surrounding the site. Only three policemen were in evidence for the festival - two in a car by the cart track and one in the village directing traffic. Access was difficult; along a three mile pot-holed cart track that was not suitable for use by cars and vans'.*

After that first year the festival's free thinking values took the logical twist to incorporate the polar musical opposite to the prog and hippie mantra; punk rock.

Chris Hewitt: "We'd had Rockslide in '76 who obviously came back as The Drones in '77, and we had Physical Wrecks in '77 and we had Hit And Run which contained two members of The Ruts and their road crew. So they formed in a tent in '77, they had the idea... they saw Physical Wrecks and The Drones and went back to Southall and thought they'd start a punk band, so the whole idea of The Ruts was formed in a valley above Rochdale."

The festival started to gain momentum and the crowds swelled each year, from approximately 300 at the first one in 1976 to 20,000 two years later. It was also the only festival that Mark E. Smith expressed positivity towards, The Fall played there in 1978 and 1979. What other recommendation do you need? Tony Wilson was asked if he could compère a 'New Wave' afternoon in '78, turning up in a White 'ice-cream' suit, as it was dubbed by Vini Reilly. But the hippie/punk divide was crossed over when Doug

Rawle, allegedly the king of the southern hippies, blotted the peace and love copybook by physically launching the lead singer of punk band Wilful Damage from the stage, as he was unhappy at the young upstart swearing at the audience. Luckily the ground broke his fall, along with his arm, but he got back up on stage to finish the set. That act of unhippie behaviour brought the two opposing music cultures together, eventually mutating into the 'crustie' scene many years later.

Grant Showbiz summed the festival up thus, '*Deeply Vale was created out of nothing by disaffected and discarded people with no influence. The organisation was brilliant, from people who had been thrown out of school, told they were shit and could never do anything. Deeply Vale was one of the first punk festivals*'.

One group of musicians took the DIY attitude to its logical conclusion. Here & Now were the archetypical hippie/punk crossover band and stalwarts of the 70s free festival scene, and a band that probably played more free gigs than any other in history. They fused free-form psychedelic hippy rock with the attitude and raw sound of punk, and crossed paths with the ultimate pot head pixie, Daevid Allen of Gong. The band would be involved in future ventures with Mark Perry, originator of *Sniffin' Glue* and Alternative TV, as well as The Fall.

Chris Hewitt: "After Deeply Vale, Here And Now took The Fall and Wilful Damage... and I don't think that The Fall would have been as successful had they not done the Here And Now tours, because that took them basically all over. All Here And Now did was hire a venue, there was no admission charge, they just passed a bucket round. So you'd get Here And Now, The Fall, Graham Massey's Danny and the Dressmakers, and Wilful Damage, plus sometimes Alternative TV. There was such a mixture of hippies and punks in all of it you know?"

Perhaps most importantly of all, the Here & Now ethos challenged the music business establishment by cutting out the 'middle man' between musicians and their fans. By selling albums to record companies they funded their own musical equipment, PA, and tour bus. This allowed them to do free tours with collections from the audience each night to cover running costs, and albums were sold at gigs and through shops at roughly half the price of normal releases. Their ultimate goal was to establish an alternative free gig circuit run on a co-operative basis with a shared equipment pool but this never happened. The politics of free tours and the determination to challenge the music industry status quo were certainly connected with the punk attitude of the time, and Here & Now tours were typically accompanied by a host of punk bands on the bill. But Here & Now were never able to shake off the hippie tag to become anything more than the "crustie's concert party", garnering at best, some media indifference.

The Deeply Vale festival would carry on growing until 1979 when it relocated to Pickup Bank until 1981.

6. the sound of music

"Musical innovation is full of danger to the State, for when modes of music change, the fundamental laws of the State always change with them."

Plato, The Republic

So for young people in the mid seventies who had been watching Top of the Pops and listening to their records at home, the next logical step was to go and see their favourites in the flesh leading to yet more life changing experiences.

Mark Windsor: "I grew up on a council estate in Audenshaw, passed my 11 plus and went to the local grammar school but left with no 'O' levels. Basically I went to see that Bowie gig he did two weeks before he 'retired', and it just changed everything. I'd only ever been to one gig before the year before, T. Rex, who I was obsessed with, and that was fantastic but it wasn't like the Bowie gig, because I didn't know much about him. My mate got a ticket for me and was like, you know, in my teenage tribal head nothing would be as good as T. Rex but fuckin' hell! I said to my mate, 'I'm not sure he's human' It was then that I realised that you were allowed to like more than one thing, you know? Bowie was de-programming you, putting things in your head. He was saying that it doesn't have to be like this."

Brian Johnson: "I was invited by the two coolest girls in school, I'm not sure how or why, to go and see David Bowie at Radio City Music Hall. This was November 1974. My mom encouraged me to go, I'd never been to a concert before, and had only seen David on TV: The Last Ziggy Show and the 1980 Floor Show. I was a little freaked out to go to the show – Bowie wasn't that popular in the US yet, and I thought I was going to see this "Glitter Monster"! My mom bought me a cool suit for the show; The Great Gatsby was the current movie and I felt pretty good. I was on the twenty-fifth row at Radio City and even just sitting in the crowd was overwhelming – all sorts of creatures in assorted dress were walking up and down the aisles. The girl next to me started screaming, "It's Mick Jagger, it's Mick Jagger!" at the top of her lungs. I turned my head to see a man dressed in an all-white tuxedo, white top hat, with a white feather boa and a cane walk down to the first rows of seats. Man, my adrenalin was pumping! Suddenly, the announcer came on the microphone and announced David. The lights went off, screaming ensued, and a man popped out of the floor, at least that's how I remember it, and started singing. I was gobsmacked. Here was this skinny guy, with flaming orange hair, like tangerine, with some blonde at the front. I also remember two pink sparkles on his face, but that might or might not be true. I was pretty close. And then he started to sing! And madness happened everywhere… So, this was where I learned that it was okay to be different, and as a matter of fact, it was better! I bought my first LP, David Live, and everything changed."

Martin Ryan: "The first band I saw was Deep Purple in 1971. Then Creedence Clearwater Revival. Actually the one thing for me was the generation divide, I didn't really want my dad to like what I liked, but that wasn't the point. He liked Buddy Greco, Benny Goodman, Oscar Peterson, and there's nothing wrong with any of those people but…"

Stephen Perrin: "The first gig I went to was Rory Gallagher at the Free Trade Hall in 1972, which would have made me about fifteen. From that point on, going to gigs was my social life. There were some bands that seemed to be playing all the time – Gallagher, Mott the Hoople, The Groundhogs, Status Quo – and others that were more of an event – Wings, The Rolling Stones – but I'd go to see anybody. By the time I met Mike Finney in 1974 we bonded over Roxy Music and saw them quite a few times."

Una Baines: "We were dead lucky, at 14 we were going to the Free Trade Hall/Lesser Free Trade Hall and seeing [the likes of] Genesis, T-Rex twice, Bowie twice. It was expensive - £3 to see Bowie and £1.50 to see the others. We saved our pocket money to do that."

Ian Moss: I saw Lou Reed at the famous gig at The Palace where he was that out of it he had to be supported by the roadies, just held up to the microphone. Plus The Tots who were a bar band basically, they weren't accomplished musicians. That would be '71 I think. His second gig in Manchester at the Free Trade Hall ended up in a riot, so he didn't come back to Manchester for 12 years after that."

One obstacle that would be have to be overcome was parental acquiescence.

Juliette J. Williams: "I wanted to go and see Alice Cooper, I wanted to go and see Bowie and T. Rex, but my parents were like, 'no you're not, no you're not, no you're not'! They'd seen people like Donny Osmond and David Cassidy on the news, and how fans had reacted at gigs, so they said; a), 'you're too young'; I was 12, b), 'how are you going to get there and back?', and c), 'you're not going to be part of that screaming mass'."

But not everyone went to 'see' the band, some actually wanted to hear them too.

Una Baines: "T. Rex was a bit disappointing. Me and my friend went to see them and all we could hear was screaming. We were a bit inhibited but we were also annoyed because we wanted to hear the songs. It makes you wonder what that was all about. Is it because girls aren't supposed to express feelings like excitement and wildness? Bring your knitting to the gig! (*laughs*)"

Deb Zee: "I went to a gig with my boyfriend at Salford University and that's where I met Woody Woodmansey and we got friends with him. I've still got a notebook with his home address and telephone number in it. I remember that his wife June was expecting a baby and I used to go to the phone box and speak to him on the phone. I also turned up at the backstage door at the Free Trade Hall and I just said, 'I'm Deb and I've come to see Woody', and I got a backstage pass. He was playing in his band U-Boat supporting Uriah Heap. You wouldn't be able to do any of that now. I thought Dave Ronson was Mick Ronson's cousin, but apparently it was his brother, and I remember him phoning me on the land line at home. He asked me if I wanted to come to Sheffield, but I said no because when I went to the Uriah Heap gig, Dave Eager, I think that was his name, was the DJ and he had this flash sports car and Dave Ronson offered me a lift with them. So we went back to his place and he was very gentlemanly, nothing happened, he made me a coffee and didn't try anything. We listened to The Eagles' 'Hotel California', which put me off a bit, and he took me home to Flixton. But he tried to kiss me when I got out of the car which scared me so I ran for it! Looking back I wish I'd have kissed him now, Mick Ronson's brother! But I wasn't like that so when he phoned me I just said no."

Fran Taylor: "We went to see Genesis. We thought they were great you know, with Peter Gabriel. We went to see a guy who ended up joining Yes called Patrick Morales or something, and he was a massive synthesiser freak, because that's another thing we were into; synths."

Martin Ryan: "Immediately before punk I went to The Phoenix and El Patio in Stretford. We did go watching bands every Thursday at The Phoenix, just your standard rock bands. Son of a Bitch were probably the biggest one, who became Saxon, they were the only ones that made it I think."

Mike Keogh: "I remember going to Slade gigs and you'd see these kids really with no musical fashion. With Slade it was tartan keks, a waistcoat, top hat if you could get one, and stacked shoes and all that.

These kids would be turning up, with tatty clothes on, and I'm thinking fuckin' hell there must be some right poor cunts around here you know? Things just evolved."

Such was the obsessive mentality of music lovers, it meant that anything unauthentic wouldn't be tolerated, a fake could be spotted a mile off.

Ian Moss: "There was a band called Silverhead. They put out an album in '73/'74 called '16 And Savaged'; Michael Des Barres was the singer, and Nigel Harrison, who went on to play with Blondie, was the bass player. They played at Stoneground in Gorton and I went to see them. I didn't like it, mainly because Michael Des Barres was doing a very bad impression of Iggy Pop. Anyway he ended up coming into the audience, and I would have been 15 or 16, so as he was doing all this posturing I went up to him and punched him right in the solar plexus, took all the wind out of him! Weirdly enough four or five years later I did the same thing to Billy Idol for exactly the same reason when they played Rafters. Ha! Ha! It was quite embarrassing because the week after I found myself standing next to him at Bingley Hall watching David Bowie."

Fred Carr: "We went to see David Bowie at Earls Court but it was really disappointing, because he was just an ant on the stage, the place was that big you know?"

All that was about to change, the barriers between artist and fan were about to be torn down. The immediate pre-cursor to Punk was 'Pub Rock', which had been getting some coverage in the music press and was just that; rock music played in pubs, with the audience on the same level, as there weren't stages in place, but also within touching distance of the bands. The music was standard rock and roll or r 'n' b fare, but played at a fast and furious pace.

Ian Fawkes was a 14 year old boy growing up in the small Derbyshire Peak District town of Chapel en-le-Frith.

Ian Fawkes: "In 1973-'74 I was an avid reader of the *NME* and in the back of the paper they used to have something they called 'Teasers'. They started to mention this band Dr. Feelgood playing at the Nashville or wherever, and then reviews started appearing, tiny little reviews you know? For some reason I was drawn to all this, because everybody at school was into Prog Rock, Sabbath, Deep Purple, but at 14 it just wasn't happening for me that style of music. I kept going back to Dr Feelgood and eventually pictures started appearing with the reviews, even though I'd not heard any of the band's music at this point. But they referenced

The Yardbirds as an influence and that struck a chord with me."

Stephen Perrin: "My favourite band of the time were Dr Feelgood. Obviously they were a huge influence on punk - short songs, short hair and sharp suits that look like they'd been slept in. Early photos of The Distractions reveal me to be a Wilco Johnson clone. I first saw them on the Naughty Rhythms tour at the Free Trade Hall in 1975 (I think). During the opening set by Kokomo, the hippy sitting in front of me asked me to stop tapping my foot to the beat as I was disturbing him. I think the Feelgoods disturbed him even more."

Since their inception in the 1950's the music press was the only place that you could get information on new bands and read interviews with your favourite artist. Radio 1 just played chart stuff, Radio 2 catered for the stay at home housewives, playing music to cook and clean to whilst the man of the house was hard at work. *New Musical Express*, *Sounds*, and *Melody Maker* were arguably the top three publications of the early 1970's. Very broadly speaking, *Sounds* normally tended to the rock audience, *New Musical Express* covered slightly left field artists, and *Melody Maker* was somewhere in between. Others were out there, just not in the mainstream. At the same time that a small number of curious kids were splitting their nights out between The Ranch and Pips in Manchester city centre, there were murmurings of a new band from London who had been slow burning their way into the minds of young people through tiny articles in the music papers, which in those days played an intrinsic role in the development of new sounds.

Ian Fawkes: "Once again, little snippets in 'Teasers' kept appearing about this band called The Sex Pistols or just Sex Pistols. Now I thought this was outrageous, I mean who calls a group Sex Pistols? The singer was called Johnny Rotten, totally negative and unusual."

Ian Moss: "I was also an avid reader of the music press as most kids with an interest in music were in those days. You felt that something was coming along, and the need for something to come along. I'd seen Dr Feelgood, I'd seen early Graham Parker gigs, Heavy Metal Kids and Kilburn and the Highroads. I don't know if it was the first time I read about them but the one that Howard Devoto talks about, the 'Don't look over your shoulder but the Sex Pistols are coming' one. I'd seen that and it was a tiny piece with a picture at the top, and I remember liking the fact that they played a Stooges song, which was incredible because, not only were The Stooges the most important band to me, but I was the only person I knew who liked them. In fact I was the only person I knew who had heard of them. It's not like you could turn on the radio and 'hey it's The Stooges' you know? You had to go out and hunt a record down, which was no mean feat. And so listening to The Eagles isn't the soundtrack that's appropriate, do you know what I mean? It was primed for punk; dissatisfaction; questioning. If you'd have had this peace and love music scene, nobody would have got anywhere. I'd read all the snippets about the Pistols in the music press, so when I heard they were playing I absolutely had to be there."

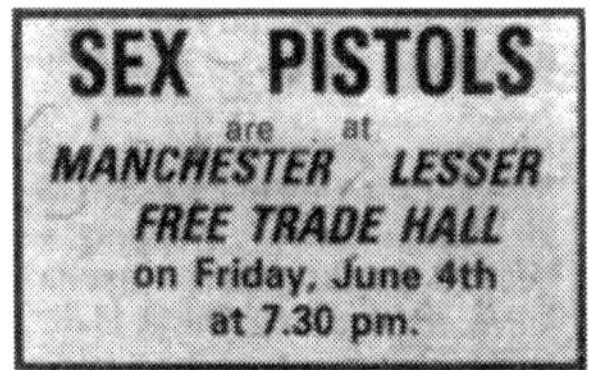

FRIDAY JUNE 4TH 1976

Sex Pistols/Solstice. Lesser Free Trade Hall, Peter Street.

Manchester's musical history is both illustrious and diverse. The Hallé Orchestra was founded in the city in 1858 by pianist and conductor Charles Hallé, and took up its first residency in The Free Trade Hall on Peter Street in the city centre, a building whose place in Manchester's musical heritage would become a recurring theme. Just over a century later on 17th May 1966 one of rock music's most iconic moments took place. Bob Dylan was nearing the end of his world tour when the controversy of his 'electric' shows came to a head at the hall. Just before the last song of the night, a disgruntled audience member shouted out 'Judas', as a derogatory exclamation of Dylan's new direction as being the ultimate betrayal of his folk roots. John Cordwell was the man eventually held responsible for arguably the most famous heckle in history, I say eventually because the bootleg recording which captured the taunt was originally credited as being from a concert at The Royal Albert Hall in London. At the time Cordwell assumed it was a copy-cat heckle. Then, a decade later, it was the turn of the Sex Pistols, who entered the building as an unknown quantity, only to leave it as the future of rock and roll.

The Free Trade Hall was built between 1853 and 1856, and is situated on the site of the 'Peterloo Massacre' on St. Peter's Field. On the 16th August 1819 the Manchester Patriotic Union organised a demonstration protesting against the introduction of the Corn Laws, along with the wider issue of parliamentary reform. The idea of the laws was to impose restrictions on imported grain, which in turn kept the price of domestic foodstuffs expensive to buy, and with fewer than 2% of the population having the vote, resistance was futile which meant that hunger was rife, with the disastrous corn laws making basic foodstuffs such as bread unaffordable. Supported by the Conservative landowners, who were set to gain from the ruling, but rejected by Industrialists and workers alike, this led to anger against Parliament and the Manchester demonstration at St. Peter's Field was the culmination of that ire.

Between 60,000 and 80,000 people were alleged to have been in attendance when, under the local Magistrate's instruction, the cavalry charged in an effort to disperse the crowd. It's estimated that between 15 and 18 people were killed and up to 700 injured in the mayhem. The dead included four women and a child. The name Peterloo is a bastardisation of Peter Street, where the Hall was situated, and Waterloo, the battle from the Napoleonic Wars which were still fresh in the memory. The government hastily introduced increasingly repressive acts of Parliament, including the passing of what would later be termed the 'Six Acts'. The events of that day led directly to the founding of The *Manchester Guardian* newspaper, and the building's history of protest continued when the Suffragettes Christabel Pankhurst and Annie Kenney were ejected from the hall after their repeated interruption of a political meeting there which included Winston Churchill. They continued to protest outside until Christabel was eventually arrested and put in jail. So perhaps it was fitting that many years later, a modern version of protest and insubordination should issue a fresh rallying call against apathy and drudgery in its environs.

On Friday 4th June 1976, what would become one of the most lionised music events in history took place in the Lesser Free Trade Hall, when the Sex Pistols came to town. At the time, there was nothing to suggest that this was going to be anything other than just another gig as the band were virtually unknown outside of their native London. Also their route to Manchester that night wasn't straightforward because the Lesser Free Trade Hall hadn't been the first choice of venue. Initially the band had been invited to play at the Bolton Institute by two of its students, Howard Trafford and Pete McNeish, after reading a small article in the *NME*. The pair had driven to London to seek out the band and perhaps catch a gig, without having heard their music; their interest was based solely on the band's perceived nonchalant, aggressive attitude. But the Bolton Institute wouldn't grant them the gig so an alternative venue had to be found. The Lesser Free Trade Hall was cheap to hire for a night and it was situated in the city centre so more accessible to a larger audience. Except that the audience didn't really turn up.

Ian Moss: "I went on my own, and that was... I could have gone with mates, if I'd phoned mates they might well have come along but I didn't. This sounds horrible, and it is in a way, you know what your like as a teenager, but I thought, 'this isn't for you, the fucking hippie rubbish that you like. I'm not taking you to this.' But by the same token I didn't want to go on my own, so I spent the afternoon at the phone box ringing various girls and asking them out on a kind of date you know. 'Do you want to come and see a band?' and they'd be like 'Oh that sounds interesting what are they called?' 'It's a group called the Sex Pistols', 'Erm, I'll give it a miss thanks'. So I went on my own, yeah!"

Dawn Bradbury: "I was 12 and it was in the early seventies and I was a big Lou Reed fan, a Bowie fan, not so much Roxy. Then I starting seeing somebody and ended up becoming a bit of a new age hippie, when hippies weren't particularly popular. But I have always tended to do the opposite to what everybody else does"

It was through this hippie route that Dawn came to be at the gig. She had just turned sixteen the week before the Pistols played there, which meant that she was the youngest person of the first collection of punks in Manchester.

Denise Shaw: "Dawn was the youngest out of all of us, she was 16."

Dawn Bradbury: "Everyone that I was knocking around with were all in old hippie bands, and that's how I ended up at the gig because Harry, the drummer out of Solstice, was one of my best friends. So my first punk experience was at that gig, which has since been done to death, the one that everybody was at, that nobody was at, and I didn't pay, I went in on the guest list with Solstice."

Howard and Pete had been trying to get a band together earlier in the year, and now this gig that they were promoting would be the perfect opportunity to get there arses in gear, and so they decided that they were going to be the support band under their new name, Buzzcocks. There was one slight problem; they wouldn't be ready in time. So a new support band was found via a distant acquaintance of Howard's who played in a run of the mill heavy/prog rock band. Solstice were totally unsuitable for the night but they were the only band he could find at such short notice. The choice of support band was purely down to logistics and good old market forces.

Dawn Bradbury: "They were after a band that had a bit of a following and were fairly local, Solstice were from Bolton, and they knew people would pay to see them. The audience consisted of quite a lot of ageing hippies and one young whippersnapper of a hippie which was me. It was just a combination of things; I knew about it through the London scene in the *NME*; Solstice got the gig. Just a case of right place right time I guess"

But for that young hippie this happy accident was to change her life forever as the Pistols crashed into her consciousness.

The Sex Pistols ambled on stage after Solstice had done their bit, to no applause or rousing introduction, and to a confused audience who were witnessing their first sight of the lead singer, who just stood and stared while the band got themselves together. There are a number of contradictions concerning this gig, of which one is that people have said that the band were shambolic and lacked talent, and some who thought that they were powerful and competent musicians. Tonight though, it would be their agitating indifference towards the audience and the sonic overtones of the music that would inspire the attendees to embrace what would soon become the next musical and cultural youth movement.

Dawn Bradbury: "I was blown away, yeah just blown away, because it was just something which I'd never experienced before. I could imagine what it must have been like probably when Elvis first played, that complete and utter mind blowing, you know, like… what's going on?"

Ian Moss: "I was an avid gig goer. I was at those Pistols gigs, famously, and I was 18. At that stage I'd seen hundreds of bands, that was what I did on a weekly basis. By the time I'd seen the Pistols, I'd seen The Rolling Stones, I'd seen The Who umpteen times, The Kinks, Lou Reed a couple of times, Bowie 4 or 5 times, Led Zeppelin, and Emerson, Lake and Palmer. So I'd seen all these influential and big bands. What amazed me was that seeing the Pistols was completely different from seeing any of them. I'd seen chaotic gigs, but it was the intent, there was an urgency about it and they were my age as well, and that… I wasn't looking up at somebody's cast offs. This was completely my thing."

Such was the band's impact that the audience didn't quite know how to react.

Ian Moss: "When the Pistols came back on to play an encore and they played 'No Fun' again, I'd been the only person stood up through most of the gig, everybody else had been sat down. After four or five songs I was squirming around in my seat, and I thought 'this is fucking ridiculous' so I got up and danced around on my own; there is a snippet, about two seconds, in David Nolan's film. By the time they came on for the encore everybody had got up by then, plus Jon the Postman was shouting out, 'The Seeds, what do you think about The Seeds? What do you think about Shadows of the Night' you know? And he got a dialogue going with Johnny Rotten about all these bands."

Steve Shy: "You know the Pistols bootleg from the Lesser Free Trade Hall… it was Dawn… she had the cassette in the top of her stockings, with a mic coming out to record it, and it was her that did it."

The biggest contradiction from that night is the number of people in attendance. An attendance ranging from 30 to 150 people have been written about with a healthy dose of conjecture, but the general consensus is that 45 people were there, and the list reads like the future Manchester musical hierarchy, although the alleged proportion of influential figures in the crowd that night has been met with doubt and scepticism from some.

Brian Grantham was the drummer for Slaughter and the Dogs and his own memory of that night is difficult to corroborate, but is still valid and gives another slant to the evening.

Brian Grantham: "The way it is… we were coming home, me and Mick Rossi and we bumped into Stuey George at Piccadilly Station. Stuey George was Bowie's bouncer, who we knew. We had no money to get back to Wythenshawe so Stuey gave us a tenner to get home, but we decided to have a bit of a stroll. We saw a white van parked up outside the Free Trade Hall, and the doors were open so we just walked in. There weren't a lot of people in there. The support band, who were a heavy metal band and I remember that they were doing a cover of… John Pilger? I used to watch World In Action, which might sound strange as a kid but I did. They were doing the theme tune to that [it was actually the theme music for Weekend World] and they finished [Nantucket Sleighride] and the Pistols came on after very quickly. There were four guys on stage and it was strange, I couldn't understand it. Caroline Coon was there I recall. I wouldn't have known anyone because I didn't know their faces, but it's pretty strange how the (music) industry in Manchester decided they were all going to be there, so how can that be? It can't be right, it just doesn't work out like that… there was maybe two of them. I know I was there because McLaren came out and Jonesy came out and me and Rossi went, 'We've got a band we'll organise a gig and all that, sort it out... so we did. Buzzcocks might have organised the gig, but it was me and Rossi who stood at the back of that White van going, 'We've got a band, here's the phone number. Forget the Pistols and Buzzcocks, and we did our own tickets because that's what we'd do.'"

Whoever was responsible for it, a follow up gig was sorted straight away.

Brian Grantham: "A date was set, but me being a mad Stones fan was going to see the Stones at Earls Court that day. So I said that there was no way I was able to play, so that gig, the date was moved. We did the gig and that was it. That's all I remember."

Odgie: "I didn't do the Free Trade Hall gig; I was probably the only person in Manchester who wasn't there Ha! Ha!"

The impact of that night has gone down in music folklore. Despite the collective amnesia that surrounds the gig, it not only changed the city musically, but also stylistically.

Ian Moss: "My hair was cut within the week. That was the most visible sign, and within a couple of weeks, and, what proved to be really difficult, I'd hunted down some trousers that weren't flared. I took a bunch of people to the second gig in July; which presumably everyone else had because the numbers swelled that much."

TUESDAY JULY 20TH. 1976

Sex Pistols/Slaughter and the Dogs/Buzzcocks.
Lesser Free Trade Hall, Peter Street.

46 days later the Pistols were back. Only this time the place was packed. Slaughter and the Dogs brought their own style, their own motley crew, and as promised they even produced their own tickets and posters, which not only contained no mention of Buzzcocks, but put Slaughter at the top of the bill! Word had obviously gone around town and you had the different factions, each there to see 'their' band.

Steve Shy: "You had your 'normal' pub band followers, then there was the Bowie and Roxy lot, and then you had all these fuckin' hooligans from Wythenshawe.'

But for anyone outside the immediate environment of the city, it took a keen eye to be there. Especially out in the sticks.

Ian Fawkes: "Back then of course there was no internet or You Tube, absolutely nothing, so to get information of a gig happening in Manchester you would have to buy the *Manchester Evening News*. You'd get all the listings for bands playing at the Palace Theatre and so on, then one day there was a tiny advert for Sex Pistols at the Lesser Free Trade Hall, July 20th 1976. I'm not trying to claim that I went to the first one because I didn't, I must have missed it in the music papers for some reason".

Andy T.: "The second gig where Slaughter were playing I was pretty sure I was away in Wales, it was the last time I ever went on holiday with my dad, that's why I missed that one and completely missed the first one, I didn't know it was on."

For others it was also more luck than judgement.

Steve Shy: "I ended up going to the Pistols gig because Wayne Barrett worked for the same firm as me. I was a Glazier by trade and I didn't get on with the blokes there… it was just boring and they were all arseholes. What they used to do was leave me in town and I'd deliver all the glass to these places – one pane here, one pane there – and sometimes they'd put Wayne Barrett with me. He was a 16 year-old painter and he used to come and paint the windows and that. He used to go into The Ranch and he kept saying, 'we've got a gig, you've got to come and see us', so I bought a ticket off him, and that was Buzzcocks, Slaughter and the Pistols. I'd never heard of the Sex Pistols before I went."

Ian Fawkes: "On the night we just decided, right at the last minute, to go down on the train. It was the red hot Summer of 1976 and we didn't have a clue what we were going to see, no idea at all, it could have been the biggest flop we'd ever seen and we'd return home disappointed. We turned into Peter Street by The Midland Hotel and we were fairly early and there was a decent crowd already outside. We were there with our long hair and flares along with, I wouldn't have called them punks, they were just different; short hair, tight jeans you know, just different. It could have been the Bromley contingent, the original crew but I couldn't swear to it. We were quite nervous as it was all new to us and it was quite an intimidating look. We wanted to get inside so we followed this bloke in and the security guard stopped him and told him that he couldn't come in, and the guy told him that he was the manager of the Sex Pistols and then turning to us he said the security guard 'and I think these kids want tickets'.

"We went back outside and were nudging each other excitedly

saying 'bloody hell that bloke was Malcolm McLaren! We've read about him in the *NME*.' So now we felt part of it. I also seem to remember Nils Stevenson (the Pistol's road manager at that time) and Helen Wellington Lloyd being there as well"

Una Baines: "Malcolm McLaren was on the door taking money. I do remember that really clearly."

Ian Fawkes: "When we eventually got in we weren't allowed to go upstairs, the Lesser Hall was above the main one, as the bands were still sound checking. So we went to the bar and wandered around for a bit, and we ended up stood right in front of the doors of a lift. All of a sudden the lift opened and there stood all four of the Sex Pistols, and Johnny Rotten looked at me and said 'Get out of my way!' So of course I got out of his way. They walked past us and they looked brilliant, just fantastic and they went over the road to the Berni Inn, just the four of them. We eventually got into the theatre upstairs and it was all seats just like a cinema. So foolishly we sat near the back, mainly because we were still a little wary of what was going on, we were just kids from the countryside you know?"

The fact that the Pistols and Buzzcocks were such an unknown quantity only added to the earth shattering impact that both bands would provoke.

Ian Fawkes: "The curtains opened and with no announcement Buzzcocks came on. Straight away I thought this is different, I'm not going to say it was fantastic, it was just different. It was like watching a school band, but it was just so much fun. There was no proper PA and no proper monitors, I seem to remember two Fender amps propped up as monitors. At the end Devoto and Shelley had a mock fight, with Devoto pulling at Shelley's guitar, there's some cine film footage of it I remember seeing. Obviously this was a set up because Shelley had swapped his 'better' guitar for the last song to a cheap crappy one and it got broken in this mock fight. Then at the end, instead of just walking off to the side of the stage they all ran through the audience which once again was great you know?"

Steve Shy: "As soon as Buzzcocks came on it excited me. Even though I was from a different thing than anybody else in there. So yeah, Buzzcocks really excited me, and I thought this has been really worth coming just to see this band, even though I'd never heard punk or whatever."

Ian Fawkes: "All the way through Buzzcock's set we stayed sat down, there was nobody pogoing or anything like that, I don't think it had been invented at that time. Bear in mind that most of the people there were just normal regulation bods like me just trying to work out what we were witnessing. There was an interval and then Slaughter And The Dogs came on. At that time they were more into Bowie and Glam Rock, and Wayne had long hair and they wore floppy hats and were a bit posy and a bit Mott The Hoople. They'd also brought their own crowd from Wythenshawe with them so they were ready established, whereas for Buzzcocks it was their first gig."

Wispa: "We met a guy called Dave Bentley who was knocking around at the time, a bit of a hippy. You maybe be aware of him as he did a couple of bootleg albums; the Pistols album and The Clash album at the Circus, and made a lot of money out of it. Anyway he turned round to us and said that there was this gig that he wanted us to go to this one night, Sex Pistols are playing…we were like, who?... it was at the Free Trade Hall…not the first one obviously, it was the second one. Slaughter and The Dogs were on it and Buzzcocks. I just couldn't believe it, I couldn't believe what I was seeing. It was so raw, the playing was a bit rough, but it was so good. We thought, we've got to get a bit of this you know? Buzzcocks came out, couldn't play and fumbled through it. Then Slaughter came on flying about like Spinal Tap. It was a great contrast, it was an unbelievable night it really was."

Ian Fawkes: "There would have been about 200 there maybe? It was full anyway so whatever the capacity was really, you know?"

According to Slaughter and the Dogs drummer, Brian Grantham, the band wanted to come on to a specially chosen piece of music, although it didn't quite produce the dramatic impact as he'd hoped.

Brian Grantham: "So we're all in rehearsal for this gig at the Free Trade Hall, bearing in mind Rossi's dressed up as Mick Ronson, Wayne Barrett's Bryan Ferry and I'm just me. I'm a Stones fan so I collect everything by them right? So when Jagger did Memo From Turner, the movie, I didn't just want the film, I had to have the soundtrack as well. Bearing in mind I'll nick it from Boots or someone will nick it for me, because Boots was the main record shop at the time. Now the last track on it comes in with classical strings, right? So we say to the sound guy on the night, I can't remember who it was, 'When we come on, you put that track, the last track on, right?' So what does he do? He puts the wrong side on! It's embarrassing and I'm going 'Turn it over!' Ha! Ha! Ha! So you've got the Sex Pistols; Buzzcocks have been on with half a chopped guitar playing real, original punk; and then you've got us; a mixed up Mick Ronson, and Bryan Ferry, you've got Howard out of Camel, and me who's still into Zeppelin and he put this wrong track on. It's miles away!"

Steve Shy: "Wayne that night was wearing like a Satin bib and brace. They did like a Mick Ronson cover, a Velvets cover, but they also did a Camel cover, you know?"

Once they got their set underway, Slaughter's theatricals polarised opinion, not just on that night but in the aftermath of what came next as punk grew.

Ian Moss: "Obviously I saw Slaughter with the Pistols. I could have thrown up. They clearly knew what was going on, they'd clearly seen a bandwagon they could get on, but they'd got it so wrong; blouses and throwing flour around. Paul Morley famously threw a Jelly Baby at Slaughter and the Dogs. I didn't know who he (Morley) was at the time. Anyway he's thrown this Jelly Baby and it's hit the singer and he stops the gig, and has a bit of a tantrum. Morley said that he'd never done anything like that before and since, but he felt compelled to do it because they were so inauthentic."

It seems confectionery projectiles were a common theme in the early days of the band.

Brian Grantham: "We were getting sweets thrown at us at the Tatton Cinema, when we'd be doing the Saturday Matinee."

Ian Fawkes: "I didn't really like them or what they were playing, and of course they turned into a different band after this gig. Anyway they finished the set and there was a big cheer, but the cheer was for them finishing the set if you know what I mean? Not a positive cheer."

The diverse mix in the audience created a hostile atmosphere and it seemed that the end of Slaughter and the Dog's set was the spark to light the touch paper and the place exploded.

Steve Shy: "It was like three different lots; there was people throwing pint pots against the wall, they were smashing and coming down on you and stuff like that."

Ian Fawkes: "All of a sudden there appeared in the audience about ten or so greasers, where they had come from I've no idea, I'd not seen them during the gig before. An almighty fight broke out between these Greasers and the Slaughter fans, and I can remember somebody lobbing one of the old style pint pots with the handle on it, and it flew over everyone and smashed against the wall. That was the cue for most of the crowd to run for it, including me, and so I ran back down the stairs. I got to the bottom and thought to myself, 'I ain't going back in there'. Then someone announced that it was okay, it's over, the fighting's finished.

I mean this is a rock concert, you don't get fights at gigs! Half of me wanted to go home and the other half was saying, no this is exciting, this is something else, unheard of you know? We went back upstairs and the Greasers had gone, and I maintain that it was a stunt pulled by McLaren to get some publicity."

Once the wild west shenanigans had ceased and the Cowboys had calmed down, the main event was ready to roll.

Ian Fawkes: "The curtains opened and there stood the Sex Pistols, and they kicked off with 'I Wanna Be Me'. In between songs Rotten kept antagonising the audience, and I can remember him saying something along the lines of 'What's up? Have you all got glue on your seats or something? Have you come to just sit on your fucking arses?' The audience were shouting 'Fuck Off!' back at him you know? Then someone shouted out 'Substitute' to which Rotten replied 'We'll play it when we're fuckin' ready!' I mean I'd been to gigs before and people were thanking the audience for coming and they had peace signs around the place, but here was this young guy just giving the audience a load of aggro."

Steve Shy: "So you've got all these head bangers and all that... Rotten just came on and sneered at everybody, and so everybody in there, it was full for the second gig, and you thought he was just staring at you."

Ian Fawkes: "As the gig went on, the atmosphere got more and more electrically charged, and although we were now stood up I didn't dare go to the front! I'm sure we weren't alone in that, you know? We weren't quite sure what was happening here, I was a sixteen year-old lad and this is... it's easy to say that this was a revolution that was happening, but it wasn't a revolution, it was just a group called the Sex Pistols doing a gig"

Steve Shy: "When the Pistols came on it was kickin' off all over and what have you. I just came out and that changed my life."

Stanley Vegas: "For me... you know the gig that everyone's supposed to have gone to? It wasn't that for me. We were at the second Lesser Free Trade Hall gig, where Buzzcocks played their first gig at. That was my grounding in punk, that little era you know?"

Ian Fawkes: "I've got a cutting of an interview by Jonh Ingram which was from the gig and it was a full page review in *Sounds* called Anarchy For The U.K. That night was the first time they played it I think, a new song it said and I can remember listening to the words; IRA, UDA. I can remember thinking 'who sings songs about the IRA? This is crazy, you know? You can't do that and get away with it!' Nobody did that, it was all peace and love wasn't it? All of a sudden towards the end this bloke came leaping down the aisle, and I mean he was taking massive strides and stood in front of the stage. A long haired bloke going nuts! He was joined by another person and then another and so on until there were about 20 people at the front of the stage going absolutely nuts, but we were just rooted to the spot in total wonder. By the time they finished the place was absolutely bouncing. We couldn't put it into words what we'd just seen. I'd spent most of the gig sat down, there'd been a fight, the band are on stage swearing at the audience and goading them, I wanted to go home and I was missing the cosy surroundings of Chapel en-le-Frith, but at the same time it was exciting and since that night I've never been to a musically more frightening, exciting gig since, not even the Feelgoods in their pomp. After the gig I felt like I knew some kind of secret but as soon as Punk got into the mainstream it sort of lost something. Too many people got to know about it."

7. man in a box

"Bakunin would have loved it"

Tony Wilson

WEDNESDAY AUGUST 4TH 1976

So It Goes featuring Sex Pistols, Studio 6, Granada TV studios, Quay Street, Manchester.

Just over a fortnight after that second Lesser Free Trade Hall gig, the momentum was ramped up another notch as the Pistols were about to enter living rooms across the wider Shires of Northern England. On 4th August, Sex Pistols made their first ever television appearance in the studios of Granada TV in Quay Street. So It Goes was a regional 'magazine' devised and hosted by local news reporter/presenter Tony Wilson, aided and abetted by Australian journalist (and punk hater) Clive James. Wilson's fashion sense ranged from geography teacher, to silk-tied, flared jeans clog wearing hippie, the overall look completed with his long hair, so despised by the band he was eager to promote. That juxtaposition in styles would not have been exclusive to Wilson, as many who were yet to see the Pistols, or be engrossed by the punk scene, dressed in a similar fashion, or with no fashion at all. For instance, Paul Morley went to the first Lesser Free Trade Hall gig on 4th June with shoulder length hair, but after witnessing his musical epiphany, that was promptly rectified.

Tony Wilson, as he referred to himself then, has always been the proverbial 'Marmite' character, but for all his faults and foibles, his heart was firmly in the right place; his heart was firmly in Manchester.

Chris Hewitt: "When he first went working for Granada they seconded him to the *Liverpool Echo* to learn the ropes about going out to do local stories. He used to go into Probe with his shoulder bag on and say to Geoff Davis, 'Hi Geoff, what's hip this week?' Geoff said that he 'just used to get all the shit that I couldn't sell, and sell it to Tony'. So he'd go back to Manchester and show all his mates these great albums that he'd bought, and all it was stuff that Geoff couldn't get rid of."

Although Wilson's musical tastes were firmly entrenched in American west coast country rock, he was looking for something that would shake up the music scene in the U.K. His initial introduction to the Sex Pistols had been a cassette sent to him by Howard Devoto before their first Free Trade Hall gig. He believed they were the future of rock and roll and vehemently campaigned to get them onto So It Goes. Peter Walker was the studio director on the show.

Peter Walker: "In all honesty it was Tony's show, so whatever he wanted on the show was okay with us. I mean we put up resistance against the Sex Pistols, but we generally went along with whoever he wanted on because he was so enthusiastic and that came over. He was the one that made it happen. I loved Tony to bits, he was a brilliant presenter, but he was so bloody arrogant, that was his problem as far as I was concerned. He wouldn't take any advice off the director or producer."

Wilson's partner at the time was June Buchan and she worked on series one of the show as production assistant, as well as being involved in the filming of the live punk gigs that would be aired in series two.

June Buchan: "He was pretty much the same person all the time. He would shout you down. During that first series he was still long-haired, wearing jeans and a scarf; a West coast hippie. I was actually with Tony, we were an item from the end of 1975 until the end of the series. We were both big fans of Kurt Vonnegut and when we were talking about the programme I remembered his phrase and said 'What about so it goes' and he said 'Yeah that's it'.

Peter Walker: "Bob Greaves recounted Tony making an entrance into the offices of local programmes. He walked in wearing black leather trousers, a cowboy hat and leather jacket. Everybody stopped working, thinking 'Who the fuck?!', and he'd announce himself, 'Hi I'm Tony Wilson'. Greaves and Wilson developed a great friendship after that initial introduction. He soon realised that Tony had a big heart and a great journalistic style."

The show went out late at night and was only transmitted in the North West region of England incorporating Lancashire, Cheshire, Cumbria, along with parts of Derbyshire including Ian Fawkes's parents' house in Chapel en-le-frith, on the edge of the Peak District.

Ian Fawkes: "About 2 weeks after the second Free Trade Hall gig, they appeared on So It Goes which was their first television appearance, and I can remember telling everyone I knew that this new group the Sex Pistols were going to be on television. Nobody else seemed interested, telling me that they couldn't play and all that rubbish, and I was there saying 'I've seen them, and they can play!'"

Peter Walker: "The format of the show and the way it ran came entirely out of his (Wilson's) head. The audience was dotted around the studio, they weren't situated on one bank, you didn't really see them."

June Buchan: "It was ahead of its time, although some of the stuff is dated."

Peter Walker: "Right from before the first programme even started, Tony said to Chris Pye and I, 'We've got to get the Sex Pistols on' and we both said, 'You must be joking, they're absolute rubbish, we can't have the Sex Pistols on, they can't play anyway! They can only play three notes and they can't sing' and I remember saying to him, 'I thought you wanted to do a music show which had a bit of depth to it? There's no depth to them, they're rubbish.'"

But Wilson was like a dog with a bone, he could see something was happening with the band and was obsessive about getting them on the show.

June Buchan: "He absolutely loved the Sex Pistols. I think what was interesting about that time was that Tony was, up until then, a total West coast music fanatic. He was on the verge… he knew that 'something' was happening, it was a crossover point and in television terms he thought he could marry the two together."

Peter Walker: "Tony plugged and plugged and plugged away until eventually Chris gave way and we had them on the last show. We didn't know how they were going to go down, and I was in fear because I'd heard about the bad behaviour and swearing. All I'd got was a White label from EMI with 'Anarchy In The UK' on it. I didn't know anything about them, I'd not seen them. So come the day, at the sound check, to my utter delight they were absolute rubbish. I'd proved my point, 'I'll do the best I can but it's going to be absolutely crap', you know?"

The band turned up and played 'Problems' as a sound check with Matlock breaking a bass string at the end of the song creating panic among the bosses because of the time constraints. They were fearful of having to pay overtime rates to the cameramen and floor staff. Perhaps all that accumulative tension was the reason for the statically charged performance that followed.

Johnny Rotten shouting "GET OFF YOUR ARSE!" remains one of the most poignant and intimidating introductions to a song ever seen on television. Aimed at an apathetic audience, it had the capacity to inspire and offend in equal measure. The words were spat out by an angry young man reminiscent of a Victorian street urchin.

Peter Walker: "They came down for the gig... they blew everybody away. The cameramen went apeshit, giving me shots that they'd never given me before. I always liked to plan the script, I didn't like to wing it, you've only got three and a half minutes to get it done, there are no retakes because it was 'as live'. So that was it; in the can, gone. I couldn't believe the difference between them playing in rehearsal and doing it on the night. I don't think they were high, they certainly didn't look it but they played beautifully and they gave absolutely everything and they really enjoyed doing it, and that really came across I think."

Tony Wilson: "They were meant to do three and a half minutes, they agreed that and rehearsed it, there was five minutes left, and they just kept playing for seven minutes... two days later the director edited it down to three and a half minutes. He did a good job, but someone threw away the original take, which was a shame."

Although won over by their performing prowess, the director did take umbrage at something he thought overstepped the boundary of bad taste.

Peter Walker: " The only thing that disconcerted me was the young woman, (Jordan) who had a Swastika on her arm and was dancing around at the side of the stage. I was like 'for fucks sake don't get her in the shot whatever you do', otherwise [Granada chairman] Sidney Bernstein would have axed it straight away, there was no way they would let that go out."

It got past all of the censorship with a little editing, camera trickery and luck. But it was a happy mistake.

Peter Walker: "I couldn't hang on to the full length shot, which I wanted to do because it was overrunning, and I had to edit it to get rid of the lady with the Swastika. They did a sort of mini Who type of thing, destroying stuff at the end and she (Jordan) suddenly appeared on the stage throwing microphones over and kicking chairs and all the rest of it. I didn't use any of that, all I did, and I'll remember this until my dying day, was get a shot of Johnny Rotten, he'd just finished singing and he's looking dead into the lens and that shot just summed up for me what they were about. We had a 'Green Room' just across the courtyard. A tiny little room and there were always a few drinks and a few sandwiches after each show, and we went over and we were thinking Oh God there's going to be trouble. They're going to be like 'What the fuck was all that about, we didn't like any of that', but they were just sitting on the floor in the lobby outside the 'Green Room' drinking cans of beer. I invited them in but they said 'We're okay here thanks, we'd sooner stay here, no problem'."

This was like nothing else that the youth of the day had seen or heard before, a visual and aural assault of the senses, this was their Elvis, their Beatles, their Stones. As the end of the song descended into a chaotic cacophony, the final scene became the defining snapshot of not only Johnny Rotten, but for the overall attitude of a new generation; A laser beam stare cutting through your television screen into the (dis)comfort of your living room.

Ladies and gentlemen, boys and girls, say hello to the Sex Pistols and punk rock.

8.1976 and all that.

"Play before you get good, because by the time you get good, you're too old to play."

Joey Ramone

The term 'punk' had been around for hundreds of years; in the Middle Ages, punk was a term for a prostitute or harlot. In the 20th century it was the American generic term for a worthless individual or 'bum'. Musically it had been used in reference to the sixties 'garage' bands, referred to, in hindsight, as proto-punk, a far cry from Sex Pistols et al style punk rock that was about to gain recognition in the U.K.

Fran Taylor: "I used to buy, instalment by instalment, a part work called 'The Story of Pop' and it also used to be on the radio every weekend. There was a whole section called Punk Rock and it was written by a guy called Roy Carr, who was one of the great writers for the *NME* at the time, and it was all about Sky Saxon, The Seeds, the Mysterions, Sam the Sham and the Pharaohs; you couldn't hear anything more different than what we were calling 'punk'. The word punk was being used over here early on but it had started in the States for The Ramones. The Ramones really were as near to a 'punk' band, as we understood it, as you could get, because what we had been into was 60's garage punk. So 'punk rock' had been around for a long time before 'our' punk rock came along."

Una Baines: "It's like Blondie and Talking Heads and all the CBGB's stuff were 'punk'… there's like a punk sound isn't there? The Ramones, that type of thing. But that's just one sound out of lots of different sounds and some people were just copying those sounds and I thought it was really boring. For me it was the philosophy and the politics that were the essence and that was projected through the music. It was quite political."

The American magazine *Punk* was published in January 1976 and featured a mixture of old and new rebellion; Lou Reed, Marlon Brando, Ramones and Talking Heads and it wouldn't be long before news sailed across the Atlantic, inspiring already established UK based magazines.

Andy T.: "I used to read *Zigzag* magazine. Kris Needs took it over from John Tobler. John and Pete Frame used to do the family tree stuff, and they wrote good stuff, they wrote about the hippie stuff. Then when the punk thing came, they sort of half embraced it, and they passed it onto Kris who ran with it."

Those who had been influenced at the Pistol's Free Trade Hall gigs were now joined by more converts who had witnessed their television appearance. The remainder of 1976 was taken up with people starting bands while established bands adjusted to the seismic aftershock of the Pistols. The race to get gigs was on. Manchester was spoilt for choice when it came to venues and the growth of pop music in the fifties and sixties had led to hundreds of bands needing places to play, and many unsuitable places were adapted so there was an outlet, plus some money to be made of course, from this new teenage movement.

In the sixties, Variety halls and bingo palaces, pubs and clubs, along with jazz and blues clubs, and even council owned buildings had modified their music policy to cater for the city's many 'beat' groups. Places such as The Corona in Gorton which was converted from a cinema to a dance hall in the 1950s, which in turn changed its name to The Southern Sporting Club which then hosted cabaret and dance nights throughout the 1960s including hosting The Beatles. It eventually turned into The Mayflower Club and became another legendary post-punk venue. This tradition of playing unusual and sometimes unsuitable places would carry on and incorporate some of the first punk gigs in the city.

THURSDAY AUGUST 12TH 1976

Buzzcocks - The Ranch Bar, Dale Street Manchester.

Buoyed by the reaction to their inaugural gig, the band quickly assembled a short set and set out to look for places to play. Pete Shelley was a regular at The Ranch so it was an ideal place to try out their increasing and improving repertoire. Although Foo Foo wasn't so sure.

Fred Carr: "I remember Buzzcocks played at The Ranch Bar but you wouldn't have known it was them; it was just four kids with no stage. They were just plugging in when we got there and they were in the corner, but punk hadn't… nobody had heard about punk then so we didn't really think anything of it."

Denise Shaw: "I went on a Thursday night one night in August '76. I don't know why I went on a Thursday because I worked full time but I did this particular night. When I got there they said that there was a band on and I was disappointed you know? 'Oh God a band! You're joking'. It was Buzzcocks. They only played 2 songs because Foo Foo cut 'em off because they were too loud but by then I was totally hooked"

Alan Keogh: "I was at that gig. That was fantastic."

Fantastic but short lived, as drummer John Maher points out.

John Maher: "The first of two planned gigs at The Ranch. Plugs pulled after ten minutes, someone came up and said 'Foo Foo says you're too loud!' The second gig was cancelled."

WEDNESDAY AUGUST 18TH 1976

Sex Pistols (support unknown) - The Lodestar, Ribchester, Ribble Valley, Lancashire.

Although not strictly Manchester, this is still an important gig and its random location illustrates the dearth of places to play. Ribchester is an old Roman village in between Blackburn and Preston.

Juliette J. Williams: "The Lodestar had a very enterprising female owner called Margaret. She also put The Boys on there. They also had a Bowie night which I used to go to on a Saturday with a friend from Great Harwood. She was into Soul and Disco so we'd alternate the weekends where she'd stay at our house and we'd go out to the local Soul and Disco places, then I'd go to her's and we'd go to the Bowie night at The Lodestar.

Odgie: "My first exposure to punk was when the Pistols played at The Lodestar at Ribchester, everybody thinks that the Free Trade Hall was *the* Northern gig but this would have been about February '76 because I remember it was cold so it was Winter at the start of '76. The Lodestar was a little club tucked away in the hills of Lancashire and it was run by Ma Grimshaw. She was sound but she was like a proper landlady you know? You didn't mess with her, but we got on fine with her. Anyway she was asking us for bands to play the Tuesday or Thursday nights or whatever. It was my mate Biggles who suggested the Sex Pistols, I'd never heard of them and nobody else had heard of them; this was pre-Free Trade Hall, pre-Grundy, pre-everything. He'd come across them from his contacts in London. Sex Pistols was quite a provocative name as well at that time; so she booked them. There were 10 or 12 people there, a typical quiet midweek night. There was a tiny stage and then these guys came out and it was just this wall of noise - BANG! What the fuck's this kind of thing, you know? It was chaos and random and just absolute noise for about 30 seconds and it morphed into 'Flowers Of Romance'. Anyway after about 3 tracks and we're all sat down with our mouths open and Rotten was like, 'You're all fucking boring' and so they went off into the back room. Ma Grimshaw's banging on the door, 'come out and play some more songs!' so they eventually came back on and did some more and then off they went. The next day I painted Sex Pistols on the back of my leather jacket. It was entirely random, entirely by chance, no design."

After quite a lot of digging around and trawling of a fair number of the Pistols related internet websites, I have found no evidence to corroborate Odgie's memory, although they did play there on Wednesday 18th August 1976 (not the 15th September as previously thought, it seems there is a lot of confusion about this gig!) There was also the added caveat of 'punk rock' in brackets underneath their name in the advert in the local paper.

Andy T.: "I went to The Lodestar and it was definitely August because it was definitely after the second Pistol's gig. They were just on, no support band, unless we got there too late. It wasn't overly busy, and I can't remember if there was even a stage. It was just at the end of a room, the bar was in another bit. They played their set and that was it. Basically there was me and a guy called Steve who used to go everywhere on his motorbike, loads of gigs, it got us everywhere except the Pistols gig in Huddersfield because of the snow. The Lodestar was a weird little club in the middle of nowhere. They used to have quite a few bands on. I think we saw The Vibrators there, and we definitely saw The Boomtown Rats there. They used to have like a Thursday night rock night and there was quite a few from Bolton who used to go, but it wasn't overly busy."

Alan and Ian stood out from the crowd.

Juliette J. Williams: "There were these two guys who didn't look quite the same as the others, who used to bring their own records which sounded quite strange; it was Ian (Odgie) and Allan (Deaves). One of the records must have been 'Anarchy…' The DJ, whoever it was, would mix in these few records in with the Bowie/Roxy stuff. I used to think, hang on a minute, what are those guys wearing? I think they had a padlock each on a chain around their necks, and we were wearing like cocktail dresses and a fox fur and a pillbox type of hat; a kind of 40's style, because that was what we were into at that time. Whereas they'd got their hair all messed up and when one of their records came on they'd jump around grappling each other. When I started going to The Ranch I saw them again, and they really stood out because Allan was really tall, mind you everybody's tall compared to me, so for me punk started in the middle of nowhere just outside Blackburn. That's where I first started hearing this stuff that didn't sound like everything else that you were listening to."

SATURDAY AUGUST 28TH 1976

Buzzcocks. Commercial Hotel, Melbourne St., Stalybridge, Tameside.

This gig was advertised as a double header with the Stalybridge gig on the 28th plus the 'Screen On The Green' gig in London the following day. It was the first piece of artwork that Linder Sterling designed for the band.

John Maher: "This was the first of two consecutive gigs over the Bank Holiday weekend. On Saturday 28th we turned up at the Commercial Inn, Stalybridge. Howard arranged it via his contacts at the *New Manchester Review*, Manchester's version of *Time Out*. The Commercial was a biker's pub. We did two twenty minute sets in front of a small, but hostile audience."

Martin Ryan: "The Commercial was one of the pubs on the Manchester pub rock circuit in '76. The bands on that circuit were mainly serious rock, with Yes and Genesis being a common influence. I suspect that it was their lack of familiarity with 'Fragile' or 'Trick Of The Tail' that turned the audience against them!."

John has another theory.

John Maher: "Howard's green glitter socks and red leather carpet slippers weren't appreciated by the long haired, leather-clad clientele. Neither was our performance."

Martin Ryan: "Towns on the edge of the countryside like Stalybridge or New Mills always had a biker element, although in their defence, I rarely if ever saw any trouble in biker pubs, unlike the jacketed 'smoothie' pubs."

Denise Shaw: "It was a great biker's pub, but it was for hardcore bikers who accepted nothing else!"

The rawness and inexperience of the band wasn't confined to an incompatible audience choice.

John Maher: "Earlier in the day I'd been to a music shop in town and bought a brand new snare drum head. I didn't realise there was a difference between the head that went on top (the 'batter' head) and the one fitted on the underside (snare head). I fitted my brand new snare head to the top side of the drum. Halfway through our first set my brand new snare head was completely caved in. Fortunately I kept the old one and refitted it during the interval."

But if the Stalybridge bikers weren't digging Buzzcocks' ethos, the following night's gig was a gathering of kindred spirits, and another landmark gig as this new movement was gathering momentum.

John Maher: "Once we'd packed our gear back in the van, we headed south. In 24 hours we were due on stage at the Screen on the Green, Islington - with the Sex Pistols and The Clash.

A few weeks later and back on home turf, the next gig would be a catalyst for change, gradually engaging more people into a scene that wasn't really a scene at the time.

MONDAY SEPTEMBER 20TH 1976

Buzzcocks/Eater. Houldsworth Hall, Deansgate.

While the first night of the 100 Club 'Punk Festival' was happening in London, Buzzcocks were warming up for their appearance there the next day with another gig in Manchester. Houldsworth Hall had been used in the past for a variety of events including wrestling matches and Jazz concerts and was even a makeshift Synagogue during the war, after the Reform Synagogue in Cheetham Hill was destroyed by German bombs, but the lack of suitable venues to play meant that the band's options were limited, and any place that would let them play was gratefully seized upon. As for Eater, at the tender age of 14 years old, it was a trip into the unknown. In 1976 Manchester was logistically a lot further away from London than today, and a journey up the spine of England was made without any accompanying familiar faces.

Andy Blade, guitarist with Eater, remembers it as a trip into the unknown.

Andy Blade: "Nope, it was totally a kamikaze gig, just us on our own. We caught the National Coach up there, with the drums in the hold! Initially, the gig was organised by me and my brother, then we got help from the Buzzcock's camp, regarding posters and PA hire etcetera. It was our first 'real' gig, beyond our bedroom. My brother lived with my dad in Salford so they helped out. On the whole my dad was appalled at the whole idea. He whispered to me about Pete Shelley after we'd picked him up from his parents house to give him a lift to the hall, 'be careful of that man, Andy, I think he is a homosexual' (*laughs*) Oh yeah, and we had no bass player."

The band were well aware of Manchester's very early significance in the growth of the new musical movement of punk.

Andy Blade: "That's why we chose it, and when the Buzzers offered tactical support for a place on the bill, we jumped at it. That, and the fact my dad and brother had just moved up there from London."

Buzzcocks were starting to burn their way into the consciousness of the wider local music-loving community, they were no longer the property of just the fledgling Punk *cognoscenti* in the city and beyond.

Fran Taylor: "I got back from university and my mates are raving about having gone to see this band the Sex Pistols, and more importantly a band from Manchester called Buzzcocks. They must have seen Slaughter and the Dogs obviously because they were on the same bill but nothing was said about them until much later. Suddenly Buzzcocks have got a gig coming up at Houldsworth Hall in Deansgate, now that was part of there being nowhere to play. It's like the Lesser Free Trade Hall, I'd never heard of it before, I'd been to the Free Trade Hall but I didn't know anything about the Lesser Free Trade Hall. Some smart guys have thought 'that's a good place for a gig' and as we know that was Howard and Pete. So they've done the same with this one. I'd been in Manchester and Salford all my life and I'd never heard of Houldsworth Hall. So we find where it is and we rock up, and we're told that there's going to be no booze on, so we go to the pub until it's time for it to kick off. So we go in and it's this big old Victorian vaulted ceiling type of place, quite a big place but with a very high ceiling. There's a stage and people scattered around; people I don't know as yet, and some very strange looking people I have to say. You've got to remember that I'm coming from a sort of heavy rock background, so me and my mates, we're all 'longhairs'. We all usually go and see bands like the Quo, but we're into Iggy Pop and MC5 but it's still very much 'longhair' stuff. I was a big Bowie fan but never got the haircut or anything, it was just about the music."

Things were about to change for Fran and his mates in the following minutes, it was a pattern that would continue for the following months, as the impact spread throughout the city.

Andy T.: "It was all seats, because they used to have bands like

Humble Pie play there, completely different to what the Circus was like, which was just a scabby room. It was there that I met Wispa from The Drones for the first time."

It was also Richard Boon's first gig as Buzzcocks manager. In the true spirit of punk, it's been (wrongly) documented that a coin was tossed to see who was going to headline the gig and that Eater guessed correctly.

Andy Blade: "The 'flip a coin' story; we've been hearing it for years and it niggles a bit, because it's totally false. We advertised the gig before the Buzzers were on board as a 'Punk Rock Special with guests'. When they confirmed, after we met Richard Boon who was helping with the promotional stuff, we were very happy to have them play. But the posters read; Eater + Buzzcocks, so the coin toss story is definitely bullshit. That myth has been around too long! I don't mind that they nicked all the door money, but I'd like to get the details right! I wished they'd suggested to me the folly of us headlining, but alas they probably took us for guys that knew what we were doing!"

So Buzzcocks took to the stage first after a memorable introduction.

Fran Taylor: "This girl comes on stage, with like a Bowie haircut, and she just screams 'THE BUZZCOCKS ARE GONNA FUCK YOU!' and on come the band, who are a rag-tag looking bunch; skinny singer, a lot of sequins and too much eye make-up. They get into it and fucking hell, I was blown away. I'm like, 'what is this?' Then they do a couple of songs that I recognise, one is a Monkees' song, which at the moment I can't remember the name, and the Beefheart song 'I Love You Big Dummy'. I'm totally overwhelmed, this is amazing, things are starting to warm up and people are starting to bounce around a bit. They're singing about taking lines, friends, and it all resonates with me, and my mates are going bonkers, and the next thing I know, bang they're gone. There's a bit of a lull and then this bunch of kids come on, although I don't really remember much about them, and that was Eater. I came out of there on a massive high. Then it was all about 'when's the next one?'"

Andy Blade: "To say we went down badly would be an insult to 'badly'! Our set was, literally, verging on a riot, thanks to my decision to start baiting the audience as 'northern wankers' and slagging off Manchester United. Overtly hostile would be an understatement. Our whole set consisted of us being showered with missiles, including sandwiches; I mean, who brings sandwiches to gigs? I thought it might have been a northern thing! The only one time I ever met anyone who attended that gig was at the Pistol's gig at Notre Dame Hall. A guy came up to me and told me he thought we were 'shit hot'. It took me a while to comprehend that this meant he liked us! I just heard the word 'shit' and agreed."

The overwhelming factor of the night was just how young some of the members of the bands. Especially Eater.

John Maher: "It was back to school for me the next morning."

Andy Blade: "Even 16 was way too old for us!"

MONDAY 8TH NOVEMBER 1976

Buzzcocks/Bob Williamson/ The Phantom Band/C.P. Lee
Band On The Wall, Swan St. Manchester.

This was billed as the *New Manchester Review's* second anniversary gig.

Mark Windsor; I went to see Buzzcocks at the Band On The Wall and it was rammed. They were rough as a dog's arse and looked nervous and it seemed feasible. I wrote in my diary; 'Decided to become a punk band. Wrote three songs tonight. They're really good. I think one of them was 'Speed Freak', and I remember thinking, 'It can't be this easy can it?"

WEDNESDAY 10TH NOVEMBER 1976

Buzzcocks/Chelsea - The Electric Circus, Collyhurst, Manchester.

Fran Taylor: "I think the first punk gig at The Electric Circus was Chelsea supported by Buzzcocks, so we all went to see Buzzcocks. Chelsea were basically Generation X with Gene October singing. That would have been November. I don't think that there were thirty people in the place, including the bands. It was pretty sparse. I'm not sure if that's when I first saw Denise but you started to notice the same faces popping up. People made their own connections in various places. Jon (The Postman) was a face you'd see. People used to recognise Jon because he would never keep quiet at any gig, he'd always shout, whether he loved or hated the band he'd still shout his head off."

Denise Shaw: "All I remember is getting to this place in Collyhurst and going in. There were about 20-30 people at most in there, and then I got talking to Linder Sterling. She came over to me and started chatting. That was the night I met Jon The Postman as well. That's when I took the photo of Howard sat on the stage. He must have been thinking, 'My God, 30 people' you know?

SUNDAY 28TH NOVEMBER 1976

Slaughter and the Dogs/The Damned or Buzzcocks/Slaughter and the Dogs. - The Electric Circus, Collyhurst, Manchester.

There is an air of confusion about this gig. According to posters of the night, The Damned were playing support to Slaughter and the Dogs, whereas it's also documented that Buzzcocks played this night, supported by Slaughter and the Dogs! On the White Rabbit website, which documents a comprehensive Damned gigography, this night is listed as being correct. Although whether that information is based solely on the poster is another matter. Martin Ryan's book 'Friends Of Mine' states that it was in fact a Buzzcocks/Slaughter double bill. Ambiguities and 'ghost' gigs would be quite a common thread throughout the early tenure of Punk.

Andy T.: "There's loads of flyers on the internet, but a lot of those (Slaughter and the Dogs) gigs didn't happen; you'd get there and it would be a different band on you know? Unfortunately I didn't keep a diary."

The rumour mill in those early days was rife with misinformation; it was a musical version of 'Fake News'.

Fran Taylor: "There was a huge rumour that went around town that the Sex Pistols were playing at a teacher training college in Didsbury. So we all traipsed down to Didsbury, it never happened, some shite band turned up. We never quite knew if it was a con just to get people down there or whatever, but we wouldn't take no for an answer. Even when people told us 'No, Sex Pistols aren't playing here', we still bought tickets and went in just in case. We'd pretty much go and see anything because we were caught up in this thing of not quite knowing where you were, so whatever came along you listen to it."

Gail Egan: "What used to happen was that the bands often played in Town Halls, then right at the last minute, I mean we didn't have mobile phones then obviously, the caretaker or whoever would try to cancel it or the Police would get involved, so it was all word of mouth. So some things were on the last minute, because if you advertised them, they wouldn't happen."

Fran Taylor: "There was another gig near the end of '76 where Buzzcocks played with Slaughter and the Dogs at the Circus, just before Howard left. We went along and like I said Jon The Postman could never keep his mouth shut and he wasn't keen on Slaughter and the Dogs. So he started shouting out 'Pop band' and giving them a hard time, and

Mick Rossi's brother came down and went for Jon in the audience. My mate Tony just smacked him across the head with a Newcastle Brown bottle."

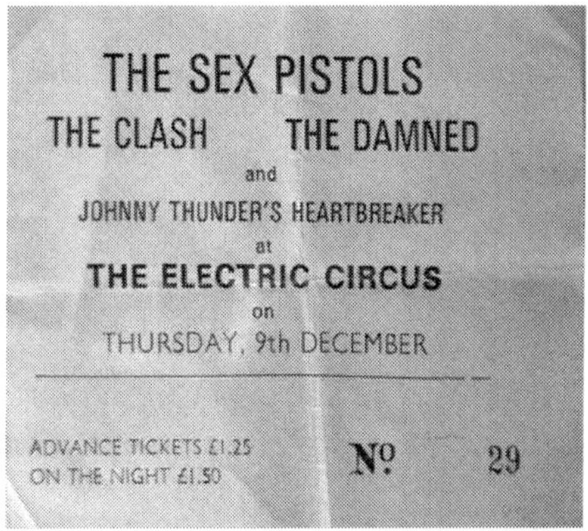

THURSDAY DECEMBER 9TH 1976

Sex Pistols/The Clash/The Damned/Buzzcocks/Johnny Thunder's Heartbreaker (sic) - The Electric Circus, Collyhurst, Manchester.

The nationwide paranoia that the Sex Pistols had instilled into the great British public's minds on the Bill Grundy show led to many places refusing to let them play but The Electric Circus became one of the few venues to allow these pariahs of society their freedom of expression. The band played at The Circus twice in quick succession in December 1976, the first time was on Thursday the 9th just over a week after their infamous Bill Grundy interview had made them both a musical curiosity and public enemy number one.

Martin Ryan: "I knew people in Marple who knew Bill Grundy, and he was an alcoholic and the most loathsome, obnoxious man, and he lived in Marple Bridge. Me and Mick (Middles) went into his local, The Midland, one night between Christmas and New Year in 1976, and we both had straight jeans on, and I think Mick had an orange cagoule on which I thought was quite 'punky'. We went in to try and wind him up but it didn't work because he carried on talking to his mates and ignored us."

Ian Moss: "The first night of the Anarchy tour rivalled Cardiff v United for violence. It was horrible because it was just after the Grundy thing, and the press had cast a very prejudicial eye over proceedings and so when you're going into an area like Collyhurst and it was no fun."

They certainly had form for this, a few months earlier on April 23rd the band were supporting the 101'ers at The Nashville in London when, unimpressed by the lack of audience reaction, Vivienne Westwood instigated a fight which eventually saw McLaren and the rest of the band joining in. Fighting at Pistols gigs would become the norm with the band themselves instigating something if things were getting too amicable. It was all part of the pantomime. Unfortunately this would have tragic consequences when a girl was partially blinded by a glass thrown, allegedly by Sid Vicious, during The Damned's set on the second night of the Punk Festival at the 100 Club on September 21st 1976.

So for the third time in six months the Pistols were back in Manchester.

Fran Taylor: "December 9th comes around and the Pistols turn up. This was just after the whole Grundy thing and things were kicking off on their tour, and they couldn't get gigs. So we went to The Castle to meet up and only two of us turned up, me and my mate Dave. We sat there in the pub looking at each going, 'Are we gonna go? Yeah fuck it, let's go'. So we went for a few beers and got tanked up before we went, and it was rammed in there."

The place was packed out alright but the crowd that turned up were there for a variety of reasons.

Alan Keogh: "I would say the audience that were there for the music may have been less than 50-50. They'd built up an infamy, so a lot of people just went along you know? Plus Manchester United's firm were in."

Denise Shaw: "I hated it when it got to that stage because of all the media, all these people turning up just to see the Sex Pistols. They didn't want the music, they didn't dress likes us, they were there to either cause trouble or just gawp."

Martin Ryan: "The Pistols on the Anarchy tour, it was a bit of a mixture, there was curiosity at that one. They got a fair reception but they weren't hardcore punks, they were just going for curiosity. Which to an extent I suppose I was you know."

Chris Lambert: "Moral panic.....just there to see what it's all about, a freak show."

Andy T.: "It was like everybody had heard about them because it had been in the papers and on the telly, even though we didn't get to see the programme. That was a couple of days after almost. It was your parents that were talking about this band that you quite liked the idea of, and mentioning these punk rockers. They were saying to me, 'You know some of them don't you?'"

Mark Windsor: "My mate Dave, who was the singer in V2, had been to one of the Sex Pistols gigs at the Free Trade Hall, more likely the second one, and we were on the bus going into town and he was describing this band. I'd not heard of punk rock or anything and he was telling me about the band; the lead singer had holes in his jumper and he was wiping his nose and spitting and the sound was just... I was thinking, this sounds horrible!"

Stanley Vegas: "The first time that I went to see the Pistols was at the Lesser Free Trade Hall, the second one. Then I saw them at the Electric Circus on the Anarchy tour that pretty much got cancelled apart from a few gigs. I went to that one with Wayne Barrett and Wayne got me into the sort of VIP bit upstairs. Johnny Thunders was there, he was off his fucking tits on Nembutal. I'm pretty sure that they must have just had a big payout because Johnny Rotten was at the bar ordering loads of drinks. Wayne knew him pretty well so he goes, "Go on then, me and Stan'll have one'. So he ordered them up but he didn't get himself a drink, so Wayne said, "Aren't you having one yourself?" And he said, "No, I've bought my own", and brought out a bottle of Night Nurse from his pocket!"

Stephen Perrin: "My first trip to the Electric Circus was to see the Anarchy Tour in December 1976. It was bloody freezing and we all had to queue up outside while the bands sound checked and local kids threw half bricks at us. Once we got in, however, there was the sense that something had changed and that our time had come. We were going to do it our way and it was going to be different and better. We were going to colour in the picture with different crayons."

Fred Carr: "We heard that the Pistols were on at the Electric Circus. Me and my mates, a guy called Paddy and guy called Sparky, were like... I think that one of The Drones' girlfriends named her three cats after us! Anyway, so we went down to the Circus and Buzzcocks came on first and Howard Devoto had this dummy with him, and one of their songs was 'I Love You Big Dummy' and he was singing to it. The Heartbreakers came on and they were just like any other band and The Clash were the same, I don't think that I was taking much notice to be honest. As soon as the Pistols came on, there was this bright light as the lights came on and someone threw a full pint pot of beer into Johnny Rotten's face. The music started and he was just like, fucking hell. He wasn't expecting it and he was so annoyed and he was just staring, he had this manic stare. The night was amazing; it was just crazy and everybody was jumping about. They were being spat at as well, I'd not seen that before. To be critical of your superiors was not acceptable, in terms of society, and I'd never seen someone be so blatantly critical of society as he was. But to be so openly in your face, I'd never seen anything like it, it was like 'fuck you'. It changed my whole philosophy. To be honest I don't remember any of the music, it all sounded exactly the same to me. My mate Sparky took loads of great photos at the time, but someone nicked them and sold them. From that night my life changed, just that one thing. I'd gone from being a weirdo to someone who's part of something you know? It was like... fuck off, just fuck off, you know?"

Fran Taylor: "In the early days of The Electric Circus, when they first started doing punk gigs, the top bar used to still be open, the balcony. They had to shut it, because it couldn't take any weight, but I can't remember when they did shut it, but there came a point when you no longer went upstairs to that top bar. It was definitely open at the first Pistols gig there, because that's where the bands used to hang out quite often because the dressing room was a shithole, I mean literally it was like a toilet.

"You had to go through the crowd to get to the dressing room, so the bands would tend to be hanging about on the balcony waiting for their turn to go on. I remember going up, must have been the first gig rather than the second and they still had the old cinema seats, and I was walking down the aisle and Paul Cook was on one side and Steve Jones was sitting on the other side and as I walked back down I acknowledged them. 'Alright lads?' and Steve Jones just went, 'Fuck off'!"

Una Baines: "I remember 'Anarchy In The U.K.' coming out and I remember hearing it on the radio for the first time and how amazing it was to hear that song on the radio with those lyrics. It was just so exciting, and every time I hear the beginning of that song... wow! I loved the record but I didn't like the name Sex Pistols; a bit phallic."

Mickey Tait: "Somebody told me about a gig at the Electric Circus, which was the Sex Pistols. I think that Subway Sect were on (they weren't), Buzzcocks with Howard Devoto, The Clash, who were absolutely brilliant, I thought that The Clash were better than the Pistols – the way they dressed and their whole attitude."

Andy T.: "I'd seen Buzzcocks before at the Circus and the Band On The Wall. They were brilliant, they were really good, they were much more impressive than the Pistols were. I don't know... they were... different. The Pistols were a standard rock and roll band really. I mean I'd been listening to music since the early 60's because I had two elder sisters, and I had inherited a little Dansette record player and some records, so I always had music around. Consequently the Pistols didn't really blow me away quite so much musically. The first time that they played at the Circus, they were much better than they'd been at Ribchester, they came across really well. So did The Clash and the Heartbreakers were just out of this world. I'd missed seeing the New York Dolls. I was into them since the first album because I had a girlfriend who worked in a record shop in Rochdale, and it was a chart return shop, so they got everything in early. They got all the posters and all that stuff and basically we got to take stuff home, probably weren't allowed to but… so we'd tape it and take it back the day after! That first Dolls album, you look at the cover and think 'Yeah that's the sort of thing I'm into."

By the end of the year, the hardcore number of 'punks' was growing slowly, but it was a case of quality over quantity.

Fran Taylor: "In '76 there were various faces we got to know. There was this one guy called Barney who always wore a short-sleeved White shirt and tie, very smartly turned out and not very punky at all. One night we were chatting away and he says to us, 'You might not see much of me in the next few months, I'm starting a band.' So we go to this Sex Pistols gig and there's Barney, and he sees me and grabs hold of me 'Where's Jon The Postman?' and I told him that he'd bottled it, he wasn't coming. So he goes 'Right come on, you're with us' and he pulls me into this crowd of fellas he's with, including a couple of his old mates who I'd seen before; one was a bloke called Peter Hook and another guy called Terry Mason plus a guy who I didn't know at the time but turned out to be Ian Curtis. So you've got Joy Division right there, or Warsaw as they were then. So I spent the evening jumping around with them, enjoying what was probably the best punk gig ever. You're talking about Buzzcocks starting, Clash next, Johnny Thunders and the Heartbreakers, Sex Pistols. It was £1.50 on the door to get into that. Mind you £1.50 was a lot of money then; it was pretty much 10 pints in 1976."

FRIDAY 17TH DECEMBER 1976

The Drones/Generation X/Martin Ellis. Houldsworth Hall, Deansgate

Once again Houldsworth Hall was the venue for Punk as the scene gathered momentum around the city, and it was another Manchester/London double bill.

Fran Taylor: "Generation X did a gig with The Drones, it must have been one of their first gigs after they'd left Chelsea, at The Houldsworth

Hall again. I can't remember if I went to that, people tell me that I did but I can't remember that I did."

Wispa: "The first major gig we did was with Tony Davidson, who was our manager at the time. He put us on at Houldsworth Hall with a band from London, and it was billed as 'Hi Energy Punk Night'. There was no alcohol on sale, just soft drinks, the support band were Generation X, their first gig outside of London; Billy Idol on vocals and Brian James on guitar, it all went on from there really. I don't think ours were the best songs at that time but a lot of thought and a lot of meaning went into them."

Denise Shaw: "I can't remember when I first saw The Drones play, they must have played somewhere before because I remember going to the Houldsworth Hall one because I've got the poster for it. I knew them before then, so where we'd met I don't know - whether we'd met The Ranch or at one of the gigs? They were a bit showy, I remember thinking that Mike was a bit of a poser, whereas the rest of the band looked the part, Mike never seemed to fit in even though he was a good singer."

As for the Sex Pistols, the furore over the Grundy incident had escalated to the extent that it resulted in the 'Anarchy In The UK' tour becoming even more disrupted and shambolic, and this led to the band playing The Circus again on Sunday the 19th. This hastily arranged date was due to the scheduled gig in Guildford being cancelled but this time the appetite for the hype had waned and it was just the music that drew the crowd.

SUNDAY 19TH DECEMBER 1976

Sex Pistols/The Clash/The Damned/Johnny Thunders and the Heartbreakers. - The Electric Circus, Collyhurst, Manchester.

Fran Taylor: "The Circus started doing the odd punk gig in '76 but not regularly. When the Pistols came back on 19th December we all went to that one... nobody there. It was practically deserted compared to the first one, because a lot of curious people turned up for the first one and went 'that's not for us'. The early punk gigs at The Circus weren't exactly packed out. Some were and some weren't."

Mickey Carr: "I went to the two Sex Pistols gigs at the Circus... they did two didn't they quite close together.

Mickey Tait: "I went to the second one as well. So yeah, went to see the Pistols and that was me then... I was a proper, you know... White spiky hair, leather gear on, ripped T-shirt and ready to rock and roll."

Chris Lambert: "I can remember the second time Lydon came on and said, 'we've got rid of all the tourists'"

Ian Moss: "Weirdly, when the Pistols came back two weeks later, or 10 days later, whatever, it was already over by then, you know. There was less than half the number of people there, there was no hint of trouble, it was all... it was back to normal, back to how it was before."

Andy T.: "The only reason we knew about it was that there was a poster stuck up in Virgin Records. It was the poster for the first gig, and someone had put a 1 in front of the 9 on the date. They didn't have any tickets because it was 3 days before."

Fred Carr: "The Pistols couldn't play the rest of the country so they came back two weeks later. But it wasn't the same, it was flat as a pancake. I remember some of the band's entourage being at the bar and Johnny Rotten was on stage calling out to Malcolm McLaren, 'Get me a drink Malcolm', but it wasn't the same."

Andy T.: "After the second Anarchy tour gig, people just dissipated and you were left with the ones who were properly into it rather than come to see a spectacle."

Despite the fewer numbers this gig attracted, it was the night that Joe Strummer felt that The Clash had surpassed the Pistols as a live act. He noted that the Pistols, 'had a really hard time following us, we blew them off stage'.

Steve Shy: "I remember when the world's press were looking for the Pistols, they're on the front of every paper, it was the Anarchy Tour. They were at the Midland Hotel, press everywhere, but they'd fucked off, they were getting absolutely legless in Tommy Ducks. They loved Tommy Ducks because it had about 400 pairs of knickers hanging off the ceiling. If you were a girl and you went in there, if you took your knickers off and give them to 'em you got a free drink. Also, they had a table and it was like a coffin with a glass cover and it had a skeleton in, stuff like that. It was a really weird pub, but they loved it in there. Anyway they got kicked out of the Midland that night and finished up at the Arosa in Withington."

All the attention was now on the Pistols, they were all over the newspapers, their notoriety was beginning to overshadow the music and they were in danger of becoming pantomime villains.

Dawn Bradbury: "Malcolm used to milk it for everything he could get out of it."

Brian Grantham: "I think from the start, with Vivienne Westwood and Sex shop in London and all that – he had a vision anyway, Malcolm. He'd had the New York Dolls which the Pistols in a kind of way came from. He wanted to make money, and he did make money, plus he wanted to make it global, and he made it global."

Ian Moss: "I don't think a lot of that went on in the early days of the Pistols. McLaren would claim things after the event to make it look like he'd managed or mismanaged it. Like the Grundy thing; by all accounts he was horrified, and it was only the next day that he sees that it was gold."

SPIRAL SCRATCH EP

Tuesday December 28th 1976
Indigo Studios, Gartside Street, Manchester.

In another first for Manchester this was a truly independent punk record release: self-financed, self-promoted, and even self-assembled. The band had already recorded their expanding set in Revolution Studios in Stockport in October, putting down 12 tracks at breakneck speed, 11 of which would be infamously bootlegged as 'Time's Up', all for the princely sum of £45 for four hours work. The initial idea behind it was basically just to get something recorded for posterity, a piece of work which would be left behind once this new, exciting musical direction had blown over, as the band's manager Richard Boon explains.

Richard Boon: "There was a group of people in Manchester with a community interest that was very different to anything in London. People found that they had friends with a common interest, and would just socialise outside these sporadic, key events. People began to hang out together. No-one was really sure if this was going to become a career, it just seemed worth documenting the activity, perhaps as the end result, perhaps the only result."

The record was also a community effort, financed by a number of individuals who were prepared to put their faith in the band.

Fran Taylor: "If I remember correctly they needed £500 to print the first run of Spiral Scratch; nobody had it. Pete Shelley's dad put some money in, there was a girl called Sue Cooper who was one of Richard's old university friends, her dad was in the film business and she put £200 in, and basically they scratched together the £500. That's how difficult it was to get £500 back then, it was a fucking fortune, an absolute fortune. Don't forget, the records were cheaper to produce than the covers. When they did the first run they had more records than covers, so they actually sat in a back room in Broughton and hand quality controlled the ones that were going to go in the covers. They made sure that the best ones went into the covers."

The band had also picked a local 'producer', someone who wasn't the standard, run of the mill thinker when it came to sounds.

Chris Hewitt: "Martin Hannett produced 'Spiral Scratch' and he also produced an album for a left wing theatre company from Sheffield, and an African band. Martin was around for years before punk. Martin was a Grateful Dead fan, a Steely Dan fan. He was listening to Jazz at 11 and he was mad on hi-fi and sound equipment, you know?"

That grounding was paramount to Hannett's ideology of how to experiment, and he brought this obtuse angle to how a band should sound, and it would go on to turn his work into something approaching cult status. A conventional 'rock' sound wasn't in his psyche at all.

Martin Hannett: "When you play it (Spiral Scratch) loud, it sounds exactly as if you're right in front of the stage at one of their gigs. I was very disappointed when the Sex Pistols album came out with seventeen guitar overdubs."

Fran Taylor: "Independent records had been made before by a number of people, but it was the first of the punk movement, and the movement that was coming along followed that blueprint."

The record was well received by the music writers, with *Melody Maker* gushing, "This is fast, sparse, and red hot with the living spirit and emotion of rock 'n' roll". But perhaps more importantly, by their friends and peers.

Fred Carr: "What a fucking great EP that was. We used to play it all the time before we went out, fucking brilliant."

Mark Windsor: "Buzzcocks put Spiral Scratch out and it was on Granada Reports and I was like… fuckin' hell some blokes have put their own record out, and they're writing their own stuff, and they're from round here?"

Una Baines: "We (The Fall) used to meet at my flat and listen to music, and I remember when we first heard Buzzcocks first single, that two note guitar solo… what it sounded like, and I'll always remember this, it was like a signal to tell everyone, it's time for action. That was the feeling I got and I can't even explain it."

John Maher: "We'd ordered 1000 copies, having no idea whether they'd sell or not; they were all gone in four days."

Pete Shelley: "We rejected about 25. It was a memento. It was early days, there was no record company interest or anything like that."

Steve Shy: "Buzzcocks had a flat on Lower Broughton Road. I can remember putting Spiral Scratch in the covers and that, and we'd go down like... I'd be going home and Richard (Boon) would be going to Red Star at Piccadilly Station to send another 100 copies to Rough Trade, on the train overnight."

Gail Egan: "I remember sat helping them sell it in The Ranch. It came in a plain cardboard cover and they were all, what would they have been, 50p or something?"

John Maher:"Spiral Scratch was delivered to us in plain white sleeves. Being new to the game we'd ordered the picture sleeves separately. A couple of weeks prior to the release date, we spent a Saturday afternoon in the back room of Lower Broughton Street transferring all 1000 copies of the EP into the picture sleeves. We learned our lesson; we made sure the pressing plant had the proper sleeves for the next 15,000 copies."

Fran Taylor: "There was no shortage of people who would help with the basics of getting a record made. There were guys out there ready to print anything. A lot of thrown together magazines were made in Tib Street, there used to be a company that used to print these things; pamphlets, that sort of thing. Whatever was the latest fad they'd print up a 20 page booklet or whatever. They did it for Bowie and loads of people and flogged them at gigs. If you went to a Bowie gig they'd be outside selling posters, it was just about making money and riding on the back of whatever new thing was going on. Morrissey wrote a book for one of these companies about the New York Dolls in 1981, which is very much a collector's piece these days. Manchester was a centre for printing, there was a company called World Distributors and they would print anything. If you look at the tickets for some of the early punk gigs, they were printed by the same company who did wedding invitations. Tickets for The Ranch were on this curly edged paper with Purple edges; exactly the same as 'Rita and so-and-so invite you to their wedding'. They didn't fucking care as long as they were making money out of it. Manchester was a centre for do it yourself stuff, it was just a matter of marrying the individual bits."

The single was reviewed in February's issue of *Sniffin' Glue* with the complete lyrics to 'Breakdown' being reprinted next to a grainy picture of Howard Devoto. The review read, "*This group IS the new wave. Buy it. If you don't, you shouldn't be reading this mag.*" It also gave the mail order details for those who couldn't buy it in their particular part of the UK. Spiral Scratch received its first airplay when John Peel played it a few days after release.

Fran Taylor: "I remember going round one time and there were piles of records sitting on the mantelpiece and shelves. This was way after the record had been released, and way after Howard had left, quite late into 1977. I asked Richard what they were and he told me that they were the rejects, the ones that couldn't be put into covers, and they were just sitting on the shelves in piles."

Mickey Carr: "When Buzzcocks released the Spiral Scratch EP they did a promotional thing, where they released balloons with a tab on, and if you found one you could fill it in and take it, or post it back and you got the EP. Of course we were straight behind the counter weren't we getting a load and when we got home like, we'd fill them in from various addresses so we all got the record, a result really."

Mickey is right in saying that there was a promotional stunt including tagged balloons, but this was for their debut album 'Another Music In a Different Kitchen'. According to Tony McGartland's book, 'Buzzcocks - The Complete History' the *Daily Mirror* Pop Club released balloons from various Virgin record stores and whoever found one would receive a free album.

Meanwhile the 'Time's Up' bootleg would be the most extensive outlet of those early songs, and there was a roaring trade in the city to be had.

Fran Taylor: "Bootlegs in Manchester was quite a thriving trade and it was based around Tib Street. Dawn's (Bradbury) boyfriend of the time use do all of that. Dawn would do a lot of taping and her boyfriend used to make bootlegs. I believe he was responsible for 'Time's Up'. They were made from the original demo tapes, so I'm not sure how he got hold of them but they used to get Linguaphone to press them."

Andy T.: "I collected bootlegs but never actually recorded any, I wish I had now, but some people did record certain things."

It would be eight months until their next official release, by which time Buzzcocks were one of the main players in Punk.

9. the electric circus

"Manchester was way ahead of everybody in the first days of punk. Why? We had a marvellous meeting place called The Electric Circus"

Tony Wilson

Collyhurst was a down at heel area on the north-east side of town, one mile from the city centre, and a million miles from the future ghastly trends of 'gentrification' and the fake cosmopolitan bullshit of the 'Northern Quarter'. In the 60's it was the age old cliché that to get out of poverty and improve your chances of a better life and prevent yourself from becoming factory fodder, you either had to excel at sport or be able to make people laugh, which did have a ring of truth to it as Collyhurst was the birthplace of the mercurial footballer Stan Bowles, Manchester United's 1966 World Cup winner Nobby Stiles, and curmudgeon-faced comedian Les Dawson.

Its other redeeming feature was the distinctive red sandstone from Collyhurst Quarry which was used in the construction of Manchester Cathedral and St. Ann's church in the city centre. The Industrial Revolution brought chemical, dye, and gas works to the area which enveloped the streets and houses with a thick black smoke, and the living conditions were squalid and cramped. By the 1960's Collyhurst was still experiencing some of the worst deprivation and living conditions in the country. A newspaper reporter visited the area of Livesy Street in 1964 and wrote of a dystopian scene: 'vagrants and prowlers scavenge in the streets by night, with those remaining residents unwilling to go out, and small fires burning on the ground'. It was still a challenging place to frequent just over a decade later.

The original Electric Circus was the Andy Warhol-run East Village discotheque in New York in the mid sixties where The Velvet Underground performed as the house band as part of a multi-media experience known as the "Exploding Plastic Inevitable". In March 1970, a bomb went off on the dance floor of that Electric Circus, purportedly set by the Black Panthers. Though never proven, it was enough to tarnish the club's image and keep patrons away. It finally closed its doors in 1971. The original 'Electric Circus' in Manchester was initially the title given to Sunday nights at Mr. Brown's, a nightclub on Brazil Street in the late

60's and early 70's. In 1970 a 21 year-old John Cooper Clarke performed his poetry there, situated eloquently between the usual progressive and hard rock bands of the time. Those Sunday evenings promised 'Poets, Dancers, Lights, Rock Disco, and Surprises'.

The Electric Circus in Collyhurst opened as a Rock venue at the end of October 1976, and was run by Business Manager Allan Robinson and Entertainments Manager Graham Brooks. The pair had been involved with the aforementioned 'Waves' club on Dantzic Street but after a rift with the management there they decided to open up their own place. Their opening night's entertainment being supplied by a band from Liverpool called Supercharge, who drew a reasonably sized crowd despite their only chart success being a number 3 hit in Australia earlier in the year, although they had opened for Queen at a free concert in Hyde Park the previous month. Ironically the band was signed to Virgin Records, who would go on to add a number of groups to their roster that emerged out of the punk era.

Fran Taylor: "Shortly after that Buzzcocks gig, one of my best mates Ged says to me 'you know those two guys who've got Waves? They've opened up a new place. It's out in Collyhurst and it's called The Electric Circus. That's why the logo for The Electric Circus is like a heavy 'hairy' with a microphone; because it's the same two guys, Graham and another bloke who had Waves."

Martin Ryan: "Graham and Allan, who managed it, were serious rock fans, in fact Allan played drums in a band. They opened it to put on kind of mid-level bands between the pubs and somewhere bigger."

Wispa: "I knew the two guys, two ex-students, who ran it, Allan and Graham. They were just mates and they saw punk slowly drifting in... they were just about getting the Circus going, they were getting a few heavy rock bands in there, like The Enid and people like that, you know? I think Beefheart played there at some time as well (he didn't), and there were odd midweek gigs. The wheels of punk were just starting to turn and they'd gone down to The Squat on Diva Street and The Stranglers were playing. [They didn't have a] record company at this stage, nothing, in fact I think that at the time they were still The Guildford Stranglers. Alan and Graham approached the band after the gig and told them that they were trying to get this venue off the ground, and would they consider playing the next summer, I think this was in 1975. So they said 'yeah, yeah we'll give it a shot', and so they signed them up to play for £200 there and then. When they eventually played the place was full and it was a great night, and that was how we got to know The Stranglers. We got on really well with them."

Although it's surroundings may not have been the most salubrious, the building itself had a Gothic charm.

Denise Shaw: "What an amazing venue, you look at those windows. The architecture on that building was amazing. It was an old cinema and an old music hall."

Fran Taylor: "It used to be a place called The Paradise or The Paramount, and it had been a Bernard Manning kind of cabaret place, and it had also been a cinema at one time. We went down the first night, it must have been October '76, and it was a heavy rock disco. It was pretty much the people who used to go to Waves; greasers, women with long dresses all the way down to the floor etc. We didn't think too much more of it."

Andy T.: "I think it was still a club in '76, but you had bands like Deaf School and Doctors Of Madness playing there. Come to think of it Doctors Of Madness was my first gig at the Circus, before the Anarchy tour."

Initially there were no Punk records to play so the choice of music would still be the staple diet of standard rock fare.

Chris Lambert: "The only records they always seemed to play were 'The Boys Are Back In Town' and Lynyrd Skynyrd."

Andy T.: "They used to play all kinds of bits and bobs. I remember that Doctors Of Madness were quite popular."

Martin Ryan: "You could hire it in the week when it first opened."

Although it started out as a Heavy Rock venue, it soon became an important home to the burgeoning punk scene in the city.

Andy T.: "I first got to know the guys at the Circus because the local music shop, Tractor Music from Rochdale, supplied the PA. There was one of the gigs in '76 where this guy turns up with a PA and I knew him so I helped him to take it in, and basically through that I ended up with a membership card."

That guy with the P.A. was Chris Hewitt.

Chris Hewitt: "I'd been working with Ian Dury when it was Kilburn and the High Roads, in '75/'76, I was working with Carol Grimes and the London Boogie Band, a French band called Little Bob Story, and an English soul band called Sheer Elegance. So I was doing PA's for them in London, so then I thought I'd start a PA company in the north, so as I came up it just so happened that The Electric Circus opened, so I ended up doing the sound at The Electric Circus. I could be doing

The Lurkers or The Adverts one night, and Stray, Strife or Motörhead the next night, and in actual fact you'd see the same people quite often because there weren't enough punks to fill a punk gig and there weren't enough hippies to fill a hippy gig. So the battle lines weren't drawn like they were in London, and I think that the hippie/punk crossover happened more in the north than anywhere else.

"I worked with The Damned, I did the first Adverts tour and obviously there's lots of punks in the audience but we had this soundman called Kieron and he was a Hell's Angel. Gaye Advert used to borrow his studded belt and, as I said, there were lots of punks in the audience but all the crew would be... I mean most of the sound crews for the punk bands were hippies. A lot of the punk bands were quite young and had been thrust into this situation where they were doing tours, and a lot of the people who were touring with them were hippies anyway, so it was all a bit of a mish-mash"

Martin Ryan: "We saw The Damned in January '77 on a Friday. They just totally died a death, they got booed off because it was a heavy metal/rock audience."

Not only did the venue's insalubrious interior and hostile surroundings reflect the gritty drabness and morbid violence of Manchester in the 1970's, it required a concerted effort from punters to get there. But that was just the start of it.

Deb Zee: "You had to get off the bus at... was it The Orange Tree? I can't remember which bus I used to get from Manchester centre, and you had to walk over to the Circus. It was a bit dodgy getting in wasn't it?"

Alan Keogh: "The Circus was mental... those kids would be like, throwing stones at you. We'd be queuing up and the kids would be picking you off. So you've got them outside, plus you would have had to get to Piccadilly on the bus, and then walk across Piccadilly... it was like running the gauntlet. It was horrible."

Kevin Stanfield: "It was like running the gauntlet there. The chances of getting jumped, or your head kicked in were pretty high."

Mickey Carr: "It was in a dead rough area, just down the road from where I lived. It did get a bit naughty around there; it was the locals off that big estate. But it would have been naughty with us anyway because they were all United fans, and we were City's punks going up there."

Dawn Bradbury: "There were a couple of bouncers who mainly used to watch out for the cars because of the kids outside"

Denise Shaw: "Yeah a bloody fine job they did of that as well! That was where there was the most violence, outside with the kids from the flats opposite. '10p to look after your car' although you weren't paying them to look after it, you were paying them to not smash it up. There was this one kid who had red hair, I think he was the ringleader, and he used to carry an axe or a hammer and every time I went I'd see him and give him the money. But one night Kevin Cummins turned up with his equipment, and they'd gone up to him you know, 10p and all that, and he just went 'fuck off I'm not paying you!" So he went in and the next minute it came over the tannoy, 'will Kevin Cummins please come to the door'. So we all legged it outside and this kid with the Red hair was stood in the tower block with Kevin's camera swinging it over the balcony, they'd smashed his car and nicked all of his equipment. We were in hysterics but not only had they robbed his car, they'd also filled his petrol tank up with sugar!"

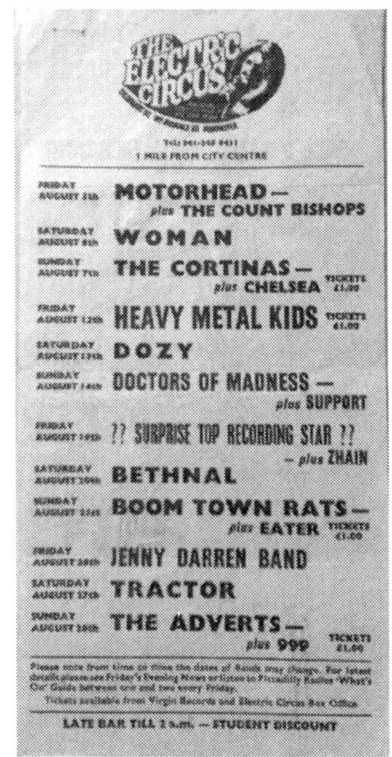

The fun didn't stop there, though. Once inside it was a dank and cheerless place, starved of light, dispossessed of comfort; the perfect venue for the new breed of the disaffected. After all, if you'd got that far...

Ian Moss: "It was an absolute shithole, a death trap. You wouldn't be able to get away with it now."

Ken Park: "Yeah the Circus was another place which wouldn't pass the Health and Safety test. The place would hold as many people as would turn up. So on big nights it would be rammed, you couldn't move, they just let everyone in, it couldn't possibly be safe."

Chris Lambert: "It was a dive, the Circus. You know you'd walk in..."

Deb Zee: "I always thought it smelt fusty, but Steve said that was the weed. I didn't know what weed was."

Andy T.: "I didn't find it too bad to be honest. Some people remember it as being like Beirut on a Tuesday night, but from where we were coming from in Rochdale mostly we'd get on the 17 bus, and it wasn't much different to where we lived anyway. You'd get United and City fans and other football fans clashing on a Saturday afternoon. The Circus gigs were mainly on a Sunday, so they were a bit quieter really, most of them. You'd hear stories of people throwing bits of concrete off the walkways, but I only remember people chucking bottles and bits of rolled newspaper! It used to be quite hairy going back on the night bus back to Rochdale. There were what you'd call football casuals nowadays. They used to call themselves 'soul boys' but they didn't have any soul as I remember, they were the closest things to nihilists I'd ever seen."

Although the place wasn't opened as a specific punk venue, as opposed to The Roxy in London, it soon began to put on Punk bands; The Electric Circus pre-dates The Roxy by a couple of months as a place where these young upstarts were allowed to play their noise, and this led in turn to it being a location where a small group of like-minded, disaffected kids had somewhere to go to see this new musical phenomenon. There had been the two gigs at The Lesser Free Trade Hall and at various unconventional venues around Manchester but now here was a place which they could adopt as their own. It was a decent size, it could 'comfortably' hold 600 people, with the added bonus that it could be hired for the place for £70 a night.

Denise Shaw: "The Electric Circus was massive. It was an old dancehall, and the second time I went to see Buzzcocks, I can't remember who the support band were, but I walked into this massive dancehall and there were about 20 people in. That's how it was in the early days".

For those initial gigs it felt like an exclusive club for those in the know; exciting, challenging and curious, unlike the shiny discos and nightclubs in the rest of the city. But its exclusivity didn't last for long.

Dawn Bradbury: "We went from having the place pretty much to ourselves, maybe 40 or 50 people or whatever, you know, and then when it started to get really packed the manager reserved a little spot at the edge of the bar, and that was where we sat."

Daniel O'Sullivan: "I remember the first few times I went, it was fucking quiet. But that grew as the reputation grew you know what I mean?"

Dawn Bradbury: " The Circus loved us because we were the only ones going in spending money, I mean when they opened the Circus, the first band they had on, the first night it opened I was there, and it wasn't done up properly because that all the workmen's tools were on the balcony. There were six people in there that night. Then the punk bands started using it and they loved us because we were filling it up."

Because everything was new and exciting there was an accessibility and connection between the new bands and the audience at first, it was the antidote to the aloof, distant Pop stars of the time, another form of rebellion.

Denise Shaw: "We didn't see these bands as being... oooh it's The Clash you know, because we just used to go and sit in the dressing room with them. I remember Wayne County, he was fine, I remember talking to him in the dressing room at The Electric Circus, but it soon expanded from it being 30 people, to it being full. So all that was lost."

Dawn Bradbury: "We were more like mates....most of the time."

Una Baines: "We saw the Pistols quite a few times, and at the end of the gigs John Lydon would be sat on the stage chatting to everybody, and it got rid of that... there was a level playing field for a short period of time. It felt like we had this really great balance between creativity and political conversation; everything went into the mix."

Even some of the London bands who came up to play in Manchester didn't have a pot to piss in, so the camaraderie was extended further.

Chris Hewitt: "I was asked to do The Lurkers' first tour, around the north-west, and they actually slept on the landing in my music shop on Oldham Road, the original Tractor Music. So I had all The Lurkers sleeping on my floor because they couldn't afford a hotel. We did such luxurious places such as upstairs at Bold Street Working Men's Club in Accrington, the room was known as The Lakeland Lounge. That place had always been a heavy metal Sunday night thing, but when The Lurkers played there, a lot of these clubs had moved over into punk by then."

But the barriers that had been temporarily lifted between band and audience were already showing signs of coming down again once the scene started to develop.

Stephen Perrin: "A few months later I was talking to a friend who was in a successful band. He seemed to have lost all interest in changing the world and told me that he was considering sacking one of his roadies as the guy had refused to carry his cocaine through customs for him. Oh, well, I thought, back to square one."

But as the scene began to grow, so did the band of believers.

Andy T.: "You met people... someone would have a badge on and you'd get talking to them, because they've got a Slaughter badge on.

Fran Taylor: "People started drifting into the circle. We all used to meet up at The Castle on Oldham Street. There was this guy who was there, and I remember that he was the first young bloke I'd seen who'd got a shaved head. He was wearing these godawful jumbo cord trousers, I'll never forget them. It emerged later on that he was Gaz Callender,

'Gus' out of The Drones."

Andy T.: "Gus (Gangrene) from The Drones used to have a flat near the Circus, on the other side of Rochdale Road, and a few people would go and stop there. The Drones were usually there even if they weren't playing. They were almost like the house band at the Circus, if a band hadn't turned up or they needed a support band, they'd normally ask The Drones to step in."

The adrenaline rush of those early gigs outweighed all of the trauma and trepidation it took just to get into the venue. The few people in those early days of Punk in Manchester knew that they were witnessing something monumentally life changing for them, and not just another shallow fad or manufactured musical phenomenon.

Chris Lambert: "The first band I saw was The Damned. It would have been a Sunday night in '76 I think at the Circus and I went in there, I had my (Oxford) bags on and whatever, I can't remember and by Monday evening I had drainpipes, a shredded jacket you know? I think they did New Rose three times!"

Deb Zee: "There was spitting and people chucking beer at the back."

Ken Park: "When they played New Rose just as the drums come in… da da da da!... everybody jumped. I think I felt like I'd jumped a world record! It was such a rush you know? Just fantastic. Right at the very start the audiences would be quite small and I can't remember the spitting. It would be like walking up to someone and spitting on them in the street. As the audiences got bigger and I suppose it was like the origins of the mosh pit, I never did it and anyway I never had any spit left because I was dancing so much, sweat was pouring out of me."

Fran Taylor: "Back then a band couldn't go into their bedroom, make something and stream it within 20 minutes. You had to go and see them to find out what it was about because they didn't have any records out. But when the Ramones first album came out… wow! It's on adverts now… then it was revolutionary."

Carol O'Donnell: "The Circus was for gigs and The Ranch was the place to go."

Fran Taylor: "In the very early days when we were Punks, we were the new thing, we hated the old farts, and it had to be guitars, drums, and a bloke screeching out at the front, that's all you needed, just like The Stooges. The MC5 didn't need fucking synthesisers."

Stanley Vegas: "The first time I heard the Ramones, the DJ was playing some stuff before the band came on. I can't for the life of me remember what the tune was, but it was off the first album, and I was like 'What's this?' So I went out and bought it the next day."

Deb Zee: "They always played... oh what were it called? I've forgotten... .oh God I can't remember now... Roadrunner... Jonathan Richmond that was it... I still love that song! I went out with a lad who was in a band called Microwave, then after that I started going to the Electric Circus with Richard Wild and Simon Topping who later on were in A Certain Ratio who lived in Urmston/Flixton."

If travelling to, and entering into The Electric Circus was fraught with danger, getting home could be the most hazardous part of the evening.

Daniel O'Sullivan: "There were always fights, always, but you just got accustomed to them. Because we used to go in such big groups we were never singled out or anything like that, you know? Coming out of there was always a bit hairy, particularly coming from the other side of town. I think I used to walk back into town, I lived in Longsight at the time."

Mickey Tait: "The walk back from the Electric Circus into town was well dodgy, because you had to go through Collyhurst."

Ken Park: "We used to walk home, we'd missed the bus, so we'd walk and the first 20 minutes getting out of that area was the worst, it was like that film 'The Warriors'."

Ian Moss: "Men in their 30's and 40's would be out in packs beating up any waifs and strays that they could find basically. Assaulting the door to get in you know? It was nasty yeah."

Mickey Tait: "That was a right rough gaff. There were some nut-cases in there... I remember someone giving me a dig. The guy was huge, and he must have been about 25-28... I'm 15, he could have picked anyone... it was like David and Goliath but without the sling."

When the fights weren't being instigated in the crowd or outside, then occasionally the band on stage would get involved.

Wispa: "I used to dive out and get in a bit of a ruck and all that with someone who I thought shouldn't be there. Somebody who'd paid his money to get pissed and start throwing beer at me, and I thought 'I'm not fucking having that, you know what I mean?"

Alan Keogh: "There were fights every single gig... I don't remember going to a gig where there wasn't a fight. It might have only been a small one."

Janine Hewitt: "I don't remember seeing any police involvement on my nights out. Or bouncer intervention either.

Fran Taylor: "I never had any problems at the Circus. But then again I'm from Salford so why would Collyhurst scare me? Where I grew up on Liverpool Street in Salford in one of the terraced houses there, before they knocked them all down, Collyhurst looked quite posh to me.

Fred Carr: "We were from Harpurhey so Collyhurst didn't seem too rough to us."

10. you're not going out dressed like that.

"The individual has always had to struggle to keep from being overwhelmed by the tribe. If you try it, you will be lonely often, and sometimes frightened. but no price is too high to pay for the privilege of owning yourself."

Friedrich Nietzsche

Most music cultures have their own wardrobe and hairstyles, and it's usually measured by an attention to detail and a rigid uniformity. the same could be said of the subcultures of the 70s: Skinheads, Mods, Teddy Boys, Rude Boys and Girls, but not so much with the punks in those early days. before the identikit tabloid portrayal and perception of the punk style of motorbike jacket (with the name of the wearer's favourite band on the back), studded belt, wristband, and multifariously coloured mohicans, the dress code in 1976 was distinctly homemade, bought second hand from the local Oxfam or Army and Navy shops, along with some rudimentary alterations to an existing article of clothing. The practice of deconstructing and recycling followed the familiar footsteps of the past when, unable to afford the 'off the peg' designs being modelled by Ferry and Bowie, fans created their own budget alternatives. Like music, the clothes we wear are indicative of our personality and individualise us, and for some that manifested itself early on in the lives of future Punks.

Deb Zee: "I was always into music and I was always different to my mates. I think I was about 12 at the time, I went to, it could have been Stolen from Ivor in Urmston I'm not sure now, but I bought a Ben Sherman top and some Two Tone pants and some brogues. I was well chuffed."

Juliette J. Williams: "I wanted two things for my 12th birthday; one was the 'Electric Warrior' album on Fly, and the second was a Ben Sherman shirt, the short sleeved girl's version. I've still got 'Electric Warrior' now and it's like new."

Even though Punk wasn't really about the clothes, wearing things which would antagonise and mark you out as different, typified the original Punk attitude of non-conformity and rebellion, and reflected the music which was inspiring this new found freedom of expression. Plus, because it was still an underground scene and exclusive to only a few like minded people in town, there wasn't a commercialised uniform with which to adhere. The transition from dressing up to dressing down was starting to filter through slowly.

Wispa: "It sort of changed from the Bowie/Roxy element, although it didn't drift away altogether but they started going to Oxfam and buying their clothes, safety pins in their ears and outrageous gear."

Brian Johnson: "It was a natural progression from where we were to that scene. It all happened at Pips and Belle Vue, very seamlessly. But punk took it a bit further. Cooler hair, ripped up clothes, razors and safety pins. So Punk was woven into our Bowie and Roxy, and it was okay."

Carol O'Donnell: "When I first started going to The Ranch I'd be wearing like satin and silk dresses you know, trying to be Jerry Hall. After a bit I was wearing my dad's cut off pants and stripey shirts. My dad would moan a bit but he used to say 'If you're not in by two o'clock I'm locking the door!' Of course the clubs didn't close until two so I was never back by then. I've lost count of the amount of times I had to sleep outside the house."

Mickey Tait: "Manchester was less designer punk. It was more… I even went out in a bin bag. But looking good was part of it. The great thing about it was how individual people were. We used to go to second hand shops for a lot of our gear then. Dinner jackets, suits, Trilbies, baggy pants or straight legged with brogues, and ties you know? We used to shop in places like Othello, the Army and Navy stores in town to get the latest gear. It was quite camp, not that we were gay, we loved the music and we loved the attention."

Stanley Vegas: "Our style came out of the second hand shops. The London thing was that it was all designed for them and that's why we were individuals up here. You'd go in a second hand shop and you'd be like, 'Right, if I cut that up a bit and if I sew a bit of this on it… whereas they'd go into Seditionaries and buy the top class gear off the peg. That's why we were different, we had more of a 'street urchin' style whereas they had a designer look."

To add some balance there were plenty of London punks wearing homemade, altered clothes, if you look at some of the pictures from the early Roxy days.

Chris Lambert: "Manchester had a really good scene… it was a lot more original because there weren't the shops to buy anything. Buy a shirt and stencil it. Oxfam was good… narrow lapelled jackets."

Mickey Tait: "The Antique Market in Deansgate was a very popular place. I remember buying a striped blazer to look at bit Deaf School-ish, you know? I was into the sort of 1930's Oxford scene."

Denise Shaw: "Everything was either homemade or from charity shops."

Alan Keogh: "What I was really interested in was making my own stuff, doing my own thing. I remember stitching up an old man's suit, stitching the trousers up inside so they were a bit narrower, because they were too fuckin' baggy and then stitching the jacket up."

Una Baines: "I had to wear flares in The Fall. I had to because I couldn't afford drainpipes. I used to have a pair of Black corduroy flares and I tried to turn them into drainpipes... I could hardly get my legs in them! They had big thick ridges in them! (*laughs*)"

Deb Zee: "Yeah we just did our own clothes."

But some didn't bother to follow any of the fashion rules.

Ian Moss: "Not in a London way, and even if I wanted to be, there was nowhere in Manchester where you could go and buy a pair of Vivienne Westwood trousers or a mohair jumper. I couldn't have afforded it anyway. I resorted to wearing an old suit of my dad's."

Una Baines: "The first Punks wore like white shirts, drainpipe trousers and bootlace ties, that was a kind of a look. I was thinking, 'What are the women going to wear', because you knew that something was going to come."

Gail Egan: "If you look at the audiences, not everyone was dressed up like Plastic Bertrand, were they? I can remember some of the 'London Set' coming down to one of the Pistol's gigs, she had short blonde hair, a little girl - Debbie, she was called. You used to see her with Jordan. I remember chatting with her at The Electric Circus, they used to follow the Sex Pistols around. She was dead friendly."

Stanley Vegas: "The first Punk crowd I saw was when me and the missus, who I'm still with by the way, went down to Finchley to see Slaughter and the Dogs when Eater played their gig at their school along with The Damned (Friday November 19th 1976). The 'Finchley Mob' were there, I think they used to follow The Stranglers around. It was quite shocking to see them at the time because we weren't used to it. We were used to dressing all posey in our Bowie gear and what have you."

Juliette J. Williams: "I remember I used to get a magazine that came out every month called *Honey*. In this magazine there was a double page spread in black and white, and it was all about this burgeoning scene in London. It had people like the guy we now know as Billy Idol and others from the Bromley Contingent, and they were wearing plastic sandals, mohair jumpers and drainpipe Jeans, which you couldn't easily buy, you'd get your mum to alter them on her sewing machine. But that way of dressing up here in Manchester was from the people who were into funk in '75/76. They were wearing plastic sandals, and at that time Bowie was recording 'Young Americans' and he was also wearing them. So I think it was a combination of the two that saw the early punks wearing that stuff. Looking back there weren't that many people dressing that way so early on. It was quite a provocative way to dress."

Mickey Carr: "When I left school in May 1976 I'd already been influenced by an elder brother with the Bowie thing. I was always dyeing my hair, as were other people, but we were very much in the minority. My sister had made some friends in town knocking about with perhaps about four or five who were like us, you know? They wore the gear, nothing to do with punk at the moment, just drainpipes and school blazers and we bought stuff from charity shops. So we formed like a little group and some of them were able to get in to places and some were too young. They were from Levenshulme, Gorton, Openshaw and not long after that, maybe the first few months, some other guys from Moston up the road from where we lived who I knew from the match, so we formed a group that had a number of things in common: dressing differently and liking different music and stuff – basically behaving differently. But also, you know, there was the City connection. So as the year '76 wore on I started hearing about this 'punk rock' from my elder brother, who was more clued up than me, and from one or two pals."

Mark Windsor: "I joined the Air Force when I left school, and had to act mentally ill for a year to get out. While I was still in there I went to see Bowie on the 'Thin White Duke' tour at Wembley Empire Pool on a Wednesday night, all the way from Haverfordwest, and that's when I saw my first punk. I think it was Siouxsie and Jordan giving out leaflets for Sex Pistols gigs. I mean, I thought that we were weird but it was like, 'Christ, look at them!', you know. The day I got out of the Air Force I went and got my hair dyed blonde and red, which would have been August '76. I was dyeing my hair while I was still in the Air Force but I had to leave some of it my normal colour because of my ID card. That was teetering on getting me in military prison because if you were gay you went to prison, and I was wearing make up to work and it was a bit of a tightrope I was walking but I got away with it.

"I remember Bowie saying in that Cracked Actor thing, someone said to him, 'What do you think about people imitating you?' and he went, 'Well it's a good thing if they find themselves through experimenting' and that's what I did. I tried the blonde, red, black, wearing make-up, different clothes, and eventually you end up settling on one that is actually you; although it's absolutely nicked off other people.

Janine Hewitt: "I first got into punk when I saw photographs of the Bromley Contingent in the newspaper along with reports on a new band, the Sex Pistols. I got the idea from here to buy a school blazer and customise a white school shirt, the fashion at the time was for big collars and these had small ones, along with narrow legged black school trousers, not flares. I cropped my hair and died it black. There is a photo of me in The Ranch taken by Kevin Cummins. I could sew and I made a pair of bondage pants and matching top as I couldn't afford to buy them from the shop 'Sex'. By wearing the clothes I was somehow part of a revolution, a non-conformist. The clothes were not about how much money or following a style dictated by fashion houses. No-one minded if you chose not to dress up either."

Juliette J. Williams: "It was really hard because we had no money and we didn't know what to wear, so it was all about thinking it up for yourself."

Mark Windsor: "It was ridiculous, you didn't have to do much. I mean nobody had them posh clothes from Sex or anything, you used to get stuff from the Army and Navy or a second hand shop, or make it yourself."

Mickey Tait: "I bought the Ramones album, I was really into the Ramones first album. I quite liked that look of the jeans, the baseball boots, pair of Converse, we used to get the Adidas 3 striped baseball boots with the leather jacket and T-shirt. When the second Ramones album came out, the first two came out in quick succession, there was some sort of thing, I must have read it in the music press, that there was a limited amount but if you sent a token off from the album, you got this Ramones T-shirt. It'd be worth a few bob now."

One particular person, who didn't follow any trend was Jon the Postman.

Ian Moss: "I was fascinated with it (punk), I went to a lot of gigs and bought a lot of records. You've got Jon The Postman who was on the fringe of stuff. He had his own drinking buddies who weren't at all trendy, who weren't walking around in pac-a-macs and things like that."

Fran Taylor: "I can't emphasise or say enough, how much Jon the Postman drove all this, certainly for my friends because he was very into the Flaming Groovies and they did a gig at The Roundhouse and the Ramones were supporting them. So Jon and a couple of mates went all the way to London to see them, and this is before the famous '76 gig where all the faces were there - The Clash, The Damned etcetera. He came back and he was like 'you've got to see this band, you've got to hear them they are unbelievable'."

Denise Shaw: "He was so knowledgeable about music, not just punk, I mean he just loved music, any sort of music. For instance if somebody had bought something dead bizarre from the American Deep South, he'd know about it. He was great."

We live in an age where you can buy your jeans ready ripped, with a label from the best fashion houses along with those from high street chains. But 1976 was a different world.

Ken Park: "Our distressed jeans were distressed because we were piss poor. The amount of invention that people were using was fantastic, what you'd see on the street."

Juliette J. Williams: "We knew that we had our own little scene going on, it didn't really have a name, it didn't really have a shape, it was very amorphous. It was just welding itself to Manchester as the weeks were going on."

Denise Shaw: "There was a core of about 20 of us at the most, and we never let anybody in. Even now when people from that time are introduced to me... Una (Baines) is one example that springs to mind, she said to me 'I used to be shit scared of you'. I didn't take any notice of anyone outside of us, it was just us. A bit like the Bromley Contingent I suppose"

Dawn Bradbury: "Part of that core would be the bands. So you've got The Drones, Buzzcocks, The Worst, you know what I mean... you've got all those people who were actually part of that group, and we were all mates... they just happened to be in a band. People would be like, 'where are they going? Because wherever they're all going, that's where we're going."

Steve Shy: "It was wrong because we were a clique of about 40-50 people, something like that. There would be people around us, but it would be really hard for them to get in. It was like 'we were here first', you know... it was one of them... totally fucking wrong. It was just us being a bunch of arseholes. You could see people who were on the outside, looking in, which was really, really strange but when you're young and that, you don't fucking realise."

Dawn Bradbury: "It wasn't a clique. You were in or you weren't in".

Daniel O'Sullivan: "I went to school in Ardwick and a couple of the lads who were in the first incarnation of The Fall were at our school, and they'd talk about stuff. I think it was the famous Bill Grundy interview with the Sex Pistols. I was sold on it then. In fact the school had a fancy dress or summat and I went dressed as a punk, you know? Got an old shirt, bit of gel in me hair, and then I just bought into it completely and lived the lifestyle. In terms of like, the people who I used to go out with and watch gigs with, there was probably about 20 of us, you know, who knew each other quite well and would phone each other and go to each other's houses and stuff like that. Not terribly many, no."

Deb Zee: "There would be me, Steve Shy, Carol, and I knew Denise and Dawn but they were a bit older than me, I was only 16, so yeah there was Steve and his girlfriend Ann at the time, and also then I used to hang about a lot with Carol (O'Donnell). Then there was Gavin, he used to be at Carol's a lot and Pete Shelley as well."

Ian Moss: "You see this is where I'm different than… I mean Steve (Shy) is a really good friend of mine and Denise and people like that. They embraced a scene and became part of a clique. I was never a part of that and there's probably two reasons: one is that they were probably better socially adjusted than I was but the other reason is probably because I was more discerning. I didn't want to hang about with a load of people who… I mean I'd got mates. It's their reality, and it's their truth, but I'm not saying it's better than my truth. I was 18 and I've got this world, you know? And without being funny, I wasn't thick. So I'd go to the theatre. Just look at the cinema in that era; Scorcese's films are an example. I'd go to the Free Trade Hall and watch the Hallé Orchestra before I would go to The Ranch or watch some punk by numbers shit like The Drones and Slaughter and the Dogs. What were they? You've loved all this music; you've loved all this Reggae, Stevie Wonder, King Crimson and The Velvet Underground. Why would I suddenly become a Drones fan? That would be the most regressive, ridiculous thing wouldn't it? Sometimes I hate myself for being so churlish about it, but really…"

Alan Keogh: "It's not like people were less passionate about the music but we kind of get looked down on. It was like, oh yeah there was *them* as well. But actually the scene *was* them as well, all the time you were there, we were there. There were class divisions within the group. There was this hierarchy; these are the famous punks, these are the mid-famous punks. I'm one of the no mark punks, you know what I mean?"

Mickey Tait: "I always knew, even though I was 14, I knew who was in the clique crowd, who'd go to London."

Odgie: "It was the epitome of grass roots; people who knew people."

Andy T.: "There were quite a few people who you'd see all the time. You knew them from Pips, and you knew them from Saturday afternoons in Manchester, hanging about at the Underground Market or HMV."

Kevin Stanfield: "You knew all the people in that circle. It was also a case of safety in numbers."

Mickey Carr: "I met Alan Keogh…he'd have bought the *NME* or *Melody Maker.* I remember him talking about it (punk) and it's not like you need any conversion from something like that, when you're at that age and you're all of one accord in a way. As different bands or different types of music are introduced within that group, you just readily fall into it. It's not like, right I'm going to get into it…make myself like it, there was no effort involved. Some of our crew of about 20 characters were more into it, dressing up wise. For a lot of us it might have just been the narrow jeans and the baseball pumps, or the pointy shoes that we got from charity shops."

Alan Keogh: "Punk rock was my first passion for white music. My choice of music as a young teenager was black music. The punk thing was really, really, fucking amazing. I lived in Levenshulme at the time, I was 15 years old, and then I met a guy called Ian Dalglish. We sort of knew each other but we weren't really friends; I knew who he was and he knew who I was. Then there was Adge, (Alan Frost) who ended up in World Of Twist and cockney George; We sort of fell across each other in Levenshulme when we were 15. Everyone was coming from a sense of like; this is shit, this mainstream culture we were being fed, we're being forced to consume is shit."

Mike Keogh: "When the punk scene hit, fucking hell, that was like a kick in the bollocks big time, yeah. I think that a lot of the kids that picked up on it earlier were from North Manchester as opposed to South Manchester. Moston, Clayton, the harder, poorer areas of Manchester at the time, which I didn't even know existed. Piccadilly Gardens was as far North as I ever went as a kid! It was a fascinating time for a young person to get into. To find out what the real worlds about when you've been brought up in a Catholic home where you had to go to church on a Sunday"

Fran Taylor: "I was once barred from a newsagents of all places! We went to Warrington to see Johnny Thunders, Buzzcocks and Slaughter and the Dogs at the Parr Hall, loads of us went down there. Me and my mate walked into this newsagents and this woman said 'I'm not serving you! Get Out! I'm not serving you lot in here, you rabble!' Neither of us was outrageous, we just had shorter hair and skinny trousers on, that was about it."

If the teenage male of the species was the devil incarnate and the symptom of an ethically bankrupt society, spare a thought for the girls. They had to cope with unwanted grief from all sides; parents, men, and from sections of their own age and gender.

11. dame to blame

"Blessed be she who is both furious and magnificent."

Taylor Rhodes
(Calloused: A Field Journal)

Everyone had their own way of dealing with unwelcome attention or potential confrontation, but it was especially difficult for girls, who drew a lot of animosity because of their dress sense and provocative attitude, but one of the most important things about punk was that it broke down some of the male machismo and sexist attitudes towards women. There was a great deal of courage required by females to be different and not follow the trends of the day, to dress how they were expected to dress; similar to their mother. This single-minded stubbornness not to conform meant a constant battle with those closest to them.

Juliette J. Williams: "My mum, she wouldn't even… we were both going into town shopping and I got on the bus and went upstairs, she stayed downstairs, she didn't want to know me. She didn't like the way I was dressed because she wanted me to dress in a certain way and I wouldn't conform. I mean she'd even try to drag me into Marks and Spencer to buy me a flowery dress, but I just wanted to get out there and do my own thing."

Una Baines: "From a feminist's point of view, women should be able to dress how they want and be safe."

Carol O'Donnell: "Everyone thought we were violent and something to be scared of. But it was the Teddy Boys and the Perrys who were going out tooled up looking for trouble but they dressed smart so… We didn't think of it as being brave, we just thought of it as a good vibe you know, I want some of this."

Juliette J. Williams: "My dad used to say to me, 'You look like something that stands on street corners' and that really upset me but I was defiant about it and I used to say to him, 'You know I'm not like that and I'm going out like this anyway'. He grabbed the back of my plastic mac and it tore all the way round, so I just tied it up and said, 'Thanks dad, it looks even better now' and walked out of the door. My mum was like, 'Where have we gone wrong?'."

The vitriol was occasionally severe and the slurs clichéd and unimaginative.

Denise Shaw: "The amount of times I'd get asked how much I charged, just because of the way I dressed..."

Sarah Mee: "Being spat at was commonplace and being different wasn't acceptable."

Janine Hewitt: "On the whole I think that people's reactions were based on fear, due to lack of understanding. Of course you stood out more in those days and that got you some unwanted attention. But we expected it I suppose."

Juliette J. Williams: "I never felt part of something integral in terms of being part of a 'girly' crowd. The early females who got into punk seemed to be as much outsiders as some of the guys did."

Deb Zee: "I remember being in a supermarket and these two elderly ladies were looking at me as if to say, you look disgraceful, but I turned round and they were like... they both had purple rinse hair and bright red lipstick, leopard skin pants... I was like, I just couldn't believe it. they were dressed like me in a way, but they looking at me as if I was some sort of a scumbag."

One of the most photographed female Punks in Manchester was Denise Shaw (nee Lloyd). A tall, strikingly provocative young woman who is still featured on the front covers of anniversary punk books to this day, especially ones about London!

Una Baines: "I used to wonder what are the women going to look like when they first started into punk, and then Denise turned up and I was like 'Fuckin'hell!"

Martin Ryan: "Denise was quite outrageous."

Denise Shaw: "I was into David Bowie, Roxy Music that sort of stuff so I used to go down to Pips the majority of the time, and I was always on my own because I lived in Rochdale. I was always a little bit weird. So I'd been into the Bowie/Roxy thing for a good few years and it was starting to get where when I went to Pips I were bored, you know? It was just getting monotonous; they were playing the same records, so when The Ranch opened I had a choice then, even though it was still a predominantly Bowie/Roxy type place. Then of course Buzzcocks played there, and that was like listening to Lou Reed all over again. After that, that was it for me, The Roxy/Bowie thing was gone; I was just into punk."

Wispa: "Denise was on the scene very early on, although I don't remember seeing her at that Pistols gig, but she was there very early Circus era with Joan, who unfortunately passed away. They were great mates and I was part of that, I was mates with them both, and I'm still mates with Denise now.

Denise Shaw: "Literally after I'd seen Buzzcocks at The Ranch is when I started to dress more punk. When they played at The Electric Circus, I've got a picture of the back of me, I don't know who took it but they must have used my camera. I just got a Black T-shirt, ripped the sleeves out, got some glitter and wrote 'punk rock' on the back of my T-shirt. That was the start of it."

That very basic start was how nearly everyone took their first tentative steps into punk, just by doing something as straightforward as cutting your hair short was deemed radical, particularly for a woman. Soon Denise would ramp up the provocation stakes, and her extraordinary attire would inspire both hostility and admiration.

Dawn Bradbury: "My mum had been out shopping with my Auntie Jean one Saturday afternoon, and when she came home she was like 'Oh my God, you're not going to believe me, I've just seen this girl today. Absolutely fantastic I wish you'd have been with me'. So I asked her to describe her; 'Dead tall, black leather pants on, great big black stilettos, with a black silky shirt. Her hair was really short and at the front it was purple and as it went towards the back it washed out from purple to cerise, then pink into a blonde at the back'. So I said 'right, okay… that'll be Denise', my mum went, 'oh do you know her, love?'. I said 'yeah it's Denise who I go out with', to which she replied, 'oh, *that* Denise! Isn't she gorgeous?' Everyone was stunned by her and kept looking round at her."

Denise Shaw: "I used to look through these seedy little magazines for anything that was black patent. I got these trousers, they were amazing. There was a flap at the front and one at the back, and they fastened together with Velcro. They looked amazing. Then I dyed my hair black and started doing the black make-up. I couldn't go to anybody's house because their parents would be trying to stop them from seeing me. You'd have thought that I was the biggest drug addict in the world, you know? Just because of the way I looked"

Dawn Bradbury: "My mum, in her little bubble, was thinking it was fantastic while everybody else was like 'What the hell…? What do you look like!' So I explained that she would be coming round to the house at seven and she would also be stopping the night. My mum just said 'Okay, in that case I'll put some extra tea on for her'. Meanwhile, my dad was, you know he'd worked all week, so Saturday night he'd be sat in his chair, with a newspaper, glasses half way down his nose. He just looked up from over his glasses and went, 'Y'alright love?' as Denise introduced herself, 'Oh I know who you are' he said, then without missing a beat said, 'Get the kettle on, tea and two sugars for me, darlin'' and carried on reading his paper without batting an eyelid!"

Andy T.: "I used to know Denise because she was from Rochdale and quite often she would get the same bus into Manchester everyday. We used to talk to each other on the bus and she was one of the first people who actually dressed like a punk but at that time most people didn't. I don't think I ever did, I put henna in my hair and had a bit of a Bowie cut but that was about as far as it went but Denise always stood out and she'd dress like that during the day.

Juliette J. Williams: "I used to know The Worst and Denise was very friendly with Ian, I'm not sure if they were in a relationship but they were very good mates, and I thought, 'Shit, I'm staying away from her, she looks scary! So I never really got to talk to her because I was always… because she was older, because she was taller, and because she had all the make up, as did we, but I didn't have the height, or a car and she was older than us. She just seemed further on down the punk line than we were."

It turns out, the reason for Denise's imposing and intimidating stare was quite innocent.

Denise Shaw: "I was short sighted but I refused to wear my glasses when I was out. Dawn told me that I had this stare, with all that black make up because I had green eyes it really stood out and I'd look straight through people and I wouldn't know that I was doing it. I just couldn't see people's faces."

The number of women who were coming out of the Bowie look into the punk style was growing, and the amount of invention and imagination that went into those early incarnations of Punk clothing was extraordinary. As with the Bowie era, the girls were taking conventional garments, or classic fashion accessories of the past, and updating them into something more relevant and reactionary, and in some cases quite unique.

Juliette J. Williams: "I went into the Market Hall in Bolton and bought lots of dishcloths and sewed them altogether to make a top. I got a snappy sandwich bag from the kitchen drawer and somehow stitched it to this dishcloth top and I used to pick cigarette dog ends off the floor from wherever I'd been and put them in this plastic bag! I thought it looked really cool, but it just looked bloody ridiculous. I'd be at college, I had no money, I lived at home, no job. So I'd nick one of my dad's shirts that he never wore any more, rip it up, I used to put black eyeliner on it if I couldn't find a marker pen to write all over it. I also used my mum's ridiculous silver hairspray to dye the front of my hair, and it stunk and made my hair really greasy. I had this long black tabard which had matching trousers that were flared with frilly elasticated bits and a belt. It looked really hippy-ish, so I sacked the top off and I cut the trouser legs shorter and tied the ends up with string and wore them with a pair of fishnets and stilettos."

There were plenty of outlets to choose from, all of them were at the lower end of the retail ladder.

Carol O'Donnell: "Clothes-wise I used to get nearly all mine from the Army and Navy stores. The best you could buy would be drainpipe jeans and that was it, then you'd just improvise by ripping a few tops and your jeans. I used to wear a pencil skirt for school. Then it was my dad's best shirts, I ripped the arms off, and I wore fishnets and I bought these really nice stiletto shoes with studs in them. I had different types of styles; I'd wear drainpipes with Kickers, dad's ripped shirt with rope wrapped around it as a belt, sometimes it would be high heels, stockings and a short skirt. I had a bondage top but can't remember where it came from. I think it was from Gavin, he was working for the BBC at the time I think. I used to get tied up on a regular basis in The Ranch!"

Gail Egan: "We met this couple who were opening a shop in Longsight. When we went upstairs it was full of shoeboxes of old 1950's Stilettos and they were selling them for 50p a pair. So of course, I was earning £11 a week as a hairdresser at the time, so I had really cool shoes."

As well as the deconstructed attire, accessories were also inventive and unique.

Deb Zee: "I had a kettle as a handbag; it was one of the old fashioned ones with a pointy spout, I don't think that went down too well. I had leopard-skin pants on, bright blue hair, sunglasses on, even though we were inside, black lipstick. We were very peaceful but they still chucked us out. I don't think that drinking snakebite through straws helped! I used to wear men's overcoats and I had a flasher Mac. I've spoken to people since and they were like, 'I would have loved to have done what you and your friends did but we weren't brave enough to do it'. I guess we had balls of steel really. We weren't trying to outdo each other, there was none of that. It wasn't a competition."

Dressing like no-one else attracted snide remarks and name calling at it's most benign.

Janine Hewitt: "As a woman, no-one threatened violence to me personally. One night some girls were about to say something but one of them said 'leave her alone, she's obviously going to a fancy dress party!'"

But occasionally there was a more sinister element to the attention the girls were getting. Some men saw the stockings and short skirts as a sign that these young women were either easy or 'prick teasers'. In truth most of the blokes were unsettled and intimidated, unable to correlate the juxtaposition of what the girls were wearing and why they were wearing the clothes that they did.

Deb Zee: "A lot of lads would look at you as if you were some kind of a slut or something but they didn't understand you did they? I didn't care, probably didn't notice a lot of it. I was 16/17 I came from Urmston and nobody around there had blue hair and fishnets on at that time, getting on the bus. I wasn't really that bothered. I think that you're kind of oblivious to some of it. You'd just walk along and people would be staring at you but because I didn't think it was sexual, I just thought that I was dressing in a certain way, it was how I wanted to dress."

Janine Hewitt: "One night a girl told me that she admired my courage when blokes would shout stuff at me. I pierced my ears myself, three in each ear as I remember, they didn't do multiple piercing in the shops. I attracted stares, nasty comments and for a couple of lads I knew an actual beating, which you could take as a rare compliment for daring to be individual?"

Deb Zee: "I think a lot of the girls were intimidating really. I used to scare some of the lads, the 'pop' people, with my blue hair and stuff. They might have been more intimidated by us I don't know but we never did anything to them."

Mike Keogh: "Some of the girls used to wear white jump suits, I can't quite remember, I think it might have been the Deaf School style, I'm not sure."

Gail Egan: "We would get jump suits from Millets, which was an Army and Navy store in Stockport. Me and Pete Shelley both had a little grey army bag worn over the shoulder, I bought one for him and one for me. I'd wear army trousers, which were proper combat trousers, or we went to Oxfam shops or made stuff. It was just 'that's how I want to dress and I don't really care what anyone else thinks' you know?

Juliette J. Williams: "We used to wear fishnets and stilettos and bin liner dresses. My friends Pat and Dawn went to the same secretarial college as me, and myself and Pat used to make our own bin liner dresses.

We'd sew them onto a normal dress, cut the dress really short and put the bin liner over the top to give it a bit more longevity. But it was always boiling in The Ranch so they would get a bit stinky! Not very nice at all."

But there were instances where situations could become intimidating and unnerving.

Deb Zee: "One night this bloke followed us back to our friend Debbie's house on Warwick Road. I'm not sure where he'd followed us from but we were panicking, so we ran in the house. We were hiding under the kitchen window and we could hear him walking down the side of the house and he was peering in and it was… URGH! We were 3 girls in short mini-skirts but…"

Janine Hewitt: "I just didn't make eye contact, plus I tried to look unapproachable if I was on my own. I was robbed once by a guy who walked me to Piccadilly Bus station from Pips. He was a straight guy. I now had no bus fare home so I went to the Police and they kindly gave me a lift home in a Police car. We drove around at first to see if I could spot him, but I didn't see him. They were really polite and never mentioned my dress sense."

Another cliché at the time concerned women and their relationship with the music and musicians they loved.

Una Baines: "Being mates with the bands, that was the bias in the music world; if you're a woman who wants to be mates with a band, then you've got to be a groupie."

Dawn Bradbury: "It was a case of 'there's a punk band on, lock up your daughters!'"

Chris Lambert: "Unfortunately it turned out to be a self-fulfilling prophecy didn't it?"

But not everyone was as comfortable with dressing their own way and were fearful of the dilemma and conflict it would cause within the family.

Denise Shaw: "Before I met Dawn, my best mate was Joan and she was the total opposite to me. She dressed punk but she didn't do it from home. She'd get changed in the car and then on the way home she'd change back into her normal clothes to go back into her house, and she was like that all the way through the time we were into the scene."

Dawn Bradbury: "Joan was what you'd call a closet punk, it never sat comfortably with her to mix her social life and her home life."

Joanne Slater: "My dad went mental, absolutely mental, when I got into punk. I couldn't put my make-up on in the house, and I had to wipe it off before I went back in. 'Foul mouthed animals' he used to say. I remember going out in a black bag one night, with a pair of jeans."

Janine Hewitt: "The music and the fashion went hand in hand for me, although I admit that I was out to shock. I was brought up by a very old fashioned Grandma who hid in her bedroom until I had left to go out. I remember a punk telling me that you couldn't be seen in public without wearing your punk gear because that meant you were a 'plastic' punk. There were rules within the punk community."

The moral compass of a lot of parents was firmly pointed towards the north of higher ground, so those who were more liberal in their thinking towards their kids was a great benefit.

Chris Lambert: "They've always been happy for me to express my individuality so they weren't that bothered."

Deb Zee: "My mum didn't mind and my dad was quite chuffed with it all really, but my brother-in-law said, when I walked down the stairs in my fishnet stockings, stilettos and my dad's ripped shirt with all my hair and black lipstick, 'you're not babysitting for my kids anymore'. He just looked at me and I said 'why? I'm still the same person', you know?"

Hairstyles are another form of defiance in any youth culture, from Teddy Boy quiffs, mod short back and sides to skinhead crops and lank haired hippies. In those early days there wasn't a 'punk' style and coloured hair had been around for a while, so it was another case of using your imagination to refine an individual look but explaining what you wanted to the local hairdresser, who to be fair was more used to blue rinses and perms, was a challenge in itself.

Deb Zee: "I went to the hairdressers, there's a picture of me with Woody Woodmansey and I've got like a Joanna Lumley cut. I went into a hairdressers in Stretford and I said I want a Ziggy Stardust cut, and at the time I had dead long hair and he told me; 'your hair will never stick up', so I ended up coming out with this bloody Joanna Lumley haircut! When I first did me hair like Ziggy, I bought this Harmony hair colour, but when I went punk and progressed I bleached it. I used to use carpet dye and clothes dye. When you put cochineal in, you know the food colouring, it all ran down your face when it rained so I used to put Kingfisher Blue clothes dye in my hair. We didn't have Crazy Colour then."

Janine Hewitt: "I heard about coloured hair dye in London (Crazy Colours) but couldn't afford that so I used food colouring or a silver spray. I'd heard of someone using Nivea to spike it up."

There was a lot of trial and error (and effort) involved in acquiring the desired effect and then maintaining it so that it would last for a whole night out.

Terry Slater: "Some of the punks used to say to me, 'You're a hairdresser, what's the best setting agent?' I told them that it would probably be too dear for them, and so I used to say, 'Do you know what you're best using - Coca-Cola."

Deb Zee: "I used to use soap and sometimes sugar and water. I went to a club, The Swinging Apple in Liverpool. I had white hair but I had all this sugar and water in it and the lights in there showed up all the black bits, you know, like when you lie on something and it gets a bit mucky."

Gail Egan: "At the hairdressers where I worked they shaved all my hair off so I had a No.1 all over, with strands hanging down. My dad was an accountant, middle class, and he was not impressed. I came home from work and it was also dyed black with bright red bits in it, Crazy Colours I think it was, and he looked at me and he said, 'You will not be sitting at the dinner table tonight, and I'll be consulting my solicitor in the morning!'. Dad just went absolutely mad, but the more they did, the more rebellious I got."

Juliette J. Williams: "That image was at complete odds with the image I had, so I started to grow my 40's perm out and dyed it black. It wasn't spiky because nobody had spiked hair in those early days. I blame Sid Vicious for starting that. You either had short cropped hair or long hippy-ish hair."

Una Baines: "I had mine cut like Brian Jones. I wanted it cut like Brian Jones."

The men were also partial to a bit of coiffure culture.

Mickey Carr: "I had this Ramones T-shirt, and I was going out with a girl, she was beautiful, probably for about 18 months summat like that, but it's forever then isn't it? We were both besotted with each other you know, and we used to listen to Bowie and all that, we'd listen to Patti Smith and then punk. We even had our hair similar. We had it dyed that blue/Raven Black it was like a Blue perm. It sounds really not punk but that was the style we had but we particularly liked the Ramones, Lou Reed. The first album I ever bought was Transformer, and I must have bought it four or five times since then in various formats."

Andy T.: "I had a bit of a feather-cut and I had a friend who owned a hairdressers in Rochdale, and on a Thursday they used to stay open late and dye our hair. So I'd have my hair different colours but I didn't really look Punky at all, it was just normal clothes. I didn't really bother, because it made you a target."

12. where have all the boot boys gone?

"Violence is the last refuge of the incompetent."

Isaac Asimov
'Foundation'

Well before the tribal confrontations of contrasting musical cultures were threatening the end of civilised culture, a more sinister, extreme style of violence was being meted out in the dark streets of the city. In the late 19th century Scuttler gangs roamed the streets of Manchester terrorising the neighbourhoods of Manchester and Salford, and two of the most notorious were the Angel Meadow gang and the Bengal Tigers from Bengal Street just off Oldham Road. Knives and belt buckles were the predominant weapons of choice and they would create havoc in the streets or in the pubs around the area, including the George and Dragon, what would become Band On The Wall years later. Ancoats Hospital was kept busy treating seriously wounded Scuttlers as well as members of the public innocently caught up in the feuding. The inevitable result in some cases was murder or manslaughter, with one judge, just about to send a gang member to jail exclaiming, '*Life in parts of Manchester is as unsafe and uncertain as it is amongst a race of savages, with apparently no other motive than a ferocious love of fighting*'.

As with the multifarious youth groups of the 20th century, there was a dress code which was strictly adhered to that marked them out as troublemakers as well as emanating a threatening visual presence. The Scuttlers employed a meticulously detailed uniform of peaked 'pigeon-board' caps, silk scarves, bell-bottomed trousers, and brass tipped pointed clogs. The hair was short back and sides with a long fringe plastered down with soap and covering the left eye. Although the vast majority of the Scuttlers were male, there were attacks perpetrated by women. In one instance four girls were involved in a revenge attack in defence of the boyfriend of Hannah Robin, who had been 'grassed up' resulting in him being sent to the gallows. The tattoo on her arm was inscribed 'In Loving Remembrance of William Willan' in tribute to him, unfortunately this was somewhat premature as he was denied the hangman's noose on account of his age. So violence was nothing new to Manchester, if anything the ferocity of the fighting had diminished over the years. In the 1970's it was usually gender, football, or fashion related, but violence came from all avenues.

Ian Moss: "Manchester is a completely different place now, if you went back to Manchester in the '70's you would be asking for trouble if you wore either a Manchester United or a Manchester City shirt, because somebody would have a go at you. I've been in that situation myself at Piccadilly Station, it was a seedy place. I don't think that you could underplay how tribal society was, but in particular youth culture."

Fran Taylor: "What you have to remember is that violence in Manchester wasn't just a youth thing. You could go to a pub and it would kick off between two sixty-year-olds, or a man and his missus would get into a fight and be tearing lumps out of each other. The last thing you want to do is to try and stop it, because before you know it they've both turned on you! Aggro in Manchester wasn't specific, it was widespread, it could happen to anybody at any time. Anyone could get beaten up for any fuckin' reason, it didn't matter if you were a Punk or whatever but the one thing that marked you out to get more hassle than most was if you looked different. So if you looked different you got belted.

"I went from having seriously long hair, so you could easily get belted for that, to having a bit of a Punky look. Now I never thought I looked particularly Punky but just being a little bit different marked you out. The threat of violence always hung heavy in the air. You weren't allowed to back down, you weren't allowed to say sorry to people. You had to make somebody stand down, that's how you kept where you were in Manchester generally. It didn't take much, a spilt drink, the wrong word, you know?"

Tolerance was in short supply in the seventies. Subjects for fervent discrimination included skin colour, religious persuasion, sexual orientation, chosen football team, haircut, geography… and trousers.

Alan Keogh: "You had to be quite brave to go out dressed the way we dressed. Adge particularly, and myself were very interested in that kind of thing. We used to make stuff, you know? We'd make T-shirts because he went to Art college in Stockport, so he'd know about printing and stuff like that. Adge and I used to wear all sorts of outrageous shit. There was no way anyone could look at us and go 'the classic punk look from the papers'. We weren't, nobody was. We wore plastic coats, red plastic sandals, drainpipe jeans, hair all over the place, dyed in whichever colour. People wanted to batter you, every time we went out everybody wanted to batter you. Manchester then was not the hipster, trendy, difference loving place with a Northern Quarter - there was none of that. Back then, you walked out and it was like 'look at that cunt there'. You couldn't even go out wearing a pair of drainpipes. Going out wearing drainpipe jeans in Manchester in those days was asking for trouble. I wore much more outrageous things than drainpipe jeans but that was all it took for someone to decide to kick shit out of you."

Mark Windsor: "They thought we were a bit psycho, you know? 'They must be hard if they can go out dressed like that'."

Janine Hewitt: "When we walked along the street people would cross the road to avoid walking past us, some people found us intimidating. It was much safer to stay in a group of say five or more as you were less likely to attract any trouble"

Terry Slater: "I used to go around all the antique clothes shops. It was fresh, it was very brave yeah. You had to be brave to walk down the street."

Stanley Vegas: "We tended to get on with everybody really, that's how we rolled, apart from the meatheads who were into their Soul and Disco. You'd come out of Pips for instance and you had to walk past this club on the corner of Fennel Street called 'Rowntrees', and that was a sort of mainstream disco. So all the guys who hadn't copped off used to come outside to fight with the punks and Bowie fans, running the gauntlet towards Piccadilly."

Alan Keogh: "I got involved in quite a bit of fighting, erm… kind of wish I didn't, but I did. I'm not a believer in violence, I would never promote violence as an answer to anything. It was very much about self-defence, it was also about, I won't deny it, it was also about a buzz you know, when it happened. I knew I was with people who weren't going to back off. I came down from Glasgow which was a tough city. I never had to fight in Glasgow, but I had to fight in Manchester."

Knives were still a weapon of choice, but this time they were smaller and sharper, and their methods of deployment became more sinister.

Andy T.: "The 'soul boys' would have two Stanley knife blades in a Stanley knife with a matchstick shoved in between them, so that when they cut you they couldn't sew you up at the hospital; the cuts were so close together you'd just end up with a big gash. Basically they'd be on the back of the bus, and I've seen it happen several times, where as they were getting off the bus they'd run past and slash people and keep running off the bus."

Among the most serious incidents of trouble, there could also be moments of pure slapstick comedy.

Fran Taylor: "I only ever got beaten up one other time, me personally, and that was coming back from the Electric Circus one night. Rather than walk back down Oldham Road, we walked back down Rochdale Road and two lads came out of the estate and jumped me and my mate. It was quite comical really because they were drunker than we were, and their efforts to beat us up were fucking ludicrous. I was standing there and this guy's trying to hit me and I'm going 'What the f…' meanwhile his mate and my mate were having a conversation while he's trying to beat me up!"

A major factor which exacerbated the violence was the licensing laws.

Mark Windsor: "Everything shut at 2am so everybody came out at the same time. I saw it kick off in Piccadilly loads of times, Police dogs and everything. I never got hit."

Denise and Dawn pinpointed the places where they found the most trouble as "*Wolverhampton, Stockton on Tees and anywhere in Yorkshire*".

Denise Shaw: "The worst ones were over in Yorkshire because the bands would be playing to an audience which were like, 'What the hell is this?'."

Andy T.: "People would come up to you and demand money, but we'd never got any money, we'd tell them that we were trying to bunk the bus home ourselves. They weren't so fierce when faced in a confrontation."

A major part in the culture of the working class youth was going to the football. It was another version of tribal fanaticism, the feeling of belonging to a movement of like-minded people, of solidarity and bonding. Music and football have consistently mirrored the fashions of the times, from The Anfield Kop singing Beatle's songs, through to the 'casuals' and Perry Boys in the 80's. It also attracted some of the worst elements in the country's demographic, whose main criteria was to cause disturbances between opposing supporters or the police all over the country but among the crowds of hooligans there were signs of the two contingents of punk and football sharing a common bond."

Ian Moss: "Famously, United always had this big London support, even then when they were unsuccessful. I was going to the away games in the south and there were these four lads from London who all dressed in Vivienne Westwood's finest by late '76. They could recognise where I was coming from and vice versa, so we talk about this transference of what was going on. They would tell me what was happening around London, they were clearly on the fringes of the Pistol's camp, you know?

I remember them telling me about the Ramones/Flamin' Groovies gig at the Roundhouse. They'd be like 'what's happening in Manchester?' so I'd tell them about the Electric Circus. So football was great it was like tom-toms."

Mickey Tait: "We used to go to the football as well… you know, with our drainpipes. I'm not sure if you know anything about where the Perrys originated from? I have a feeling that Liverpool was possibly the recognised starting point but there would have been 15 to 20 of us who used to go and see City wearing the drainpipes, and we had the flicks because we were into Roxy Music and stuff like that in '76. We used to go to the away games, plus we'd meet up at Victoria train station on a Sunday morning and go to Blackpool for the day, about 30 of us. I had it in my mind that that kind of look developed from that, then punk came along. Mickey Carr would have been around that scene at that time yeah."

Mickey Carr: "In no time at all, amongst the fans, you got a mix of people at football matches, from beer people, louts, and the more serious hooligans. We were the more serious hooligan type… we were there before, when it was just Doc Martens and stuff. Perhaps the remarkable thing is that all of a sudden City had a recognised sub-group among their hooligan element which was 'City's Punks'. Not that there weren't any at United…, there were 2 or 3 who were part of that Ranch Bar thing, and there was a cross of colours thing, they never changed their loyalty but they started coming with us. We all used to hang about at the same part of the ground and generally make a nuisance of ourselves with the Hamburger and programme sellers. It was like, who won? We were just pissing about… trying to nick burgers and that. We'd watch the match of course but we'd be out early doors to get a punch up with the away supporters."

Those warring factions of fractious behaviour weren't confined to the football terraces, the band's themselves would also divide opinions between their respective audiences.

Fran Taylor: "There was friction and the threat of violence between the fans as well. You'd hear people at gigs slagging each other off, proper tribal stuff."

Non football fans would also get caught up in some of the more indiscriminate and sinister acts of wanton thuggery.

Mike Keogh: "Terry and meself used to have some cracking nights in and around Manchester. Wherever we could get to, that either would let you in or you'd risk getting a clobbering trying to get there. One night, following the 'derby' match, the United and City fans were out for a good night. All of a sudden I felt something thud into my back... Terry just went 'fuckin' hell' and picked a dart out of my back."

Terry Slater: "I remember that. We were walking through the centre of Manchester on our way to The Ranch, and because we were dressed a little different someone threw a dart at Mike and it hit him right on the shoulder piercing his skin. They probably thought 'look at these pair of ponces'. So we dived in this pub where you went downstairs. So we ran in and went straight to the toilet and I got this dart out of his shoulder. All of a sudden the door burst open in the toilet and I thought 'Shit!' But it was a lad that I used to go to school with, and he was a bruiser, do you know what I mean? So he said 'Alright Terry? I thought it was you, what's goin' on?' So I said 'I don't know, some idiot's thrown a dart at my mate and it was stuck in his back'. So we stayed there with him for a bit."

One experience that football gave the supporters was a chance to see other parts of the country as they followed their respective teams. Many people never travelled further than a few miles from their houses for most of the year, so when they turned up in a town or city hundreds of miles away and saw the same problems, there was a feeling that the dire economic situation in and around Manchester, was a common thread linking them together; the country was in a bad way.

Ian Moss: "For a lot of young people and teenagers, there was no reason to travel... apart from going on their holidays to Blackpool or wherever...that would be the only time in the year that they moved out of their area. Quite often even Manchester was too far for them. If you lived where I lived in Tameside, Ashton would be the big night out. For 50 weeks of the year they would work in the area, they'd go out in the area, and they'd have two weeks. That was life."

This dis-United Kingdom was perfectly reflected in the singing and chanting at the matches, a distasteful verbal sparring from rival societies. Pop songs, classical works, and hymns, all bastardised into triumphant roars of solidarity, or alternatively mocking and sometimes offensive baiting of their rivals.

Ian Moss: "I remember going to Cardiff and it was like being thrust into a fucking horrible Charles Dickens novel, it was absolutely black, because of the coal, and everything was falling down. The match was at Ninian Park, I'd never seen violence like it. Both sets of fans had scabs that were raw; the United fans were chanting about Aberfan, and the

Cardiff fans were shouting about Munich. People were picking up huge slabs of concrete from the terracing that was all broken up… huge pieces of concrete were flying over. It was incredible, and very, very strange."

Eventually the first punk songs were beginning to filter onto the terraces.

Ian Moss: "I'd never give City much credit for anything but I do remember very early on, the City fans chanting 'Ay Oh Let's Go' and 'Beat On The Brat'. They'd adopted those into chants, so there was a punk thing…"

Mickey Carr: "One of the biggest highlights of the football year would be the games away at Liverpool or Everton. It was always really uncomfortable for anyone going there as it was for them coming to us. The trick was to get the service train, not the football special. It was at these games where the United punks/friends would come with us as well as some of the other City hooligans. We'd go really early, straight into Lime Street, and there's a reception committee waiting for us because it used to go on all day. So before the trains even stopped we're all off and running and some of the lads have got the make up on you know, eyeliner and that. So there's a gang of us from Moston, Harpurhey, Gorton, Levenshulme… the same lads who we'd hang about with in the week at the bowling place at Belle Vue. We'd be causing trouble there, having fights, being cheeky, you know. Anyway we're off the train and one lad had blue hair at the time, very tall, and a black kid with us called Kano, he was big and various scallies wearing drainpipes and baseball boots, quite punkish, there might have been the odd 'Destroy' T-shirt. So we're all hyped up and ready for it, and there's a load of scousers. There used to be an arcade there and word had got round that a train from Manchester has just come in, so there's going to be some early action. They thought it was great, you know? 'Look at the state of these', expecting us all to run away, but we weren't daft, we'd been going there for years. So they're all coming across the road towards us and we just stood there and we all pulled out the Stanleys (knives). Their faces changed, you know what I mean? Because they weren't expecting it off these weirdos with their strange clothes on, and it ended up in a big fight across the road and into the arcade itself. It was a sight to behold when they thought that they were going to have us and it just shocked them. Us being tooled up with the Stanley knives glinting in the sun you know? Come on!"

Ian Moss: "There were the clichés thrown about places, for instance the thing with Liverpool; most people had never been to fucking Liverpool. We'd go to the football, travel around, and you'd see what a state the country was in, and that sort of fuelled the punk aesthetic. You saw what a filthy, broken mess we lived in."

Although the punks were singled out for a bashing in mainstream society, the bonds of the football fraternity were tight, so if you wore the same colours, it didn't matter what you looked like.

Mickey Carr: "The other City fans would look out for us, just as you'd look after any of the gang, but we were a more identifiable target from our main rivals, which was United. We ('City's Punks') didn't operate in isolation, we'd be attached to the main mob, you know. They liked us you know... we'd be in the pub after and people would be sayin' 'yeah City's Punks went in their end'. Which we would do independently... 15-20 of us would find ourselves into the Leeds end for instance. United's boys would come looking for us, because of something we'd done or whatever. And they'd come looking for us as distinct from the general City fans you know... City's punks."

Mark Windsor: "The football lads used to protect us."

Stanley Vegas: "I remember going away with City, the old Baseball Ground, Derby County. At half time they played either The Clash or the Pistols, and we all started pogoing, and we pogoed onto the pitch towards the Derby fans, because there was loads of punks."

Martin Ryan: "Paul Morley was a City fan, he used to go with his dad, Kevin Cummins and Rob Gretton."

Mickey Tait: "I remember seeing a kid called Daffy at a Stockport County game against Everton for some reason. It was a freezing cold night and I remember he had a jumper on with all rips and he had a safety pin from his ear to his nose. He was a City fan as well funnily enough."

As if the standard Saturday night punch ups weren't enough, once the media embarked on their sensationalist, and in most cases fabricated headlines, there was literally a target audience for the thugs to concentrate on. Real punks were a bit thin on the ground and in any case were extremely wary of the newspapers, so they mocked up an identikit 'punk rocker'. They upped the scaremongering stakes with tales of immorality, swearing and violence, it was as if the flick-knife wielding Teddy Boys of the '50's and the Mods and Rockers of the 60's had never happened. One particular incident spelt the death knell early on.

Mark Windsor: "I think that the Bill Grundy show ballsed it all up. The straights got in and all of a sudden you were hated, people were being brainwashed to hate you. We were chased, had stuff thrown at us, and getting on the late night bus back to Denton was like taking your life in your hands."

Ian Moss: "I always went to the football, and I remember it was just after the Bill Grundy thing and I was going to Ipswich. I was on Piccadilly train station waiting for the football special, and someone said 'you're one of them fuckin' punk rockers' you know? The football was another thing that shaped me. In those days you had to learn that the Police weren't to be looked up to, you learned to distrust them and authority, because that was a lie."

Alan Keogh: "You learned to deal with the violence propagated by the media, propagated by the *Daily Mirror* - punk scum. I never identified myself as a punk, never ever called myself a punk. I like John Lydon's take on it, 'we never said that we were punks'. I didn't call myself that, never ever called myself that."

Ian Moss: "You steeled yourself for it; you'd go into places knowing that there would be friction. It was good in a way you know, going into these places, and you're exposing what bigoted, close-minded cunts they are."

Mark Windsor: "I remember there was some remark made somewhere that proclaimed, 'PUNKS DON'T WEAR FLARES!' So we all went out in flares you know, okay so you're predicting me now are you? Right then I'll go out with a Belisha Beacon on my head and flippers! We didn't walk around like we were scared, we walked around like we fucking owned the place! People would move out of your way. We had to front it out and sometimes it worked and sometimes it didn't."

Of all the places that attracted the most trouble, it was usually where there was easy pickings and a guaranteed supply of victims.

Fran Taylor: "Usually there'd be people hanging about outside waiting to ambush people. What you've got to remember about Manchester in 1976/77 is that there were a limited number of ways to get home, and they all involved Piccadilly Gardens. Basically once you got past midnight you were into a night bus situation, and all the night buses and everybody who got on them, got on them from Piccadilly. So if you wanted to meet and beat somebody up, all you had to do was hang around there long enough because people had to go there to get a bus or a taxi. Fights went off all the time in Piccadilly. Piccadilly Gardens, waiting for a bus to go home it just kicked off on a regular basis, it was mayhem. Me and Pete Shelley and a bunch of girls came out of The Ranch and were crossing Piccadilly and I just heard this yelp from behind me and Pete was on the floor. I ran back and this bloke came out of nowhere and clothes lined me, knocked me straight up in the air, so me and Pete took a bit of a kicking and then the girls came and started screaming at these blokes and they ran away. That was early '77 and Pete was getting to be known."

Terry Slater: "The scariest thing was getting the bus home after I'd finished my shift at The Ranch. I lived in Longsight then and I'd get the 192."

Joanne Slater: "I used to get the 210 and the driver used to turn off Hyde Road and drop me off outside my house to make sure I got home safe."

Denise Shaw: "One particular time I got on the bus, and the driver, as soon as I got on, you could just see it in his face, he was just like, 'Oh my God' you know. So I went upstairs and there was a group of lads on the bus and they were making comments and what have you, and every time the bus stopped and somebody was coming upstairs I'd hear the driver go, 'Eh, wait until you see 'that' upstairs', so I'd had that right up to Queens Road, and then Sarge, who used to roadie for The Drones, got on the bus. He was a Hells Angel and he was a big guy, so of course the bus driver says to him, 'Hey mate go upstairs and have a look at the state of that upstairs'. So he came up, looked at me and then he looked around the rest of the bus, 'Is he talking about you?', and I went, 'Yeah'. So he went back downstairs, lifted the bus driver out of his seat, and said 'Get up them stairs and apologise'. So this driver's going 'I'm really sorry I didn't mean to offend you' and all this, and I'm cringing thinking Oh my God this is even worse! I couldn't get off the bus quick enough!"

Ken Park: "There was a lot of violence and it came afterwards, outside the clubs. If you missed your last bus home you were in trouble if you got caught out with the different gangs. We had to run for our lives!

Stanley Vegas: "The all night bus home was never a good thing, because it had come from Manchester and it'd be rockin', plus it was full of fucking meatheads, and we'd have to get on with all our punk gear on. We were glam punks so we always wore make up as well, so it would be a bit of a shock to people on the bus."

Juliette J. Williams: "It was a violent time, especially running the gauntlet of Piccadilly station for the all night bus back to Bolton, which was at a quarter to two in the morning. It only went as far as Little Hulton precinct, so I'd have to find my own way home from there, which was a fair way because I lived on the north side of Bolton. It was a hard time if you looked different. We got chased once by these middle aged men who were throwing the old bevelled pint glasses at us because they didn't like how we looked."

Alan Keogh: "There was violence all the time. There was violence for me and Ian Dalglish and Adge. We were going down on the 192 and getting off the bus in Levenshulme, a couple of bikers decided to come after us with bike chains you know, they were shouting, 'fuckin' punk bastards'."

Sarah Mee: "It was a time of economic depression, cheesy Disco music, and if you didn't follow the pack, or the ideal of the 'norm', you had to expect the rage aimed at you for being different by the rest of society...including children as well as old folk. Not getting spat at or physically attacked was an achievement in itself. However, getting home was always a nightmare as we had to go to Piccadilly Gardens bus station to get the night bus home. On one occasion my sister and I were walking with Pete (Shelley) to the gardens and he was wearing pyjamas, my sister had shaved her hair and dyed it pink, and I was blonde and spikey so we didn't stand out too much! We had just sat down when a couple of men came over and started on him, then grabbed my umbrella and hit my sister over the head with it. Luckily it was a cheap one from the market so it bent easily. But those were the typical things that happened on a night out in Manchester."

Janine Hewitt: "A lad I was with was punched in Piccadilly Gardens, but we didn't consider reporting it. I think they just disliked the way he was dressed and what he thought he stood for. You just expected it, that was the way it was then I suppose."

Deb Zee: "Piccadilly Gardens at the bus station it was like... the Perry boys. They'd come up to you and one of them used to be a punk and they took their belts off and they would swing them at you. I was quite fearless then so I wasn't bothered but then it happened in Moston in the high rise flats; me and Gus Gangrene and somebody else. I don't know if Daniel O'Sullivan was there. Some Perry Boys came knocking at the door and they came in and I remember my Doc Martins going out of the 8th floor window in this Bradford Court estate but luckily they didn't take my records. They were hidden in this settee which was broken but it had like a false seat in it and they were all hidden in there."

Martin Ryan: "When people talk about Perry Boys, I'd never heard of them in 1977, but I've heard about them since. I didn't really encounter many Teds either."

Gail Egan: "The 'Teddy Boys', that was the big thing with punks. They used to come into Manchester and try to start a fight. I can remember me, Cath West, and a couple of other people walking back up Rochdale Road from The Electric Circus, and a load of Teds came running after us. This Transit van pulled up at the side of the road, so we had a choice; getting beaten up by the 'Teds' or jumping into this unknown Transit van. We jumped into the van and fortunately it was someone we knew so we were alright."

Daniel O'Sullivan: "It was always difficult. You always felt that you were being scrutinised, looked at, abused and all the rest of it. I just felt quite thick skinned towards it."

Carol O'Donnell: "We used to get chased a lot, we got called all sorts and everyone hated us, and thought that we were scum. I was never into violence and never into fighting, I'm still not."

Chris Lambert: "We got chased quite a bit."

Mike Keogh: "We were walking across Spring Gardens, there were four of us; me, Terry, Alison and Fenula – then this gang of Teddy Boys were coming towards us. I thought we either going to get chased or slapped but they walked past us. I thought that's a result but the next thing I remember is being picked up off the floor. It was that quick, I never saw it coming. I was a bit groggy but we carried on to The Ranch. I woke up the next day with a bit of an egg on my head."

Janine Hewitt: "The hype in the papers at the time about spitting being a punk activity made us out to be violent, anarchistic and without morals so that didn't help the public relate to us."

Una Baines: "The media said that punk was about violence, spitting and jumping up and down. That was so offensive."

Chris Lambert: "I hated the spitting. I could never understand it. It was anti-social then and it's still anti-social now."

Juliette J. Williams: "It never happened until the fall out from the Bill Grundy incident, which meant nothing to us because it wasn't televised up here, and all of a sudden... I can remember exactly where I was. I was on the No. 8 bus coming back to Bolton, I'd been to Virgin on Lever Street, and I'd been for some single or other, I can't remember what it was, and someone had *The Sun* open in front of me and I was like, what's that about? And it was going on about the spitting. This was Summer '77 but me and my friend were like, 'What's all this spitting?' There was a photo of Lydon with a can of lager spraying... looking like he was spitting. From that moment every gig you went to, you'd have globules on the back of your hair and on your leathers. It was revolting and prior to that it wasn't happening."

Gail Egan: "That was the thing that used to annoy us because we didn't. Honestly your hair used to smell, it was that disgusting."

Mike Keogh: "The best thing about it was that it was all new stuff, it was a new thing that was happening. The newspapers, parents, they hated us big time."

Anyone with a persecution complex may have had some justification for it but the opportunity to antagonise was just too tempting, every opportunity was taken. It was done predominantly to get a reaction rather than anything seriously malicious.

Alan Keogh: "When Elvis died we made these T-shirts with a coffin on. It had 'Elvis' above the coffin and underneath 'is dead'. Then we walked around town and there were all the Teddy boys, they were fucking furious - we only did it to wind them up. I mean I haven't got a problem with Elvis, he was alright. I love rock and roll for the record. I love Gene Vincent. But it was a case of, let's torment the fuckers."

Another turn of phrase from the tabloids primarily attributed to punks was 'Glue Sniffers'. There was the fanzine *Sniffin' Glue* as well which turned the insult into a badge of honour. Although to be fair there was an element of truth to it.

Odgie: "My memory is excellent about some things, I can remember things from when I was four or five years old but there are also big gaps in it, particularly around the punk period because we were doing that much Evo-Stik. We were hitting it pretty hard. It's a much maligned drug, it's a really good drug in many respects, you could stop time with it. If you used it properly it was a really interesting mindscape that you got to, but you can't get it anymore because they've changed all the fucking chemicals in it."

Deb Zee: "I didn't understand the sniffing glue thing, but we used to sit about and do some Dodo's, because we bought them over the counter and they were cheap, they'd keep you going. Me and my mate Sarah used to have Night Nurse... no, sorry it was Day Nurse... that was cheap as well."

Odgie: "Johnny Rotten got us into Night Nurse because that was what he used to do."

Chris Lambert: "Our chemist banned cough medicine."

Ken Park: "I always thought that solvents were kind of desperate. I remember when you went into a recording studio, the guys on the desk, the tape head cleaner, they'd always be sniffing that."

There was a distinct juxtaposition of looking effeminate and dressing differently, but coming from a tough background, which resulted in the bullies and 'straights' sometimes picking on the wrong people.

Alan Keogh: "We were inner city kids us, we weren't middle class, boundaries of Stockport kind of punk kids like a lot of them were. We were from Moston, Blackley, Collyhurst, Levenshulme, Longsight and Harpurhey. We were 15 year-old kids who weren't going to be knocked about physically."

Mickey Tait: "What we had to do was stick by each other, not as a gang, but we had to have a presence. Because of where we grew up it was a natural thing, so we were ready for all that anyway. I don't want to sound aggressive or anything but…"

Mickey Carr: "All the beer monsters, some of them were just horrible - just bullies. Some of them would just take the piss, but others… We were game for trouble. you know what I mean? We were off these estates in Manchester, we'd grown up with it all. I'm not saying we were hard or anything but we had this tightness. A lot of people came unstuck, whether it was the divs in town, or the Bee Gee types as we called them who'd be like 'what the fuck do you look like!' and all that shit. Well, they'd find themselves surrounded by experienced nuisances if you like."

Mike Keogh: "Some of them were real fucking 'head the balls'; they had knives, bike chains, the lot. Getting slapped by the Teds down in The Cottages; the toilets at Spring Gardens. You didn't go down there unless you were really crapping yourself. We weren't in there long when the bike chains came over the top of the toilet door, and I got a bit of a slapping. Anyway I learnt after that, just fucking piss on the street rather than go down there, and that's what we ended up doing most of the time."

Terry Slater: "People were so happy but having said that, on the way home it was dangerous, as was going out. But you were always looking over your shoulder. It could be dangerous in a lot of places then, especially going to Band On The Wall because you know where that's situated, don't you? Dale Street could be a bit intimidating too."

Daniel O'Sullivan: "I was attacked by this notorious soul boy, who used to go to Genevieve's with his crew of mates… they took a dislike to me. So I'd have to run the gauntlet with them now and again."

Kevin Stanfield: "I used to walk into the centre of Manchester from Sedgley Park, mainly because there were Boddingtons pubs all the way into town. In those days if you were a punk you were targeted so if I was pissed I didn't really care."

There was also a lot of trouble at gigs between the differing factions of society, sometimes it was literally a case of 'your face didn't fit'.

Andy T.: "There were some good gigs at the Civic Hall. So It Goes used to put gigs on there. They had Tom Robinson and Mink

Deville. There was that Damned/Adverts tour which had the poster; '*The Damned can play three chords, The Adverts know one. Come and hear all four at...*' They played at the Middleton Civic Hall at the start of the tour and at the Circus at the end of the tour. The Circus gig was a great gig, and so was the Civic Hall but there was loads of trouble after it. Middleton is one of those places that's very insular, even though it's connected to Manchester and surrounding areas, it had its own town centre. If anyone outside went in there, it was like, the piano player would stop playing and everyone would look round, and they'd know that you were an outsider. The people who were going back to Manchester had to go through the town centre to get buses and stuff. So you'd get attacked in the Bus station."

Chris Lambert: "Yeah, we'd been to see The Damned at Middleton Civic Hall and after we went to the Dusty Miller pub across the road. There were only two people in there and they left as soon as we walked in, so we had a pint, came out and the two that were in there earlier had gone out and got all their mates."

Alan Keogh: "I'm from the estates and the fighting culture. I always felt a bit frustrated, and I still do feel frustrated that a lot of the punk guys of the scene at that time really looked down their noses at what I would call genuinely working class lads. Not girls, it's a gender thing because the girls we knew were all from the same places as us but they never got it. I never went out looking for fights. It was partly about our age, very much about how we were perceived, and very much about the media. When I got into fights or trouble, it was always about protection of somebody which makes perfect sense if you knew my upbringing. It was looking after your friends you know. You're not going to do it to us, you're not going to make us your victims."

And they certainly didn't.

13. a noise annoys

"The people who make the best rock records can't really play that well at all"

Robert Wyatt
NME October 26th 1974.

By the middle of 1977 the number of bands in Manchester and around the country had been gradually increasing, giving each region its own punk scene away from the epicentre of London; The Cortinas from Bristol, The Adverts from Devon, Penetration in Newcastle, along with countless others whose career never got past the bedrooms/youth clubs/garages they practised in. The notion of not being able to play, perpetuated by the press and some of the bands themselves, broke down the barrier between artist and audience. Rudimentary skills could be excused over power or inventiveness, and just the sheer act of doing something positive and new gained a muted respect from their peers. Some took the ramshackle ideology to the limit, whilst others mutated the new found musical experimentation to produce a more individualistic result. Manchester's selection of early bands collectively fitted into an assortment of those characteristics, from poppy punk to cacophony and poetry; nothing was off limits.

BUZZCOCKS

As the first genuine punk band to form in Manchester they bought Sex Pistols to the city, and released the first independent punk single. They had their own unique style of buzz saw guitars and melodies when punk wasn't supposed to have melodies, which was one punk myth. They also wrote songs about un-punk subjects such as love, unrequited or otherwise, which is another punk myth. Pete Shelley (real name Pete McNeish) was a big Beatles fan and he met Devoto (Howard Trafford) at Bolton Institute of Technology, where Shelley was running an electronic music society. Devoto required some soundtrack material for his video projects and at that time they were unacquainted but joined forces when a mutual love of The Velvet Underground and The Stooges became apparent. The name Buzzcocks came from a review of the television drama Rock Follies in *Time Out* magazine that had the headline,'It's the buzz cock!'. On April Fool's Day 1976 the first incarnation of the band played their first gig.

Fran Taylor: "The original line up did one gig in Bolton at the College of Technology, and that was Garth, Howard, Pete, and some mate of theirs who played drums. Garth was in Pete's very first band called The Jets of Air they were at school together basically."

Some of those early Jets Of Air songs dated back to 1973 and would later resurface as Buzzcocks tunes; Love You More, Nostalgia, Telephone Operator and Sixteen Again. Elsewhere, and completely separately, Steve Diggle was recording fledgling versions of 'Fast Cars', 'Promises' and the main riff to 'Autonomy'. The dots were joined together gradually until the first recognised line up of Devoto, Shelley, Diggle and Maher played their first gig with the Sex Pistols and Slaughter and the Dogs. The addition of Steve Diggle was a happy accident because he was outside the Free Trade Hall on the night of the first Sex Pistols gig there on June 4th. He was there to meet someone about a vacant bass playing job in another band but owing to a misunderstanding he ended up with the wrong band. Or the right band as it turned out.

The dearth of 'punk' bands around Manchester in those early days meant that Buzzcocks and Slaughter's paths would cross often in those early gigs. Leading to a fractious relationship between them.

Gail Egan: "I can remember the rivalry between Buzzcocks and Slaughter and the Dogs, that was real, they really didn't like each other. It wasn't Pete, because he was dead chilled out, I don't know what it was all about."

Fran Taylor: "There was a huge rivalry between Slaughter and the Dogs and Buzzcocks. It was overhyped at times but it did erupt into some serious violence. I can remember that they didn't like supporting one another, and when they were both supporting Johnny Thunders at Parr Hall in Warrington, I heard that there was a massive ruck backstage where Garth the bass player wanted to wade in to Slaughter and bust a few heads. He always fancied himself as a bit tasty but I wasn't convinced myself."

Wispa: "There was a lot of inter band rivalry, even between the Manchester bands, you know the sort of thing 'we're better than you...' it was pathetic looking back now, really pathetic. We were at the Circus one night watching a gig and the Slaughter lads were there as well. Anyway, things were said and next thing you know they're walking out and a pint pot gets thrown at us so we chased them outside, and we're all scrapping in the street, and then half an hour later we're all best mates! It's stupid innit?"

When Howard Devoto left the band in February, just after Spiral Scratch was released, Steve Diggle moved to lead guitar leaving a space for a new bass player. Garth Davies replied to the advert in Virgin Records and reacquainted himself with Pete Shelley.

Davies's reintroduction into the band was announced in the March edition of *Sniffin' Glue*. Next to a picture of a very grumpy looking Garth was the news: "This is the new guy in The Buzzcocks (sic). His name is Garth. Happy bleeder ain't he?"

Gail Egan: "I can remember when Howard left, I said to Pete, 'Who's going to sing?' and he said, 'Well, I am'. I'll never forget that. Howard was such a prominent figure."

The new bands like Buzzcocks, Clash, Sex Pistols, and The Damned had come to blow all the established farts out of the water, with their youthful aggression and antipathy to their overblown self importance. The notion that any of those early punk bands could have musical skeletons in their cupboard was a thought too horrendous to contemplate.

Fran Taylor: "I can remember going to the house that Pete, Richard and Howard shared in Broughton and Linder (Sterling) was there at the time because she was Howard's girlfriend. As we were leaving one day, Howard was coming out of his room, and as he opened his bedroom door there was a poster on his wall... of Queen. I was devastated that he had a Queen poster on his wall. I thought, oh he's only got it up there because it's that science fiction one with the robot, it's an art thing, not because he likes Queen; he can't like Queen!"

Being the trailblazers had its advantages, and their star was in the ascendency more or less immediately. By the end of the first 12 months they were seen as one of the major players along with Sex Pistols, The

Clash, The Jam, and The Damned.

Fran Taylor: "Buzzcocks were pretty much headlining all the time, they very rarely supported bands, although they did the White Riot tour supporting The Clash. When it came to Manchester they didn't support, they were left off the bill. It just became The Clash, The Slits, and Subway Sect, Buzzcocks didn't play the Manchester gig. They played with them in Leeds but... make of that what you will."

Such was the paucity of suitable venues in which to play, trips out of town were undertaken, plus there were instances where 'a gig was a gig'.

Fran Taylor: "During 1977 I became friends with Kevin Cummins and Paul Morley. Kevin had gone to my school and lived around the corner from where I lived in Salford, and he had a car of course. So I went to a load of little clubs across the north-west, and wider ranging, to see Buzzcocks with Kevin and Paul, I used to chip in with the petrol and he'd take us. Plus we would get in for nothing at the other end. Places like The Outlook in Doncaster, Nickers in Keighley, and I think it was either Oasis or Palms in Blackburn where Buzzcocks played supporting Sad Café. What an awful fucking evening that was!"

Fran ended up working for the band.

Fran Taylor: "It built up gradually, going to see them with Paul and Kevin, we'd be there at sound checks and your face gets known. I pretty much knew Pete and Richard (Boon) by then, I first met them in Cox's Bar in Manchester. It was before the Eddie and the Hot Rods gig, late '76 and I was chatting to them, so I knew them to talk to. By the end of '77 I ended up working for Buzzcocks. I was at one gig and Richard came up to me and said, 'You come along to a lot of our gigs and we need a bit of help loading and unloading the gear, would you like to help out? We can't pay you but you get into the gigs for free plus your travel is free.' So I said 'yeah alright, I'll have some of that.

"After the very first gig he gave me a fiver, and after that I started setting up the drums and various bits and pieces until in the end I was putting together the PA, mixing for support bands, whatever. I learned as I went along, doing guitars and whatever was needed and as they got bigger they'd get a more expert person in so I mostly did the monitors on stage. I also did the out front sound for some of the support bands, Keith, who did it normally, asked me if I fancied doing it because they never usually had their own sound man. The first one I did was Subway Sect because they were managed by Bernie Rhodes, he would turn up to the big gigs; Manchester, Birmingham, London, with a sound man and the rest of the tour I would do. Vic was happy with what I was doing, so eventually Vic and the band said 'We don't want 'him' anymore, we want Fran'; 'him' was Mickey Foote, who produced the first Clash album."

Although the success of Spiral Scratch had ignited a spark of interest from record labels, they were in no real rush to sign to a major label.

Fran Taylor: "Buzzcocks didn't get a recording deal until August '77. Of course they had the New Hormones deal but that was then… there's a photo where Pete's written out the lyrics to Sixteen and at the bottom he signed it Pete Shelley, Copyright New Hormones 1977 just to protect it because they didn't have a copyright deal. As far as they were concerned they were a New Hormones band. They signed to United Artists on the day that Elvis Presley died. They actually signed on the bar of The Electric Circus the night of the gig they did with Penetration and The Jam which was recorded for So It Goes; 16th August 1977."

John Maher: "My dad had to sign for me as I was underage."

Fran Taylor: "A lot of record labels were piling in to get their punk band, they were desperate to sign a punk band, anything. Plus a lot of punk bands were desperate to sign a deal. Buzzcocks weren't desperate to sign a deal. The Clash actually got death threats for 'selling out'. I heard people shout out at the gigs, 'You fucking sell outs!' I mean, why do you start a band in the first place?"

The volatile relationship between Shelley and Davies came to a head on October 8th 1977 when the band played at the Mr. George club in Coventry. Davies's enthusiasm for the band was waning and he wasn't in the right frame of mind for the gig that night. The sound check had ended abruptly following a stand up row between Davies and Shelley, culminating in Davies walking out of the building to find the nearest bar. Eric Ramsden went with him to make sure that he made it back to do the gig. They had a meal and more drinks and Ramsden got him back just in time to go on stage. But his mood hadn't improved and shortly after the set began he threw down his guitar and stormed off stage. The band carried on without him, Steve Diggle playing the bass parts on his guitar. Once the gig was over it was time to get back to Manchester, and with Davies being *persona non grata* he travelled back separately from the rest of the band.

Fran Taylor: "I was at his first and his last gig, and his last gig was amazing. We'd gone to Coventry and they were playing a gig at a place called 'Mr. Georges' supported by The Flys who included Hazel O'Connor's brother. So Garth and Eric Ramsden, before he became

Eric Random, went on the piss all day. Eric was instructed to keep Garth out of the rest of the bands' way, because they were already falling out. Anyway they came back and Garth was completely out of his box. They went on stage and Garth's got this brand new Thunderbird bass, and I'm not sure if something was wrong with the lead or the amp but the next thing he's banging his bass on the speakers. He's not doing his vocals, he's not playing the tune and then he throws the guitar down onto the stage and storms off. This is about three or four numbers in and Pete turned to Steve Diggle and said 'Just play the bass parts on your top strings' and carried on with the rest of the set and the crowd didn't seem too bothered.

"Anyway when they got back to the dressing room they just told Garth, right that's fucking it, you're out, and you're not coming back in the car with us either. I was travelling back in this fucking horrible Leyland van and you could just fit the back line in it, so Keith and Tony, the other road crew, are up front and I always travelled in the back. So what do they do? They put Garth in the back of the van with me, all the way from Coventry back to Manchester. I'm thinking 'Oh for fucks sake!' Thankfully he was so fucked he just fell asleep after the first two minutes. I've got an image of him asleep over the bass drum, this is before John had flight cases, and I was thinking that if he wakes up I'm going to have to hit him with something really heavy before he has a chance to kick off".

With Davies gone and an album to make, moves were being made to acquire a new bassist.

Kevin Stanfield: "I used to hang around at Virgin, and I can remember an advertisement for Buzzcocks needing a new bass player. Steve Garvey got the job, and we used to travel on the same bus into town. It was quite surreal because a bit later on I'd be watching him on Top Of The Pops on the Thursday and then I'd be sat on the bleeding bus with him on the Saturday night!"

Buzzcocks didn't rely on gimmicks or sensationalism to sell records, the songs were classic short, sharp slabs of pop power that still stand up to scrutiny to this day. Although advice to the contrary was sometimes forthcoming.

Fran Taylor: "I remember sitting in the backroom of Richard Boon's house at Lower Broughton Road and he got a phone call. It was Malcolm McLaren talking about getting The Slits on the Buzzcocks tour and when he got off the phone he said, 'That was Malcolm, we were discussing the tour and then he started to tell me how I could make Buzzcocks more outrageous, do more outrageous things'. Part of Malcolm's agenda was playing up the outrage after the Grundy thing, they were making money out of it. I think they (Sex Pistols) could have played nearly anywhere if they'd wanted, but it was part of the mystique."

Buzzcocks became regulars on Top Of The Pops over the next four years, dispelling yet another punk myth that once you've been on that programme, you'd 'sold out'.

Fran Taylor: "You've got to ride the wave, you've got to take the opportunity. Opportunities for people in bands are so few and far between so if you don't exploit the ones you get, you're never going to go anywhere."

The band split in 1981, Pete Shelley returned to his earlier love of electronic music. The music world had caught up with him, as that was a time of the experimentation of what would lazily be termed post-Punk. Diggle formed Flag Of Convenience, John Maher played with Pauline Murray and the Invisible Girls, Penetration, and The Things, among others, and is now an acclaimed photographer living on the Isle of Harris. Steve Garvey worked with both Shelley and Diggle on their respective solo ventures, as well as his own band Motivation. He now lives in America. Shelley and Diggle continued to front the latest incarnation of the band until Pete's untimely death from a heart attack on the 6th December 2018 aged just 63.

Pete Shelley didn't fit into any category, the same way that Buzzcocks didn't fit into the surmised remit of punk; loud, abrasive, confrontational. He ploughed his own individual musical furrow from the start. His interest in electronics led to experimental soundscapes, recording 'Sky Yen', which he didn't release until the next decade. Pete also tried out a more conventional rock direction with "non existent group" Smash. Eventually everything came together with the new sound and attitude of the Sex Pistols and there was finally a place where his music fitted. He has been described as Punk's Ray Davies, because first and foremost he was a songwriter. Those simplistic, buzz saw pop tunes masked the craft and ingenuity that went into every tune. Buzzcocks didn't record anything throwaway or substandard, and whilst most of those early punk songs still sound of that time, Buzzcocks' songs still sound fresh today. Thank you Pete Shelley.

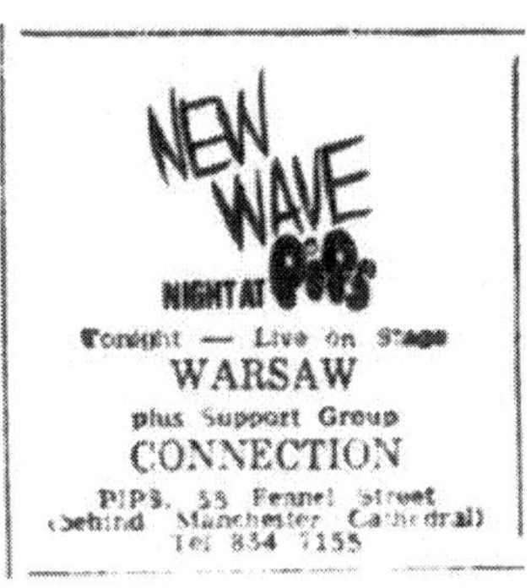

WARSAW

Inspired by the first Sex Pistols gig at the Lesser Free Trade Hall, which 'Barney' Sumner and Peter Hook attended, the pair decided to form a group. They both went out and bought their respective weapons of choice and started to rehearse together, but the missing links were a drummer and a lead singer. An advertisement was duly pinned onto the Virgin Record's notice board and after several candidates for vocal duties were given the 'Thanks, but no thanks' treatment, they eventually found the perfect fit one fateful night at The Electric Circus. Hook and Sumner had seen this kid with 'HATE' written on the back of his donkey jacket around different venues in the city, because the scene was so small at that time in late 1976, it would be the same faces doing the rounds.

The three of them had apparently exchanged words at the second Pistols gig at the Lesser Free Trade Hall in July but that was pure coincidence. Ian Curtis was a few months younger than them, he was married and living in Oldham, and he had the nucleus of a band, but whereas Hook and Sumner were a guitarist and bassist, Curtis's group only had a drummer and guitarist. That drummer was Martin Jackson who went on to play with Magazine, and then in the 80's, with Swing Out Sister. His guitarist was Iain Gray, who'd been at the first Pistols gig and was a mate of Curtis. By the time all three met up at the Sex Pistols gig at The Electric Circus on 9th December, both Jackson and Gray had left, leaving Curtis free to join up with Hook and Sumner. He was the perfect fit. Unfortunately drummers - decent, 'different' drummers that is - were a bit thin on the ground, so that final position would take a rather more protracted sourcing.

Fran Taylor: "The thing that people don't realise is that you can have a band of shit musicians but you can't have a shit drummer. The one thing that will stand out like a sore thumb is a shit drummer. In

Manchester in those early days the one thing that was in short supply were drummers. That was the big problem that Joy Division had; getting a fucking drummer. In the early days of Warsaw, Terry Mason, their best mate, said he would be the drummer, Hooky said he would do the bass, Bernard said he had the basics of guitar, Ian was the singer. But Terry couldn't do the basics so they started auditioning for a drummer. The first one they got was Tony Tabac but he was too Rock and Roll; the next guy they got was Steve Brotherdale who was already playing in a number of other bands including V2 and The Panik, in fact the first thing he tried to do was poach Ian to sing for The Panik! But he was also too Rock and Roll. Eventually they got Steve."

Before Steve Morris was initiated into the band, they had already been scheduled to play their debut gig as invited guests of Buzzcocks at The Electric Circus on 29th May 1977. With the drummer's stool still vacant, it was Tony Tabac who filled in that night and stayed for the next few gigs. As the time of the gig approached, the band not only didn't have a permanent drummer, they didn't have a name.

Martin Ryan: "I saw Warsaw the first night with Buzzcocks and Penetration at The Electric Circus, that was their first gig. They were meant to be called Stiff Kittens, some of the flyers had them as Stiff Kittens."

The name change to Warsaw was decided by Curtis just before they took to the stage. Stiff Kittens was suggested by Richard Boon and he'd put that on the posters advertising the gig. The band thought it was too 'cartoon punk' so it was ditched in true ephemeral punk style. It's fair to say that their initial efforts at song writing were a 'punk by numbers' style racket anyway, far removed from what they became, although some of those early songs survived into Joy Division set lists.

Stanley Vegas: "We knew Joy Division, well, before that when they were Warsaw. Our drummer Stevie Brotherdale was in Warsaw, and he left them to join a band called The Panik."

Martin Ryan: "I never really 'got' Warsaw, I always thought they were just a third division heavy metal turned punk band sort of thing. To be fair 'At A Later Date' was on the 10" Electric Circus album, I thought that was alright, and 'Novelty' which is on the b-side of 'Transmission' they played that back then."

With that first gig out of the way, the next one came along a couple of days later at Rafters, once again supporting a major player in the punk scene; The Heartbreakers. The band were playing for free, and most bands could only have dreamt of the quality of those early gigs. But that initial excitement would turn to frustration and disappointment as the drug habits of The Heartbreakers and their crew meant that Warsaw didn't get a soundcheck, plus when they did get to witness them play, they were less than impressed, they thought that Johnny and his mates were sloppy and shambolic; a valuable lesson learned.

Warsaw's first out of town gig was supporting Penetration in their native Newcastle, also on the bill were The Adverts and Harry Hack and the Big G. It was also their first paid gig: £20. At the beginning of June 1977, Warsaw played the 'Stuff The Jubilee' gig at The Squat, along with The Worst, The Fall, The Drones, and The Negatives. A few weeks later and they were back at The Squat, again with The Worst plus a local Reggae band, possibly X-O-Dus but that's unconfirmed; the gig was given a review in *Sounds* by Tony Moon, but doesn't mention X-O-Dus by name. It was also Tony Tabac's last gig with Warsaw. Steve Brotherdale joined for the next gig at Rafters at the end of June, which is where they first met Martin Hannett and Alan Erasmus.

Brotherdale continued his drumming duties at Tiffany's in Leicester and also when the band went into Pennine Sound Studios on Ripponden Road in Oldham, to record their first demos. They recorded 5 songs; 'Gutz For Garters', 'The Kill', 'At A Later Date', 'Inside The Line' and 'You're No Good For Me'. Unfortunately Brotherdale soon left the band to join The Panik and the search for a drummer started all over again.

Another advert was placed in Virgin Records, plus one in Jones's Music shop in Macclesfield, which was where Ian Curtis was now living with his wife Deborah. Stephen Morris saw it, replied to it and an audition was set up in Cheetham Hill, at the Abraham Moss Centre, which was Warsaw's rehearsal room at the time. His style was just what the band needed to move on from their unrefined, crude, three chord thrash. The acquisition of Morris accelerated the momentum for the band which carried on through until the end of 1977, playing at the last night of The Electric Circus and culminating at the Swinging Apple in Liverpool on New Years Eve; their last under the name Warsaw.

THE WORST

"There is no gap for The Worst to fill. The band use the most primitive techniques and riffs imaginable, and their singer squalls words about oppression, depression, and most other – 'essions with a Kevin Coyne-like intensity."

Paul Morley

If ever a band epitomised their name it was The Worst: They took musical ineptitude to another level. The band, a term used at its very loosest, consisted of Allan Deaves on guitar accompanied by Ian Hodges on Chad Valley drums.

Stanley Vegas: "We knew The Worst. They were quite unique really! Nobody could say they were shit because that's what they were trying to be! It was like, they were aiming for the bottom and they got there! We all quite admired that."

Una Baines: "They were the masters of primitive."

Kevin Stanfield: "I remember The Worst; they all wore leather jackets with The Worst written in paint on the back of them."

Gail Egan: "Wasn't he (Ian from The Worst) a trainee accountant? He also collected classic cars like Cadillacs and what have you. I remember him getting a tattoo and you know the gauze that you put over it, he put it in his ear as an earring. My friend Pam went out with him for a bit. Allan was married to Linda and they had a little boy. Linda never used to come to The Ranch, but she came one night and I remember her telling me that Allan really wanted to buy a guitar but he bought a fridge instead, which I thought was quite sweet."

Mickey Carr: "There was a group called The Worst, Woody was one of them, and there were a couple of kids from Bolton who were really into punk, they were punks before we were; Allan and Ian." Allan and Ian were actually from just outside Preston.

On Friday 3rd June 1977 The Worst played their first 'performance' at The Squat. The gig was advertised on the posters as 'Punk Rock Rules'. Also on that night were The Drones, The Negatives and Warsaw. The Fall also played that night but weren't featured on the poster, but then again the date on the poster was for 6th June!

Odgie:"Warsaw were playing a gig at The Squat and we got asked to play."

According to Dave Bentley, the manager of The Drones at the time, they just turned up on the night and asked to play, but there was no room on the stage so the offer was declined. They wouldn't take no for an answer, so instead they set up on the floor in front of the stage.

Odgie: "We didn't really have a band at all but I'd got a set of drums, they were kid's drums, a Chad Valley drum kit. Deavesy had his guitar and we were just jamming in the garage, just messing about, because we'd heard some tracks and thought 'yeah, we could do that'. He didn't play any chords, he tuned his guitar to E and took the top string off so he could get his finger across the 5 remaining strings. He was very good at making up lyrics on the spot, and there was Woody who had a bass guitar, that was the only criteria needed, so we met up at The Squat. Bless him he didn't have any sense of rhythm. So anyway we got onstage and Crash! Bang! Wallop! we did our five tracks or whatever and it might have only lasted about five minutes but we got a massive round of applause and cries for an encore. We didn't know any more so we did the set again as the encore! Woody only ever did the one gig and that was that."

Wispa: "I taught Woody to play bass... sort of. Well, I taught him the four chords you needed to play, you know? Beyond that point it was a bit difficult! (*laughs*)"

Alan Keogh: "I only went to The Squat on Diva Street once, I think it was to see The Worst. They *were* the worst band, they couldn't play and when I think about it now, they are probably the most punk of punk bands."

Stanley Vegas: "I remember when they set up, they had this drum kit, and it was sort of propped up on bricks, and it was painted camouflage I seem to remember."

Odgie: "We were fearless as well when I think about it. It's embarrassing looking back on it now just how... I don't know... you were lost in your own space, I think. There was no design to it at all, or a plan, it just unfolded in front of us and we went along with it basically. It was very much 'we're not anything special'. When Deavesy was playing guitar he'd have the audience right in front of him, and he'd show them what he was doing and reach down to get one of them to bar the fret in the middle of the track... it was very much that 'any fucker can do this', to show them that there was nothing special about it at all. It was also about getting out some of the angst and aggression that you tend to have as a young person. I've always had a problem with authority and the idea that someone can come and tell you what to do. I was always in trouble at school because I wouldn't cut my hair or wear the right shirt. I never got on with school at all, right from Primary school. They didn't like me anyway; I was arrogant as well which was unfortunate. So I was pushing and prodding at everything that came in front of me. Every so often you'd get beaten up for it or caned for it, so it was this kind of running battle for the rest of it, doing just enough to get by."

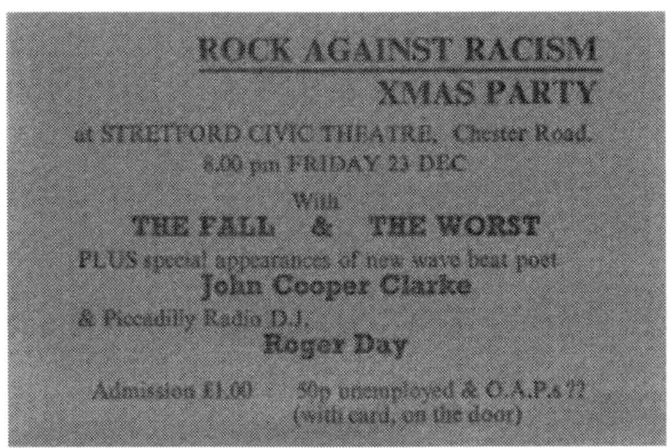

ROCK AGAINST RACISM
XMAS PARTY
at STRETFORD CIVIC THEATRE, Chester Road.
8.00 pm FRIDAY 23 DEC
With
THE FALL & THE WORST
PLUS special appearances of new wave beat poet
John Cooper Clarke
& Piccadilly Radio D.J.
Roger Day
Admission £1.00
50p unemployed & O.A.P.s
(with card, on the door)

Despite their shambolic and unique musical interpretations, the duo managed to secure some decent support slots.

Odgie: "Not sure how the second gig came about but it was probably something to do with Richard Boon and Buzzcocks, supporting them somewhere. We did quite a lot of gigs with them you know? We eventually toured with them. Not big tours, just five or six gigs, one of them was in Ireland. We got on well with them and they liked what we were doing you know?"

Decades before The White Stripes and Royal Blood perfected the art of just drums and guitar The Worst were ploughing their own anarchic furrow.

Odgie: "We were a two piece for a while, just drums and guitar. When we played The Roundhouse we were a two piece if memory serves, there were a couple of gigs where one of the roadies from Buzzcocks, I can't remember his name, could have been Fran (Taylor) but I'm not sure, he took over the last couple of tracks on drums and I got on the mouth organ. Now I can't play the fucking mouth organ, I'm tone deaf, if you heard me whistle you'd fucking cringe! So I'd got the mouth organ jammed against the microphone at, was it The Roundhouse or The Marquee? I can't remember properly but it was just another way of ending the gig in even more chaos."

Steve Shy: "I remember The Worst supporting Buzzcocks, I think it was a Tuesday. They were playing at Ilkley College, in fuckin' winter. There was a band there saying 'we're on the bill as well'. They were like, no there's only two bands on. So they asked 'can we play?' So Richard Boon said yeah, of course you can play, no problem...that was Gang Of Four's second ever gig. The following week, Gang of Four asked The Worst to play with them at Leeds University. They asked The Worst if they wanted to sound check and they were like, 'you what?' So they were in this big hall and you had students going from lesson to lesson, and they just started messing about. I think Robin was in them then... so Robin just got a rhythm going and Allan started picking at his guitar over the top... his old fella used to tune him up to an 'E' chord and he'd just 'bar' it. When they finished up there were about 250 students sat on the fuckin' floor watchin' it, all clapping at the end of it. They didn't even fuckin' notice it... they were just messin' about for a sound check."

Odgie: "A lot of the gigs were very hit and miss anyway because we were more or less making it up as we went along; they were jam sessions on stage, plus we were fucking stoned off our heads all of the time! Sometimes it just takes off and you become... there's that bit where you become greater than the sum of your parts, something's happened, you've plugged into 'Universe B'. 'Where the fuck's this come from we're away now!' you know? The audience pick up on it and it ends up being a fantastic gig. And then some nights it just doesn't gel at all for whatever reason, the sound quality's shit or you can't hear each other or it's a bad vibe."

Steve Shy: "Another time, on the same tour they played Shrewsbury. It was The Prefects, The Worst, and Buzzcocks. We got there, it was at Tiffany's, it was a Sunday, and the PA van had broken down so the gig was cancelled, they cancelled it. But outside the queue was going right around the block and that, so we just said, 'have you got a house PA?' and this bloke said, 'yeah'. 'Well can we just play?', but he was like, 'no, no'. 'But you've got all these people outside, you may as well let them in for free you know, keep in their good books and that'. So eventually they said alright and so in the end The Worst and The Prefects played, and they went round with the hat afterwards."

It certainly wasn't a glamorous or palatial rock and roll lifestyle.

Odgie: "When we were on tour we'd be in a Bedford CF van and generally we'd be lucky if someone in the audience would ask us back to their squat or flat so we would crash out there, and if not we'd sleep in the van. We had a big Maxwell House Coffee jar full of magic mushrooms; a spoonful washed down with water in the morning..."

On Friday December 23rd 1977 at the Stretford Civic Theatre, a gig took place which featured The Fall, The Worst, with John Cooper Clarke as compère and a special appearance from Roger Day, a Piccadilly Radio DJ. Advertised as a Rock Against Racism gig it attracted the attention of the local National Front thugs who briefly interrupted The Fall mid performance.

Denise Shaw: "I remember The Worst playing at some youth centre or something. I think that there was also... do you remember that mish-mash band of Paul Morley and Kevin Cummins [The Negatives], I think they were on as well. Anyway the NF or some other similar group had got in, and somebody had thrown a pint pot at Allan or Ian and of course they kicked off. Dave actually tipped a table over and we were sat under the table dodging all the bottles and for 5 or 10 minutes it was the worst I'd ever been to. We were thinking, 'How are we going to get to the door?' There was a lull, so Dawn shot out and I'm just shouting, 'My car will be trashed' because it had all stickers on it, and I was expecting all the windows are through and everything, but they weren't, it had only kicked off in the club. There were lads with their faces covered in blood, it was really bad. The police turned up and they were pulling people left, right and centre."

That two-piece had turned into a permanent three-piece with the introduction of Robin Utracik on guitar. The gigs kept on coming including playing support to the new breed of bands whose inspiration was rooted in punk.

Odgie: "So we knew Robin and he could play a bit of guitar so it was just one of those natural evolutions and we settled on then being a three-piece. It was Robin that got us the gig with The Automatics in Coventry. He'd been at college in Coventry and he knew Jerry Dammers and that's how we got the gig. They obviously became The Specials."

As well as the music being punk at its most rudimentary, The Worst's attitude to opportunists was just as brutal.

Odgie: "If we came across people who we thought were latching onto it, or riding the bandwagon, we were down on them immediately. We thought that they were just playing at it, I mean we were playing at it but we were authentic and believed in what we were doing. The anger with us was genuine fucking anger about the things we saw that were wrong, the injustice and morality of things, you know. A few years back I did a phone interview, I can't remember what it was about, but I was asked, 'What's this about the feud between you and The Drones?' I was like 'What feud? There was no feud between us and The Drones'. Then it came back to me that there was a bit of rivalry which I won't go into now, but there was. I suppose it was us just being arsey… playground stuff."

What started out as fun began to be routine. The band's reputation preceded them, so the audiences were anticipating the next stage of the group's 'development'. Although the spontaneity and initial impact of the band was beginning to wane, by the time punk had reached it's zenith in late 1977 the wheel had turned full circle. Despite their lack of commercial aspirations The Worst were courted by those who had found a way in to the current music revolution.

Odgie: "We got a write up in the *NME* or *Sounds* or whatever - Paul Morley did it I think. All the time we were a band we were getting write ups and we'd read them and think, what a pile of pretentious bollocks this is, you know? 'Sounds like a bleached out Kevin Coyne', 'sounds like Hawkwind' or this, that, and the other. Reading it back now these people were talking sense but at the time we thought that we were just kids banging about. It was a laugh that these people were writing about us. It really wasn't that serious to us, we didn't take it that seriously at all…it was all fun. But I suppose the more you got people's expectations and the more they were coming to see The Worst rather than us just being on anyway, that impacts on your ability to not give a fuck. We got some nice things written about us, I've got some of the clippings at home, which looking back now are much more meaningful than they were then. We were just enjoying it. It was a good laugh really as much as anything. When it stopped being that, when we got to the level where there was an expectation of us, once it got to that stage... we didn't stop as any grand gesture, it just got to the point where we were having more fun jamming in the garage than we were doing the gigs. It was funny because the whole punk thing had taken off by then so the guys from the record companies were wanting to sign you up without even hearing you; 'Don't you want to hear us play first?' we'd say. There weren't as many as soon as they'd seen us play [*laughs*] which was fine by us, you know? We genuinely weren't into all the kerfuffle; we were into making simple, basic music that people enjoyed… hopefully!"

Whether people enjoyed it is perhaps a matter of conjecture, but one thing is for certain, whatever they did, they did with honesty.

Odgie: "Without wishing to big ourselves up, we weren't trying to be authentic, we were just doing what we were doing and I suppose there is some authenticity in that, which is what the people who were writing about us were seeing, even though we were taking the piss out of it. We may have got as far as '78, I really don't know to be honest. The only regret of it all I suppose is that we never got any recordings of anything at all. I believe that Richard Boon would have some if anyone did because he recorded us and the Buzzcocks when we played with them, from the mixing desk I presume."

Martin Ryan: "Although there's been various reasons why they've never been recorded, apparently Dave Bentley wanted to do it, and Richard Boon said he'd fund them, and even John Peel, when he was on that Brass Tacks programme, offered to pay for them to but I would have thought that he would have just invited them for a session first of all. I wonder that it's just as well that they never did get recorded because..."

At the time of this being written, any aural evidence of The Worst is still unpublished.

THE DRONES

The Drones were right at the forefront of the nascent Manchester punk scene. The band had been playing together for a few years prior to punk, which led to accusations of jumping on the bandwagon, but to be fair to the band, they never hid their past.

Wispa: "I got into a band which was the early Drones, called Rockslide, and we were a pop band. I haven't got a problem with our history. Like I said to you, most bands started in history... I didn't get into a band to be a punk because there was no such thing as punk. I got into music like most people; it's an easy access to the female sex. We weren't born as punks, it was like a second coming if you like.

If you look back on Bowie's career, he started out in a Mod style 'beat' band, then when that didn't work he crossed over to the Folk style that was prevalent in the late 60's, until he totally reinvented himself and gave himself an alter-ego, Ziggy Stardust. Marc Bolan was also a Mod, before moving onto a more pastoral, psychedelic direction, before eventually ending up as the Dandy of the Underworld. So to criticise bands for seizing the moment is harsh. Something not totally lost on Wispa.

Wispa: "My inspiration was from the 60's initially. I'm going to be honest with you, not punk. Very little punk was coming through to the U.K. MC5 stuff, early Iggy stuff was coming through which was great, but it was bands like The Who, The Kinks, they were my early influences. I mean if you listen to The Kinks, it was like Punk anyway, you know with the guitars, and I thought that was fantastic. That's what inspired me to get into a band. I met Pete, and I met Mike, and we formed this band called Strand. That would have been around 1973-74, and things got a bit serious and we got offered a deal to go to Germany for six months and we thought we'd made it. So we get out there and we were doing the American Air Force bases, and we'd gone out there with this Shang-a-Lang pop music and we got laughed off the stage, so we changed things about after a couple of months, so we started to play heavy rock."

Like many before them, the group worked hard perfecting their set with a heavy work schedule, a steely determination to succeed, and with little monetary reward. When Punk came along it provided the band with the direction they needed to move forward.

Wispa: "We spent those six months together, we were living together, we were starving together, and we were playing about five one hour sets a night at these bases, we got tight. I'll be honest with you, most punk rockers that are in bands, and were honest about how they started… we just thought, we've got to do that, that's the way to go, so we just sat down and started writing songs around that (Punk) theme. We had the attitude, I mean we were out of work, we hated what was happening at the time, so we had ammunition to write songs. So we started getting gigs, and the first early gigs were at Pips and at The Ranch. The first gig? I think it was at Pips. I got fuckin' battered that night, [*laughs*]! We'd come off stage and it was still a bit Roxy/Bowie so they didn't know how to take us, but we ended up getting a good reception. So I'm talking to a few people in the audience and the DJ's like 'There you are, Rockslide, they used to be Rockslide and now they're The Drones' and he played 'Jump Bump Boogaloo'. He was out of order playing that after we'd just come off .So I went into the DJ booth and filled him in. Next thing I'm being dragged out into the next room by the bouncers and then the owner turned up and I ended up getting a kicking."

Denise Shaw: "From seeing Buzzcocks at The Ranch I then found out that they were playing at The Electric Circus so I started going there, and then I heard about a band called The Drones".

Fran Taylor: "Rockslide re-invented themselves as The Drones, whereas Slaughter and the Dogs didn't bother, they just carried on."

Daniel O'Sullivan: "I was quite friendly with The Drones so I saw them really early on."

Wispa: "Tony [Davidson] managed The Drones and he had his own TJM Records; Slaughter did a bit of stuff on it, and I think Mick Hucknall did a bit of stuff on it with the [Frantic] Elevators. Then he got a warehouse in Knott Mill down on Deansgate; Joy Division, The

Drones, Buzzcocks, Magazine, even Sad Café were all in there using it to rehearse."

July 1977 saw their first singe release, 'Temptations of a White Collar Worker' on OHM's Records, the band's own label. The single was recorded by their early champion Paul Morley, and came in green, blue, and black folded covers and consisted of four tracks played at 33rpm. The songs on the EP were;'Lookalikes','Corgi Crap','Hard On Me', and 'You'll Lose'. It was recorded in ten hours and perceived as being poorly recorded by Morley but the EP went on to sell 12,000 copies.

Steve Shy: "I was in the studio with The Drones – it was a studio in town where they recorded the first EP. I don't know if it was me or Morley, threw a glass and you actually hear it breaking on the record."

The band moved onto the local Valer Records, releasing the generic Punk sound of 'Just Want To Be Myself'/'Bone Idol' in October 1977. It is regarded now as a Punk classic and such was it's impact that in 2001 it was listed in the '100 greatest Punk singles' in music magazine *Mojo*. Their first album 'Further Temptations' was released in November 1977, but received lukewarm reviews.

Andy T.;"A lot of that is to do with Paul Morley. He wanted to manage The Drones originally, in fact he did manage them for a while. He thought that they were the best thing since sliced bread, and he wrote an article, I think it was for the *NME* about Manchester punk. Now at that time, Manchester punk was basically Buzzcocks, Slaughter, The Drones, and The Worst. I think that was it. So he wrote this really good article, then they asked him to go down to work in London. He reviewed The Drones album, which is a classic, it's got loads of melodies on it, you could tell they could play, they'd been playing together since 1973 or whatever, and he totally slagged it. He completely slagged it and they didn't know why he'd done it, and to this day Gus can't understand why he stabbed them in the back so much."

Morley had once referred to The Drones as 'Manchester's number one Punk band' and as previously mentioned, had managed the band for a short while before moving to London to work for the *NME*. But it wasn't just Morley who gave the album short shrift, it was also criticised by Alan Lewis in *Sounds*, describing the band as 'unoriginal, average, enjoyable but not significant'. Despite the underwhelming reviews the album went on to sell a modest amount of copies and is still held in high regard by many of the original, early scene Punks. It was recorded in London among exulted company, although the capital wasn't really to the liking of some of the band. The north/south divide was acutely felt by the band – particularly in the audience of one particular venue.

Wispa: "When we went down to The Roxy we used to feel very out of it. When we'd play at the Electric Circus with the likes of Denise, it was like a community. You'd go to The Roxy and the bands would be sat on the top balcony, looking down on everyone. I enjoyed The Marquee, The Nashville and the Red Cow and places like that, which were like sweaty pubs, the perfect punk venues. The Roxy? Stick it up your arse. The London set; I fuckin' hated 'em. I'll be honest with you, I hated 'em. It's that north/south divide; they think that we're common. We were mainly working class."

Stanley Vegas: "They didn't like the northern Punks when we went down there (London). I remember we played The Marquee with V2, with Slaughter funnily enough. Erm, hang on... before that we did a tour with The Dickies, and part of that entailed playing at The Marquee. Anyway we'd only played a couple of songs and they started throwing fucking bottles and everything at us so we stopped. We went back about a month, maybe 6 weeks later, I can't remember but we were there supporting Slaughter and the Dogs. This time we'd only walked on stage and they started throwing things at us! [*laughs*] They'd remembered us, we didn't even get to plug in!"

It's true to say that the feeling was mutual, apparently after witnessing The Drone's support slot for XTC, the *NME*'s Tony Parsons destroyed a chair in disgust! Ironically the band would end up leaving Manchester and relocating to London.

Wispa: "I used to like going to what you'd call the provinces... places like Bradford, Newcastle, places like that. I'd worked all my life and I was out of work at the time, M.J. and Gus, weren't working at the time. It's not that we didn't want to work, it was just that the band was more important at that time."

There were exceptions to the North/South divisions though.

Brian Grantham: "Like Steve [Wispa] was saying... a lot of the London crowd had attitude, they didn't want to know us Northerners. Yeah there was a bit of that like 'We started the punk thing' The Clash, The Jam, they were a bit like 'we're not interested in this... we don't want to do that... we don't want to rub sides with you because you're Northerners, as such. That was the way I thought it was but not the Pistols."

Wispa: "I thought The Clash were great, Joe was great, I met Joe a few times and I thought he was absolutely awesome. They were downstairs doing their album while we were upstairs doing ours at CBS. We were on the top floor doing 'Further Temptations…' and they were downstairs doing the first Clash album. We used to go in the boozer across the road while they were mixing down and that. We never really saw Mick Jones but Joe was anyone's mate you know and a nice guy to boot."

Chris Hewitt: "The Drones got signed by this label who had no idea about how to budget for records and Allan Robinson from The Electric Circus was involved in the management of The Drones. He had a band called The Slugs, I mean he was another hippy who got into punk because he thought there was money in it."

In December 1977, The Drones gained some musical kudos when they recorded a session at Maida Vale studio 4 for John Peel's show on Radio 1. The track listing was 'Be My Baby', 'The Change', 'Clique', and 'Movement'. This would prove to be the last recordings of the original line-up that would see the official light of day. A single version of 'Be My Baby' was scheduled for release but the record company folded before it was released.

The overriding problem with The Drones was that they weren't authentic enough for some of the more earnest and discerning punters, plus their past would always come back to haunt them. But for many, they were the epitome of punk; loud, brash, honest, hard working with no airs and graces.

Wispa: "We made so many mistakes it's untrue… record deals etcetera."

The band have since reformed, split up again, and now play as a three-piece with Wispa being joined by Brian (Mad Muffet) Grantham from Slaughter And The Dogs, and Alan Crosby.

SLAUGHTER AND THE DOGS

Formed in Wythenshawe, South Manchester, they were very briefly called Wayne Barrett & The Mime Troupe but that soon mutated into Slaughter and the Dogs. The new name was an amalgamation of 'Diamond Dogs' and 'Slaughter On 5th Avenue', two of Barrett's favourite albums. The band spent their early gigs as a covers band playing the local clubs, and were originally a five-piece with guitarist Mike Day leaving the group early on but not before he played the Pistol's Free Trade Hall gig.

Brian Grantham: "We were all at the same school at the time and me and Mick would go home on the bus and we'd chill out together.

Growing up, a lot of us didn't have anything to and obviously there was the Bowie influence and all that, and we thought yeah we'll get a band together. That's how it kicked off with the band. That would have been 1974. Our first gig was at the Greenbrow Road Social Club, Newall Green, Wythenshawe in 1975 with Mike Day also on guitar as a five-piece. The Lesser Free Trade Hall was his final gig."

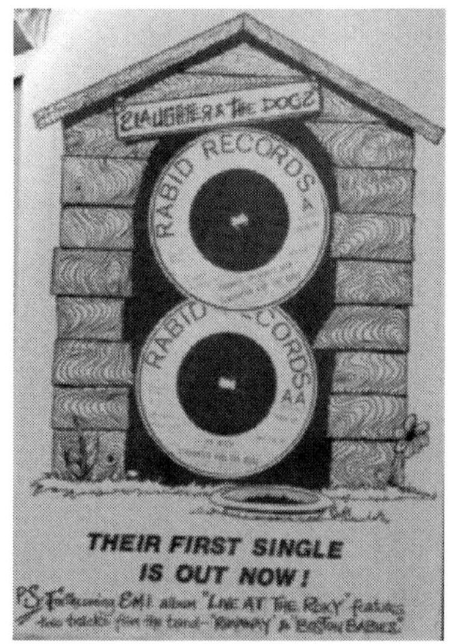

That Bowie influence would be both a curse and a blessing throughout the early days of Punk. Slaughter and the Dogs and The Drones were both targeted for their perceived act of bandwagon jumping.

Steve Shy: "I hate it when people say that Slaughter And The Dogs jumped on the bandwagon, they didn't"

Mickey Tait: "Slaughter were more glam/punk rock really weren't they? They get frowned upon, there's a bit of snobbery. Wythenshawe's a shit hole you know, like Ardwick. There's limited expectations, they were proper working class a bit similar to us, but they were from Wythenshawe and we were from Ardwick."

The band themselves didn't hide away from their detractors. Interviewed in *Shy Talk* fanzine, Wayne Barrett agreed with the backlash, but hoped that their music would rise above it. "*We really deserved the slagging we got when we started, but I think it's gone on a bit too long, we should be given the chance to see what we can do.*"

Brian Grantham: "We were doing covers; Bowie, New York Dolls, and then we started doing a bit of writing. It was me, Mick, Wayne and Howard. Then when punk happened, we sort of got into that, although we still had a bit of that glam element. I wouldn't say that we were that Punky but we had a bit of drive, you know what I mean - Rock. The chord structures what Mick was throwing down still had that driving..."

Stanley Vegas: "I met Wayne Barrett in Pips, which is how I got into Slaughter, how I got into Punk. Wayne was a mate and we were into Bowie, in fact Wayne got me into Alex Harvey. He said 'Oh I'm in a band, why don't you come and see us?'

Deb Zee: "I first went to Gilly's with my sister, I used to do Karate, and I was into Bowie at the time. This girl came up to me and said, 'You look like you'd like this gig, I'm Glenda and I'm engaged to a lad called Wayne and his band are playing at Wythenshawe Forum', and it was Slaughter and the Dogs, but I never went because I was only 15 or 16."

Martin Ryan: "My first Punk gig would have been Slaughter and the Dogs at Wythenshawe Forum. My mate had a firm's van, he associated them (Slaughter) with Punk, I can only think that he must have done that because of... do you know the poster, the Slaughter and the Dogs and Sex Pistols, where they put themselves on equal billing? I think he associated them with punk because he'd seen them on that, so he said 'shall we go and check this out, this is Punk rock'. Of course they were like a Bowie/Roxy sort of band. Support was from Wild Ram, who went on to become Ed Banger and the Nosebleeds, and a band called Mudanzas who were a serious rock band, a bit like Solstice. I only caught the end of Eddie and Wild Ram but they seemed pretty good actually, Mudanzas were like the sort of bands I'd seen at the pubs, they had a massive Hammond organ, a Yes/Genesis type of band. Tony Wilson was compère for the night, and when he came onstage we were like, 'Oh look it's Tony Wilson'."

Andy T.: "At our sixth form there was a bit of a Slaughter and the Dogs fan club going on. One of the guys who was there had come from Wythenshawe and he had this tape and they were a five-piece and still doing covers like 'Honky Tonk Woman' and Roxy Music songs. So we went to see them, but I can't remember where it was, it was a massive pub but it wasn't The Oaks, it might have been in Wythenshawe. There were all these different rooms and they played in one of them, and I think that somebody said that they had a residency there but we only ever saw the one gig there. We went down in this van, so I'd heard of Slaughter and I'd read about the review about the Pistols."

The band's exposure had exploded when they got themselves onto the bill supporting the Sex Pistols at the Lesser Free Trade Hall.

Brian Grantham: "The first gig we jumped on with the Pistols, at the Free Trade Hall, Jonesy was really cool, and so was Cook. Plus Malcolm was cool about it."

Although you wouldn't know who was supporting who on the night, that was dependent on which poster you read, the band continued to play gigs around the city, before heading south.

Slaughter and the Dogs played the first of their seven appearances at The Roxy in London on Wednesday 19th January 1977 with support from The Adverts. A provincial double header; The Advert's founder members, Gaye Black and Tim Smith were from Bideford in Devon. The gig was reviewed by Neil Spencer in *NME* 10 days later, who had nothing but praise for the group, describing them as, "*a curious blend of Bowie, through Ramones, through the East Lancs Road*". The band would go on to contribute two songs to the 'Live At The Roxy' album, 'Runaway' and Boston Babies'.

The group's first single 'Cranked Up Really High'/'The Bitch' was released on Tosh Ryan's Rabid Records label in June 1977.

Wythenshawe was fertile ground for future players in the early Punk scene: Billy Duffy, Vini Reilly, Eddie Garrity (Ed Banger and the Nosebleeds), and in particular Rob Gretton, who was an early advocate of the band. His fanzine *Manchester Rains* was all about the band, with help from Steve McGarry, who provided the artwork for it.

Steve McGarry: "We were friends from the age of 11, toe-rags from the Wythenshawe estate who passed the Eleven Plus exam and attended the posh Grammar School. By the age of 15, we were young mods, sporting French crew-cuts, Levi's jacket and jeans and shiny brown brogues, sneaking into the Firbank pub before catching a live band at St. Peter's youth club. We hitch-hiked through the night to Man City away games, and blagged tickets to tapings of the pop show "Lift Off" at Granada TV studios. When Rob became the fan club secretary for Slaughter & The Dogs, he got me to design the band's logo and fanzine. It was an Alsatian's head with blood dripping from its mouth. They wanted me to design the cover for the first single 'Cranked Up Really High' as well, so I did that along with their promotional posters.

Martin Ryan: "I remember Rob showing me the fanzine in Rafters when the Dogs gig got moved there from The Oaks in June 1977. I had spoken to him a few times when he was DJ at The Oaks about the Cranked Up single before it came out. I also bought the single off Rob at The Oaks when it came out.

Brian Grantham: "Rob was greatly involved from the very beginning of Slaughter and the Dogs' career. I have a memory of him sat upstairs in his bedroom with a typewriter, replying to fan club members."

Slaughter weren't shy about self-promotion, even if it meant advertising gigs that never transpired for one reason or another.

Andy T.: "During 1977 we went to four Slaughter and the Dogs gigs where they never turned up. We were writing to the fan club to find out where they were playing and Rob used to send us posters and badges and stuff. They were either off doing something else or they'd got a better offer, or perhaps they were just trying to publicise more gigs than they actually had. You'd quite often get a band playing but not Slaughter."

Gail Egan: "Mike Rossi was friendly with Mick Ronson back then, and I remember Mick actually coming to Manchester, which was interesting for us, being massive Bowie fans."

Brian Grantham: "We were scouted by a few companies whilst showcasing and Decca visited us a few times. Derek Rodgers and Nick Tuber were the A&R guys - Derek had signed Thin Lizzy to Decca and Nick went on to produce their single 'Whiskey In The Jar' as well as 'Do It Dog Style'".

Steve McGarry: "When they signed with Decca, they did it at the DHSS office in Wythenshawe, but they didn't actually have a contract to sign, Ray Rossi bought a gas bill with him and they signed that! Those were the kind of lads they were dealing with."

The original line up fell apart seven dates into the tour that was planned to promote the release of their debut album, 'Do It Dog Style', with the last show being at Nottingham Sandpiper.

Since then the band has undergone multifarious mutations including a very brief appearance in the band by Morrissey.

Brian Grantham: "Morrissey joined the band around the time that we were rehearsing at TJMs. My memory of him was that he was always sat down, chilled with a khaki jacket and a green canvas shoulder bag. He sat with the mic whilst singing, and I suggested that he should stand up to sing. In my opinion, he didn't have that edge to his voice to suit the band, therefore he did just a few rehearsals."

JOHN COOPER CLARKE

A native of Higher Broughton, Salford, Clarke lived on the corner of Bury New Road and Great Cheetham Street East, opposite the Rialto picture house. He embraced poetry at an early stage in his life. "*I wrote bits of poetry at school, I had a knack for it but so did a few of the kids in the class. We had a good teacher, Mr Malone, who was actually the PE teacher doubling up. He had a glass eye and when he took us swimming he'd throw it in the pool... honest... and whoever got it the first would get off early. He was a real outdoor guy, an Ernest Hemmingway type, red blooded, literary bloke. But he was a really inspiring teacher, he used to read old 19th century stuff and say 'Just do it like that but only write about what you know' which was pretty good advice from anybody.*"

His first job was as a 'Shabbos Goy' - a non-Jewish person who performs tasks for Jews on the Sabbath that are forbidden by religious law. After brief dalliances in tailoring and printing he ended up as a lab technician at Salford Tech working in the joinery department handing out power tools. That was where he was interviewed by Tony Wilson for So It Goes, the interview was interjected with excerpts of his live performances of 'You'll Never See A Nipple In *The Daily Express'* and 'Psycle Sluts'.

Punk gave him an environment to show off his caustic wit and intelligent wordplay, all delivered via a unique delivery style of a thick Salford accent, his poetic meter punctuated with a metronomic chewing gum rhythm. Those who met him couldn't help but be charmed by him. The Bard of Salford, with pipe cleaner legs and a bird's nest hairstyle, whose words ricocheting around the room from his scattergun poems at breakneck speed, was self-deprecating about his talent. "*I guess that's what I do - talk in tune*".

Punk audiences held no fear for him, he'd already served his apprenticeship appearing in the local pubs and clubs, so snotty-nosed upstarts were easily despatched with the ultimate weapon, his vocabulary. He was part social commentator, part comedian.

Daniel O'Sullivan: "I lived with John Cooper Clarke in Prestwich in 1977, he lived in the same house as us, with Alan Wise... it was his house and we shared it with various people. John was there for quite a while, he was really fucking entertaining. My memories of that time were always of John coming down in the morning for breakfast cracking jokes, which really set me up for the fucking day, and then rolling around in this old Transit van all day picking up bits of furniture and delivering 'em with him. Alan Wise ran a furniture removal business called 'Wise Moves' which he then carried on into the music sphere, so John would work with us doing furniture removals and that, because he wasn't a full time poet, you know, so we didn't have much money."

His first recorded output was the 'Innocents EP' released on Rabid Records (TOSH 103) in October 1977 and featured, 'Suspended Sentence', 'Innocents' and 'Psycle Sluts Parts 1 and 2'. He was accompanied by a backing band he called the 'Curious Yellows' on account that at the time of recording they were all suffering from Hepatitis.

Kevin Stanfield: "I moved to Manchester and I had a little apartment in Sedgley Park where John Cooper Clarke used to live. That's when I first started to be a punk. I used to go down to the George Hotel in the centre of Sedgley Park, there was no jukebox in there, people just went in there for the Boddingtons, and he and the artist Steve Maguire went in there. They were the best of friends. Steve was in a documentary about John, he was in the dressing room with him and Linton Kwesi Johnson at The Ritz. What I loved about Clarke is his memory… his mind; everything that goes in there stays in there. For instance, the track Health Fanatic; we used to sit outside The George, around the back where there was a bowling green and people used to run past there. The 'Disguise In Love' album; that was Steve Maguire's artwork, and of course the 'Open Neck Shirt' book had Steve's illustrations in there."

Wispa: "He used to do the support slots at the Band On The Wall for us and Buzzcocks. He'd get up and read for about 20 minutes with his drainpipe trousers and Bob Dylan haircut."

His debut album, 'Ou Est La Maison De Fromage?' comprised of a mix of live performances, demos and rehearsals was originally released in 1978 on the Rabid Records label as NOZE 1. The band members featured on some of the recordings are; Paul Burgess – drums, percussion, Martin Hannett, bass guitar, and Steve Hopkins – keyboards.

He signed for CBS Records in 1978 and released 'Disguise In Love', with the same backing band, now named The Invisible Girls, but augmented by Be Bop Deluxe's Bill Nelson, and Pete Shelley from Buzzcocks. Further albums included 'Snap Crackle and Bop' and 'Zip Style Method', as well as a book of selected poems 'Ten Years In An Open Necked Shirt'. He has also been awarded an honorary doctorate of arts from the University of Salford. He continues to tour to this day, his popularity now greater than ever.

THE FALL

In the summer of 1973, Mark Edward Smith was attending St. John's College where he was studying for his 'A' levels. Another student there was Una Baines, although the two of them had already met each other earlier that summer in Heaton Park. They both left the college early into their studies, Una briefly getting a job as an office clerk before training to be a psychiatric nurse, while Mark started work as a clerk on Salford docks. Whilst there he would utilise his access to the office equipment to type out short stories and poems, which would later become part of his lyrics with The Fall. As with every band's story, fate played a big part in getting the band together.

Una Baines: "I met Mark first and we used to sit in his front room with his mate listening to records quite regularly. Then Mark's sisters brought Martin and Tony round and I remember that first time because instantly Tony and Mark were sword fighting about who knew the most about music and that type of thing. Martin was very quiet, I remember he had this long brown coat and he looked like he was almost invisible. They seemed like they were loads younger than me and Mark, even though there's only six months difference between us. That was before I got my flat, so then we used to hangout there and we'd go to a club called Waves. We started reading our poems to each other, Tony could already play the guitar and Martin was learning. Originally Mark was going to be the guitarist, and I can't remember who was going to be the singer, it might have been Martin, but anyway Mark never learnt to play the guitar so he ended up being the singer. But I think no matter what, he was going to be the singer, and I was going to be the drummer but I couldn't afford a drum kit. Eventually I got a bank loan and got a keyboard. So it kind of evolved like that, and once we had all the instruments..."

Friel and Bramah were ardent music lovers.

Martin Bramah: "We were totally wrapped up in music, it meant a lot to us. The bands we loved, we loved dearly, it was our escape from what the world was offering us. Every weekend we were getting out of our faces. But we didn't see it as a nihilistic thing because to us it was a quest for knowledge, we were hungry to see different ways of being. We were all writing poetry."

Una Baines: "We were listening to The Stooges and Velvet Underground and Beefheart, stuff like that. But Mark had always talked about having a band way before we went to see the Sex Pistols. It had a number of names over the year, just ideas, but I'm sure he was writing songs in his head quite early on. We were going to be called The Outsiders or something like that which was before anybody had learned to play an instrument, like a fantasy band."

Early names were Master Race and The Death Sense, and for a while they were The Outsiders, after the book by Albert Camus, until they found out that someone else had got there first. Another of Camus's books [La Chute], did eventually get immortalised in musical history, when Tony Friel suggested The Fall.

Before Punk came to shake up the music business, local music, other than club singers and cabaret acts, were thin on the ground in town.

Martin Bramah: "The music scene was very different then. People didn't start bands in Manchester. The gigs were all at big venues and bands came from out of town and half of them were American. You didn't think you could really do it, until the punk thing happened."

Although the band themselves, particularly Smith, never really associated The Fall with Punk, it was the perfect foil for their scathing and acerbic musical attacks on the audience's aural senses. The band didn't want to be labelled with any musical genre, or conform to any style of dress code.

Una Baines: "We were anti-fashion, we wouldn't 'dress up', we just wouldn't you know?"

The Fall's first gig was in the basement of the North West Arts Association office on King Street on Monday 23rd May 1977. The building was a meeting place of the Manchester Musicians Collective, set up by two music graduates, Trevor Wishart and Dick Witts, who recalls the venue as being "*like a fashionable restaurant in the late 70s, with everything white. It was done out like a small white cave. We just took the tables and chairs out. Mark and Martin, who were taller than the others, had to bend down because of the low ceiling. It wasn't really public, the audience was just a group of other musicians sitting around listening.*"

Steve Shy: "I went to the very first ever Fall gig, it was tiny, only held about 30 people at most, but there was hardly anybody there. But the people who were there were… Una didn't play that first gig because she was still waiting for her keyboard to come out of the catalogue. It hadn't arrived so she couldn't play. At that time it was just Martin, Tony, Karl, and Mark obviously. Una was Mark's girlfriend at the time. Mark was being a bit of an arsehole, which he could be at times so later, when they split up. Una and Martin ended up forming the Blue Orchids."

Una Baines: "I didn't do the first gig, I was in the audience. My bank loan hadn't come through for the keyboard. I bought this keyboard called a 'Snoopy' and that same week *Sounds* did a review of it and they said it was the worst sounding, tinniest keyboard, which was perfect! We didn't think that at the time and I loved it. It had this fairground sound on it, which was a spinet but it sounded like a fairground. It had a tinny piano sound on it which is what I used mostly, but it suited us, it was fit for purpose you know. Mark might still have it, or he might have thrown it out, I don't know."

Martin Bramah: "The first gig was recorded, so somebody might have a tape somewhere. It was a small room and about half the audience was Buzzcocks. Mark just let fly with such venom from day one. I remember he just sort of reached into the audience and virtually poked his finger up Howard Devoto's nose."

The set included 'Repetition', 'Bingo Master's Breakout', and 'Hey

Facicst!'. The drummer was 'Dave' an insurance salesman and 'rabid Conservative' who lasted just the one gig.

By the time of the second gig, the group had changed into the first (of very many) 'classic' line-ups; Mark E. Smith, Tony Friel, Martin Bramah, Una Baines and new drummer Karl Burns. The Fall weren't even listed on the posters advertising the gig. The line up included The Drones, The Worst, Warsaw, and The Negatives.

Una Baines: "My first gig was at The Squat. I had a fuzzbox on my keyboard and because the gig was 'Stuff The Jubilee' I was playing God Save The Queen with all these explosions. I thought it would be like when Jimi Hendrix played 'The Star Spangled Banner', but people were going, 'Get off!' [*laughs*] so it was a bit of a baptism of fire!"

Although there was an unhealthy competitive and bitchy element between some of the Manchester bands, there was also a respect and a willingness to look after some of their rivals.

Una Baines: "Richard Boon really helped out, he got The Fall support on Buzzcocks gigs and he also paid for the first single to be made as well."

The gigs with Buzzcocks gave the band the chance to play to audiences outside of Manchester, where they could inflict their own brand of cacophony, so alien to the mid '77 punk by numbers bands that were cropping up all over the country. There were gigs at The Vortex, the club opened by Andy Czezowski after he gave up The Roxy, and North East London Polytechnic in Barking quickly followed, and then it was back up to Manchester and back down to Earth as a gig was set up at a local youth club. St. George's Community Centre on Livesey Street were putting on a disco and a live band. The Fall were the live act and a more inappropriate setting would have been hard to manufacture. Kevin Cummins was at the gig: "*It was a pretty pointless gig really - the kids were too young. The band played three or so songs before the guy running the place told us that 'they weren't the kind of band he was expecting'. The gig was abandoned and after a quick phone call, the gear was loaded into the van and they went to The Ranch club on Dale Street to 'finish' the gig.*"

On December 23rd at the Stretford Civic Theatre The Fall, and Tony Friel, played their last gig of 1977, with support from The Worst and John Cooper Clarke plus Piccadilly Radio DJ Roger Day. The rudimentary recording of the gig was released as the album 'Live '77' after Smith found the tape at the bottom of his wardrobe. The night was memorable for another reason.

Una Baines: "I remember we played a Rock Against Racism gig and a load of skinheads turned up and started throwing missiles at us. We hid behind our amps, being young you think that you're invincible sometimes, we were hid behind the amps throwing missiles back!"

The extraordinary high turnover of band members was a characteristic of the band over proceeding years. Una was in the band for the first 12 months, with Smith being the only constant figure throughout the whole history of The Fall. He would continue to carry the reputation of being difficult, uncompromising, with a healthy dose of arrogance. And that was just the music.

Una Baines: "We were quite insular in The Fall so I didn't have that camaraderie with the outside people. We were quite aloof I would say, we looked from the outside. The Fall were like our own little clique. In a way I felt that it would have been nice to have had some female company. But then things might have been a bit different, although I don't regret anything, but things might have been different. I also felt some slight isolation when I moved to Prestwich to work at the hospital, all my mates were Mark's mates. I mean it was great and we used to hang out and moan about Prestwich Hospital and get drunk, but sometimes I thought that it would have been nice to have some female company, because there are some things that aren't going to be instantly understood by guys, so you just keep things to yourself. I was with them for about a year. My only regret was that I didn't play on the 'Witch Trials' because I was learning the song but I had a breakdown and I had to take time out. But that was my only regret because I don't think that I would have liked to have stayed much longer than that. It was a tough training ground."

Mark E. Smith died on 24th January 2018 from lung and kidney cancer aged just 60 years of age. Another disciple from the first Lesser Free Trade Hall Sex Pistols gig, Smith's unique vocal delivery and the band's deliberate jarring rhythmic style of music was another example of the originality of those early Manchester bands. Taking their lead from punk but mutating their songs into something just as visceral and challenging but without the rock and roll bombast of The Clash and the Pistols. Smith was notoriously caustic in his wit and his treatment of band members, resulting in a revolving door of drummers and guitarists throughout the band's 40 year existence. It's alleged that the total count of Fall personnel is 66. Never interested in commerciality or fame, he was another maverick unwilling to compromise his ideals. Although there were a few commercial successes The Fall were highly revered by music critics and fellow musicians alike, along with John Peel's proclamation that they were his favourite band. 32 studio albums and two solo albums plus many live recordings, collaborations and side projects are testament to Smith's prolific output over the years. His music defied categorisation, the subjects he wrote about ran from philosophy to football with the odd ballet thrown in for good measure. We will never see his like again. More's the pity.

MAGAZINE

Formed shortly after Howard Devoto left Buzzcocks, Magazine were another completely different animal to the rest of the bands that were just cottoning on to punk during 1977. It could be argued that they were the first of the 'post-Punk' bands, the rather pithy term given to anything that wasn't a three minute thrash. The band formed when Howard Devoto met Scottish art student and guitarist John McGeogh, and was completed by Barry Adamson on bass, Martin Jackson on drums, along with Bob Dickinson on keyboards. Featuring elements of prog, pop, and rock, Magazine were nearer to Roxy and Bowie than to Buzzcocks, partly due to the Eno style keyboards, and with longer, more mid tempo songs. Devoto had grown weary of what he saw was the dumbing down of the scene and the uniform style of the new bands. *'I'm tired of the noise and short of breath. What once was unhealthily fresh is now a clean old hat"* Allegedly Howard managed to get backstage when Iggy Pop, complete with Bowie on keyboards, played at Manchester Apollo. He presented a copy of Spiral Scratch to Iggy declaring: "*I have every record you have ever made. Now you have every record I have ever made"*.

Their first 'official' gig was organised by the *New Manchester Review* on Friday 28th October 1977 at Rafters, supported by The Fall, all for the princely sum of £1. There was a brief appearance at the last weekend of The Electric Circus, but Rafters is considered to be the first 'proper' gig, as stated on the advertising posters, with the full band. And they made an instant positive impression.

Kevin Stanfield: "When Rafters first opened, John Cooper Clarke took me down, and we went watching Magazine. Never heard of them or seen them before obviously, but John said he was going to see a band so off I trotted with him. Howard Devoto came on stage and I was just stood there with my mouth open. I'd been to see Iggy Pop on the 'Lust For Life' tour and he had the same impact on me."

John Chamberlain, guitarist with The Fireplace remembers the gig for a different reason. *"I was at art school with John, Magazine's guitarist and I distinctly remember lending him my guitar for Howard Devoto to use and him returning the guitar to me the next day."*

Fran Taylor: "This was Magazine's first 'proper' gig after a brief appearance at the Electric Circus "Scanner Benefit" weekend. I recall there was a guy who lay on beds of nails as part of the entertainment."

The band signed to Virgin soon after and would release the album 'Real Life' in June 1978.

V2

Formed in 1976 by Pips regulars Mark Standley (Windsor) and David Wilks, the band were closer to the glam style of Slaughter and the Dogs rather than the archetypal punk thrash.

Mark Windsor: "We formed in November '76 but it developed into, you know, Punk I suppose. I was mad keen to be in a band, before I'd heard of Punk rock or anything. I thought that I'd have to be in a covers band, I never thought about writing songs. But the thing is, we were crap! I'd go to Working Men's Clubs when I was a kid and nobody covered the Roxy/Bowie scene as a cabaret act, it was all straight music, so I said let's do that. But it was dead hard! Of course the first few songs the singer always sings exactly what you're playing. The first gig we ever did was 15th April 1977 at the nurse's home in Manchester Royal Infirmary because I worked there in the operating theatre. There was a bloke called Johnny Washington who was a DJ and he asked us if we wanted to do a gig. We had two ten watt amps with everything going through them in this massive hall. We cleared the place! I've got a picture of us and we're like little specks on the stage and everyone's at the back of the room."

The band was eventually completed by drummer Steve Brotherdale (again!) and Stan The Man on bass.

Stanley Vegas: "I was from Gorton, Mark was from Denton/Openshaw, and Dave were the original members and we met in Pips, that was where we got to know each other and developed our liking for the unusual let's say. I was in a different Bowie gang than Mark and Dave, and we were such fucking poseurs, we wouldn't dance if they were dancing, you know, things like that! So when a Bowie song came on, it was a race for the dance floor because if we got there first, they wouldn't dance either! [*laughs*]"

Mark Windsor: "Two people left the band, I don't think they were into Punk and we got Stan, who we picked because we liked his hair, we were at the Zoo-B-Doo disco at Belle Vue, and eventually we just went up to him and said, 'Do you want to be in a band as a bass player?' He said, 'I've never played bass', so I said, 'Don't worry about that, I'll teach you, just turn up at Crown Point on Saturday with a bass and I'll teach you'. He turned up and I remember him stood there with red hair, this cheap bass with newspaper wrapped around it in an elastic band. On the newspaper was a picture of Marc Bolan and Bowie on the 'Marc' show."

Stan's recollection of the invite to join the band is slightly different.

Stanley Vegas: "At the time I was still really into Bowie, so I kept the red hair. I just changed the silver shoes for Doc Martens, you know. I knew who they were and you'd get on the same bus going home at night sometimes you know? We'd been putting a rumour about that we were a band, me and a couple of other mates, we were called Cheap and Nasty. Mark came up to me in Pips and said, 'Are you in Cheap and Nasty?' And I said 'Yeah'. 'What do you play?', I said 'Guitar'. 'Oh right' he said, 'We're looking for a bass player' So I said 'I'll do it'. I'd never played guitar in my life! I didn't even own one. There were two places in Manchester where anybody who's buying their first instrument buys them from; Johnny Roadhouse, and this place opposite Piccadilly station called Mazels, which was a second hand shop. So I went down and bought a bass, I paid about £15 for it or summit and it was a right load of crap, but I didn't know. I think they'd already done a gig doing covers, Mark used to work at the hospital and they'd done a nurse's party or something like that, anyway the bass player decided he couldn't handle it so they got me...because of my hair!"

Whatever the correct reason for joining the band, Stan's inadequacies on the bass were confirmed at his first practice.

Mark Windsor: "I didn't know any notes, it was just 'first dot', 'second dot', 'third dot', or space, space, space, and that's how he learned it. I never knew any chords all the way through V2; I couldn't even play minors, I'd tune to E major. But it did give me quite a unique sound you know?"

Stanley Vegas: "They sussed pretty much straight away that I didn't have a clue what I was doing, so Mark just said, 'Press that one, then press that one', and I think we did a gig at the end of the week. It was at The Electric Circus I think, playing with The Spitfire Boys. That was my first gig and it didn't seem too long after that when we played at the last night of The Electric Circus."

Their stage show had something in common with Slaughter…as well.

Mark Windsor: "We used to have this gimmick where we'd play 'Feel Alright' by The Damned. There was a quiet part and as we came out of that we used to throw flour over the audience and it ended up all over us as well. We used to gauge our success by how far the trail of flour went from the venue [*laughs*]. We all liked Slaughter, and were in fact quite influenced by them. It was the Bowie-esque glam aspect that appealed to us. Stan had known them since they started and used to follow them around to gigs before he joined us. I liked most of the Manchester bands, but as we started to get more known, there was a lot of rivalry which spoiled it a bit.

Gradually the band started to become part of the Manchester scene, and V2's second gig was supporting Slaughter and the Dogs, The Drones, and Fast Breeder at Middleton Civic Hall. But by the start of the new year the relationship between the V2 and Slaughter had turned into petty animosity when V2 supported them on their home turf at Wythenshawe Forum. The 'oneness' that was prevalent at the start of the year was beginning to wane and the gigs would turn into an unhealthy war of attrition.

Mark Windsor: "There was a lot of rivalry between us by then, and it was their home town. As we started, the drummer hit his drums and they all collapsed. Slaughter had loosened all the nuts. The crowd was hostile to us, and when one of our female fans passed up a box of chocolates to us, they started to hit her. Stan took his bass off and lifted it over his head charging at them. Luckily the security intervened and it was stopped. Two minutes later, Dave leant into the crowd singing and someone grabbed the mike, cut the wire with a knife and ran off with it! When we came off, I went and de-tuned Mike Rossi's guitar and took the battery out of his foot peddle, ruining their big entrance. Stupid stuff really, but we were all young boys. I had this vision of camaraderie but…"

One disgusting aspect of Punk, which was more to do with the media propaganda campaign, was spitting at the bands.

Mark Windsor: "We used to come off covered in gob. I used to go to the front and be like, 'Come on, get it in my mouth, you cunt!' The psychology was to get them to spit themselves dry... I remember one time I got a big 'greenie' hanging off my eye and a great big flob of it hanging on the neck of my guitar, and you'd be surprised how quickly it goes cold. I knew I had to go to 'F' next... Stan threw up once when he got one in his mouth."

If the puerile, disgusting habit of the audiences were beginning to get a little tiresome, then the musical direction was also in need of a change of attitude.

Mark Windsor: "I like melodies, so after a year I was getting bored of the noise. The Pistols had melodies, Buzzcocks had melodies."

Stanley Vegas: "It all happened so quickly. In less than a year we were rehearsing full time at TJM studios, he'd (Tony Davidson) signed us up, Dave Bentley, who was The Drones manager, had put out our first EP, so we got to know The Drones through Dave and being at TJM."

The first single was 'Speed Freak'/'Nothing To Do'/'That's It' and released on Bent Records. 'Speed Freak' was the first song that Mark had written. The band went on to have success with their 'Man In A Box' single, released on Tony Davidson's TJM label, which reached number one in the 'alternative" charts.

THE DISTRACTIONS

One band who tend to slip under the radar of the early Manchester Punk scene are The Distractions. Another example of a band who took the essence and attitude of Punk but morphed into their own individual style. By not following the herd, they appealed to the increasingly more discerning audience who were looking for something with more musical substance.

Stephen Perrin: "There is some confusion as to when The Distractions formed. Mike says it was 1975 and as his long term memory is okay, since his short term is shaky, we'd probably best go with that. Mike and I met on a day release course at Stockport College. Basically, the only available options for entertainment round our way seemed to be drinking and fighting. Neither of us had a problem with the former but we were no use at the latter so we needed some sort of an outlet. He just kept singing all the time and, as I played the guitar, I suggested that we form a band. There was no hope of getting any gigs as, like I said before, the small club scene had gone and the only possibility was the working men's club circuit for which we would have had to do some sort of cabaret act. We just felt the need to make a noise as the rest of our lives was so boring. We rehearsed in a Catholic primary school in Benchill with a kid called Tony Trappe on drums and a bloke called Lawrence Tickell on guitar. Lawrence worked with Mike, and his mum was the cleaner at the school. He was obsessed with The Rolling Stones so we did a lot of Stones songs, some Bowie - 'Suffragette City', 'Jean Genie' etc - Roxy's 'Remake Remodel', the Marvelette's 'Needle in a Haystack' and various Velvet Underground stuff.

"We would have liked to have played some Beatles songs but they were too complicated. I have no doubt that we sounded like shit and we were eventually thrown out for making too much noise and annoying the neighbours. I think Punk gave us the confidence to start writing our own stuff and believe that we might get to play in public. No doubt the original material was influenced by what we had been playing before. We couldn't find a bass player but Pete Shelley gave me Pip's phone number as she'd applied for the Buzzcocks job but they'd already got Garth. When Garth started acting up Pete said that he wished he'd gone the other way. We were so happy that she had a bass we didn't bother asking if she could play it. Initial gigs were done with Pip and Tony then we decided to expand. Tony went off to university, we found Adrian via an ad in the *NME* and he brought Alec with him.

The Distraction's debut gig was at The Electric Circus on August 28th 1977, quickly followed by Rafters, supporting Buzzcocks, and then a run of gigs at The Ranch Bar on the first Thursday nights of September, October and November.

The band released their debut single 'You're Not Going Out Dressed Like That' on Tony Davidson's TJM label in 1978, and went on to release 'Time Goes By So Slow' on Factory (FAC12) a year later.

ED BANGER AND THE NOSEBLEEDS

Wythenshawe spawned another band who very quickly became associated with the nascent Punk scene in the city. Phillip 'Toby' Tolman (Drums) and Eddie Garrity (Vocals) were mates at St Paul's school aged 15 when they got the idea of getting a band together. Eventually they acquired the services of fellow classmate Phil McGuinness (Guitar) along with Steve Urmston on bass and began to rehearse. Tolman explains: *"We didn't do any gigs, we just fucked about in our kitchen... rough as fuck. I couldn't play, none of us could play. We just did it for something to do at night."* They started off with Beatles songs because *"We couldn't think of any of our own"*. Finally after a period of about 18 months of bedroom rehearsals, they managed to get competent enough to get a one hour set together. Originally the band played their first gigs in pubs but it wasn't until they met replacement guitarist Vini Reilly and bassist Pete Crookes that things started to happen for the band. Reilly was a much more competent guitarist and a month after joining them, the band supported their mates Slaughter And The Dogs on Friday 10th September 1976 at The Wythenshawe Forum with a set which was more musically accomplished after Reilly's inclusion, trading under the name 'Wild Ram'.

Songs such as 'Another Ounce Of Rock' were standard Heavy Rock affairs, but were still quite raw sounding, they just needed speeding up a bit to fit into the Punk envelope. Another name change to Ed Banger And The Nosebleeds was undertaken after an altercation at the second Sex Pistols gig at the Free Trade Hall. Garrity worked the July 20th gig as a roadie for Slaughter & the Dogs. When the crowd became violent and he and a friend were injured, someone said, "You're a right bloody mob aren't you? Headbanger here and him with a nosebleed". Their name was shortened eventually to The Nosebleeds. The Wythenshawe Forum gig was filmed by John Crumpton and Bob Jones and formed part of their documentary 'The Rise And Fall Of The Nosebleeds'. The forty minute film centred around the band and their manager Vini Farl as they careered into 1977 and the Punk explosion, with footage filmed at Rafters, and a Rock Against Racism gig in Bury. The change in tack musically is striking but according to Tolman, it was a necessary evil: "*We couldn't get any gigs with long hair. The punks were like,'that's not Punk, that's Heavy Rock'. But we were still playing the three chords."*

The song titles certainly got more punk; 'Fascist Pigs' being one example. Interspersed with the live footage are interviews with the band and an anarchic appearance on 'What's On' with Tony Wilson playing their first single, 'Ain't Bin To No Music School'. There is a sequence where Wilson is explaining to the band pre show, that they have two minutes of airtime and that he wants them to do something *"strange to surprise the audience"*. They discuss with him the idea of jumping onto Wilson's desk during the song, but in the transmitted recording, Garrity jumps on Wilson instead, even getting an embarrassed looking Wilson to sing the chorus whilst holding him in a headlock. It's inconceivable to think that letting a bunch of working class urchins loose on television would happen nowadays. It might have been a case of Wilson showing us that he was at one with 'the kids', but still, it was a very brave thing to do. According to the band the song 'Ain't Been To No Music School' was written about Sad Cafe, who, after seeing The Nosebleeds at The Oaks, derided the band's musical inadequacies, but it was also about musical snobbery in general. Other songs were 'Rich Kid', 'Uptight', 'Blackpool Rocks' and 'Middle Class Suburban Creep', but the band never got as far as making an album - the relationship between manager Vini Faal and Eddie Garrity became irreconcilable with accusations of financial impropriety. The final nail was driven into The Nosebleed's coffin after a gig in London and Eddie quit the band. The appearance on television hadn't gained any interest and their musical career had stalled before it had really begun. Vini had already earmarked Eddie's successor as "*another kid who I've got my eye on*". That other kid was Stephen Patrick Morrissey. Another luminary to pass through the Nosebleed alumni was Billy Duffy, who went on to find fame with The Cult. Phillip Tolman went on to play with Primal Scream, but was known as Tomanov. Vini Reilly formed The Durutti Column, whilst Eddie went on to form Ed Banger and His Group Therapy amongst other ventures, releasing singles on a variety of labels over the years. Eddie is now Edweena and still regularly plays gigs as The Nosebleeds as well as Slaughter II.

THE PANIK

The band consisted of 'Nance' on lead guitar and vocals, 'Random' on rhythm guitar, 'Hilton' on bass, and Brotherdale on drums.

Martin Ryan: "I had one record by The Panik."

'Modern Politics' was the 'A' side of the 3 track EP 'It Won't Sell' released on Rainy City Records, and produced by their manager, Rob Gretton. It would be the only release on the label as Gretton's focus was soon diverted elsewhere to another band, Warsaw.

Steve McGarry: "When he put out a single for The Panik, the first band he managed, he got me to design the sleeve. He was working part-time for the council as a census taker at the time, and I remember that he was chased though the streets of Benchill by a pack of wild dogs when he called round at my Gran's house to pick up the artwork. A few months later he'd started managing a fledgling outfit called Joy Division, and he got me to design a sleeve for their first EP.

Stanley Vegas: "One of their songs 'Murder' was about The Ranch. The first line went 'Coming out of The Ranch Bar late on Saturday night' and then carried on the story of how they got beaten up. Anyway Steve (Brotherdale) left The Panik and joined us. There was quite a bit of intermingling, you know? I would imagine that Steve would have preferred to stay in Warsaw/Joy Division really wouldn't he? But then again he was a totally different drummer, he was basic and solid."

'Modern Politics' would be the only recorded output by the band, but it's a fine example of basic DIY punk rock.

THE SHOCK

The Rock world was male-dominated in the 1970's, women were usually denigrated to be the nubile object on an album sleeve, or associated with being just groupies that followed the stars around. Patti Smith had been challenging and provoking this orthodoxy in America and there were seeds of female emancipation being sown in the UK. There was a healthy and increasing amount of women who had gravitated to punk in the very early days in Manchester, so the next logical progression was to form an all girl band in the city.

Juliette J. Williams: "Just before I started the band I used to look at people like Una and The Slits, there's the American women doing it but it's not quite the same, because they were older anyway. I always felt a little bit jealous of The Slits because they were in the centre of what was happening in London and I suppose I wanted us to be the Manchester version. I was saying to myself 'They've got the Pistols, we've got Buzzcocks, they've got The Slits so why can't we be the equivalent of them'. I didn't have any female role models in who's footsteps I'd like to follow, or aspire to. I just wanted to put on a pair of leather trousers, a leather jacket, and be in a band with guys because I always had boys as friends growing up, because I soon discovered that girls can be bitches.

"I got into playing the bass through listening to Reggae and Dub, which came about through listening to The Clash. I blagged my way backstage when The Clash were playing, I'd seen them on the White Riot tour at the Circus, but this time they were playing at the Apollo. Me and my mate got backstage through Pennie Smith, the photographer, and we got to know them from then onwards. When Joe found out that we'd got an all girl band, they'd just taken The Lou's out on tour who were a French female band, he said 'get your act together, keep rehearsing, keep rehearsing, you can support us on tour'. But it never happened. Paul Morley used to say to us when we were in The Ranch, 'Get your act together', and I mean yes, we did play at Pips where Warsaw were third on the bill and we were second with a band called Genocide, and they were our mates; the singer used to cut my hair and the bass player used to teach me how to play bass. We supported them and we went to the gig on the bus, it was two pence because we said that we were 16. We got changed and put our make up on upstairs at the back of the bus. We were like 'we're feminists so we can dress how we want'. When we played at Pips...Jane would be onstage in just her underwear, she used to wear a bra and pants with fishnets and suspenders. So as soon as the guys saw her they'd all go to her side of the stage, there was no one on my side! But I do remember women in the audience heckling us, calling us a bunch of slags and what have you. To my shame, I'd had one over the odds because I'd got stage fright, I hit one over the head with my bass, which probably wasn't the right thing to do, but she was giving us so much hassle. She was shouting at us, 'you fucking slags' and all that, so I just turned round and looked at Julie on drums and she was like 'don't do it!' but I did, and the bouncers dragged them out. So much for solidarity! It wasn't the right thing to do but I was angry and pissed off...it was a violent time and I read somewhere, I think it was either Lydon or Strummer who said 'we were there, we earned our stripes', well we earned our stripes too!

"We did about three or four gigs in Bolton. We did a gig at The Swan in the cellar in Bolton, which was a very early venue, and you could get in for 20p on a Monday night. They had a punk night which a very enterprising chap from London called John put on. He was an old hippie. You know what it was like in the early days, there was nothing to play because nobody had recorded anything. When he first started his punk night it would have been the beginning of '77 so you had 'Anarchy...', 'New Rose', 'Get A Grip...', and 'Do Anything You Wanna Do', as well as stuff from New York Dolls and stuff like that. We did another gig at a pub in Bolton which Mick Middles came along to review, but it ended in a bit of a riot. I'm not sure why but I think it was something to do with the band that supported us because there was a bit of a ruck going on so next thing Mick is high tailing it back to the train station, so we never got reviewed. We had more gigs lined up but we just fell to bits. Our guitarist, Jane, decided to go to Spain and open a bar with her mum. I wanted to move to London but Julie, our drummer, and Vivienne, our vocalist, didn't want to move. When Jane left I advertised for a new guitarist in the *NME* and *Sounds*. I got a phone call from somebody who turned out to be Deirdre Cartwright, who was the original guitarist in Girlschool but because she didn't live in the area it was a non-starter.

"When our guitarist left and went to Spain I was like, right, who do I know that would fit in to the band, and we ended up with a guy. I was so reluctant to have a guy because it was my band and my idea and it was my sort of like say so. So we got this guy from Glasgow and he was a mad speed freak, and a mad Iggy fan. He never got to practise on time, if at all, and then there was talk of him moving to London, so I was like where do I go for female musicians? I would have just started the whole thing again from scratch with no drummer and no vocalist because when they said that they didn't want to move to London, that just felt like, 'you can't be arsed being in this band, you're not interested in moving forward, you're not interested in creating what I want to create'. So there I was, stuck in a crappy typist job working in a mail order company. So not being able to find another female guitarist and the fact that the other two weren't committed, I just gave up and I shouldn't."

The Shock never recorded any material.

PHYSICAL WRECKS

Inspired by the DIY ethos and the fact that you didn't have to be a proficient musician any longer, bands started to be formed among friends and people that they would meet in places like The Ranch. Chris Lambert, Ken Park and Alan Wild formed Physical Wrecks after watching The Damned at The Electric Circus.

Chris Lambert: "I think that was towards the end of '76. On the bus on the way home we'd pretty much made up our minds to form a band. Then we saw the Pistols and The Clash on the 'Anarchy' tour twice in December, and that just reinforced what we were thinking. But we were great at talking about forming a band, but crap at actually doing anything about it. We'd bored our mates rigid about our band ethos and what have you and they said 'you're talking shit, you're never going to do it', so in the end we were embarrassed into doing it. We'd been listening to Stooges, Velvet Underground, Roxy, Bowie, The Who, Stones, MC5 etc. Pips had started to play Ramones, but there was no punk music about until The Damned released New Rose. So we were going to clubs listening to Dr. Feelgood and Eddie and the Hot Rods. We booked a church hall to rehearse in and spent the first couple of rehearsals kicking a football about. Alan and Ken had been to school together and we knew this guy who played bass, Dave Ashworth, and a lad called Mick Atherton who played drums, so they came to the first rehearsal. We'd done about three or four and they'd gone okay, and some of our mates were in another band called Cry Tough, who were like a Rock band, they supported Sad Café, that sort of Rock you know? So anyway they got a gig at a local pub called The Rawstron and they said we could support them, we only had 20 minutes."

It didn't go too well for them.

Chris Lambert: "Our first gig… we were barred from the pub… barred for life."

Ken Park: "At the end of the gig, we were gently kicking our equipment… because we didn't have much money to replace it, it was all power chords and all the rest of it. Chris is on the floor yelling, you know? It was in a pub in Whitworth, where we come from, out in the sticks. So he's lying on the floor screaming and the landlady's got a brush and she's going; 'Get up! Get out of my pub!'"

Chris Lambert: "Also, Alan our guitarist… he tried jumping a table and didn't quite clear and knocked all the glasses over!"

The band were also the first punk group to play at The Deeply Vale Festival, but it was more by default than design.

Chris Lambert: "A bloke called Chris Hewitt came to one of our rehearsals and he was organising Deeply Vale, and he took a bold step actually asking us to play. He put us on late on the Friday night rather than banging us on in the afternoon, pretty much just below the headliner I think. I mean, there was a few thousand people there and The Drones played on the Sunday. We got a lot of abuse. I heard one guy shout out 'I've heard of Johnny Rotten, but you're just rotten'. So we legged it after we came off, just got in the van and fucked off."

Ken Park: "In Rochdale we had the hippie/punk crossover. They had the gigs, and the gear, and the experience almost. The guy that put us onto Deeply Vale in '77 he was a hippy and he got a lot of flak for putting punk bands on - we got booed on! The Ruts saw us playing, two of the band saw us and The Drones, and they went back to London and they definitely developed an affection for it. In many ways we were the classic punk band, we played very few gigs, we caused an absolute furore wherever we went, and we were more talked about than listened to. Plus a lot of people who saw us became bands; they thought, we could do that!"

Because the band were from out in the sticks, there was a fierce adversity to towing the big city line.

Ken Park: "There was a real feeling, when we got the band together we realised we didn't need London. We could make a record ourselves, we'll put it out, get it printed and we'll get it pressed. We knew that recording studios were expensive so we built our own in an old mill. To me that's what that era was about; you just go and do it. There was so much energy around then, young people just bubbling under."

Chris Lambert: "There was this attitude amongst us of, sod it, we're here. We played The Ranch in 1977, a Sunday night. It was our big gig. I took the Physical Wrecks to The Ranch Bar and it was a bit intimidating. It was only our third ever gig I think, so to come from Whitworth, and we'd been playing youth clubs 'round Rochdale, so to end up actually playing in The Ranch Bar was quite..."

Ken Park: "When we did The Ranch Bar our drummer at the time was pretty basic... a decent drummer just loud, noisy. He had a problem with his testicle - one of them blew up so he couldn't sit on his stool, so he had to go to hospital so he couldn't do the gig. So a friend of ours, Simon Brocklehurst he was in a jazz band called Howard The Duck, he was an absolutely magnificent drummer. So we said 'can you stand in?' We had about four days. Rehearsal 1; We set off, he's still doing his intro, we've finished! So it was... Stop! 'Okay it's two guitar riffs, then bang bang and in. That's what we wrote on his drum kit! He dumbed himself down basically. He was fantastic on the night"

Chris Lambert: "I ripped his shirt!"

Ken Park: "He was a bit nervous about what to wear. He turned up and Chris said 'that's no good so he slashed it!"

Chris Lambert: "When we played The Ranch... one of our mates unplugged us"

Ken Park: "I asked him why? And he said 'I'm trying to have a conversation, I can't hear myself talk!' He unplugged the back of the bass cab."

Chris Lambert: "We only played about five or six gigs but they were memorable you know, they were chaotic, people never really knew what to expect."

The band have recently got back together and continue to do sporadic, but intense gigs.

NERVOUS BREAKDOWN

London had Eater, Manchester had Nervous Breakdown. Aged between 14 and 16 the band were formed in summer 1977 and were from the inner city area of Ardwick. In an interview with *God Is A Newt* fanzine the band's influences were diverse: Buzzcocks, Yardbirds, and Eddie Cochran.

Mickey Tait: "I was in Virgin Records and this guy comes up to me and said to me, 'do you know any punk bands or anyone who wants to come on telly?', and I just said yeah 'I'm in a punk band'. I wasn't but we'd talked about it. He was from Granada Reports doing the research. Anyway we got a date to appear on TV. We'd never played, so we went to Droylsden to this girl's house, her mum and dad were on holiday, and we practised for one night. The next day we were on Granada Reports. There was a punk discussion on the programme - Tony Wilson and me were going upstairs into the studio and Elvis Costello was walking down the stairs. He stopped and had a chat with Tony and I remember Costello wishing me well, shaking my hand on the stairs. So we went on the telly, and when we heard it afterwards, we'd never played, we couldn't play. You don't get more punk than that - literally we had one night's practice. They even had to hire us some instruments! Punk was breaking and I think they just wanted to throw something together. I think some of the other Punks were a bit pissed off with us that there were better bands who could have used that time to progress. They had a couple of complaints from the public.

"Our first gig was either at The Ranch or Pips. We played Pips and The Ranch a few times. Do you remember the band Eater? The youngest band? We were younger, we were 14 and 15. We played with V2 on the first gig, played with Warsaw a few times, The Distractions several times. We also played with Suburban Studs and nearly chinned 'em afterwards because they were real arseholes. I'm not into the hierarchy of Punk, or those who see themselves as that. Even when we were playing with Warsaw... there was us, Warsaw, The Snides, and there was another band whose name escapes me at the moment. I remember Warsaw; 'we're going to be top of the bill' because there was talk of a tour around the country playing at all the colleges. I think it was Barney, 'we're going to be top of the bill', which was really important to him which was good, I mean they were doing some good stuff.

"I bumped into our first guitarist, Dave Machin, he was a Teddy Boy at first. Anyway I bumped into him about five years ago and he said to me, 'do you know what really pisses me off? We never had a mention'. There's two things on the internet; Manchester Music Archives where a girl did an interview with us for a fanzine, and also there's a club in town where we played on the same bill as Warsaw. Hooky wouldn't let Nervous Breakdown borrow some of their equipment. I got quite friendly with Ian Donaldson from Skrewdriver. I met him in The Ranch, before he was a racist by the way. He gave me their first E.P. 'Anti Social' with 19 Nervous Breakdown on the other side. He was at the Suburban Studs gig when they were being arseholes about the PA. They wanted us to pay our fee towards it so we wouldn't even have enough money for a drink. They thought they were the big I am. Anyway we didn't give them anything. Manicured Noise and ourselves, Nervous Breakdown, we used to practise in the same building, we hired a building, they'd have a couple of hours and then we'd have a couple of hours practise as well. Funny thing is, before we split we were getting really good. It was just our drummer - one day we were playing the Tower Club in Oldham, he didn't show up. We were on with the Frantic Elevators, they were supporting us, as they did a few times. From that moment on I was devastated. I was only 15 at that stage. On the Queen's Jubilee, Alan Keogh called me over to Wythenshawe to see if I wanted to join their band with him and Ian Dalglish, but they thought that I sounded too much like Howard Devoto!"

Stanley Vegas: "Nervous Breakdown supported V2 a few times. They were the same as us really, we had similar outlooks on life, we'd both had it rough."

No recorded output exists of the band.

14. fanzines.

"I had zero idea of what I was doing. I honestly had no idea where to start. All I knew was I had something I craved to say. I wanted to create art that lived on longer than I do."

Scott McGoldrick [Songwriter].

Fanzines weren't invented by the punks, they had existed a long time before that, catering for a multitude of subcultures such as Rockabilly, Psychedelia, the proto-punk of The Velvet Underground and MC5 and so on. Basically, anything that wasn't mainstream. Some of the earlier ones hailed from America including, *Denim Delinquent*, *Brain Damage*, and *Nix on Pix*. 'Blogging' would be the modern vernacular. One fanzine that sat well with those released stateside emanated from a lot closer to home.

Penetration was conceived and written by Paul Welsh in 1974, a few miles down the A6 in Stockport, South of Manchester. It primarily concentrated on non mainstream artists like Henry Cow, The Velvet Underground, Kiss, Rocky Horror, and Kevin Ayers amongst many others. In issue 8 the publication reported on Sex Pistol's Free Trade Hall gig in June 1976, with photos taken by Welsh himself, and subsequently these pictures would be used in the numerous books and features on the subject. The article gave a positive appraisal of the gig and the band, proclaiming that Johnny Rotten was 'Vocalist of the year No.1.', and the group was 'Band of the year No.1.' Fellow Stockport dweller Paul Morley would also contribute articles to it and it lasted until September 1977, with its 13th issue being the final one off the photocopier, before Welsh called it a day after conceding that it was getting too expensive to produce.

Punk's first major outlet for information, in what would kick-start a plethora of fanzines reflecting the genre up and down the country, was started off in London by Mark Perry's *Sniffin' Glue + Other Rock'n'Roll Habits For Punks!* in July 1976. There were no pictures, just words bashed out on a typewriter which Perry had been bought as a Christmas present aged 10. It consisted entirely of reviews of gigs, albums, and singles with untidy handwritten titles photocopied onto eight A4 stapled together pages. Despite the term Punk being used throughout, such was the dearth of Punk groups, bands like Blue Oyster Cult, Captain Beefheart,

Todd Rundgren and The 101'ers were all featured alongside Ramones, The Stranglers and Television. It wasn't until issue 3 in September that Xeroxed, grainy photos were added to the narrative as the list of Punk bands was beginning to grow, along with the scene. Buzzcocks got a mention in the 100 Club Punk Festival special (issue three and a half): "Their sound is rough, very like the Pistols, but that guitar sound! Fuckin' 'ell, it was a spitting, rasping monster... They've got a loyal following up in Manchester and they're hoping to get some more gigs in London."

January 1977's issue 6 featured pictures from one of the Sex Pistol's gigs in Manchester on the Anarchy tour, as well as a passing mention of the gig in July at the Lesser Free Trade Hall.

Ken Park: "There were people just putting their own magazines out, self-producing fanzines."

One of Manchester's first fanzines was *Shy Talk* put together by Steve Burke (Shy) with the first issue coming out in March 1977, and it was a case of trial and error.

Steve Shy: "The magazine came about mainly through Buzzcocks and The Drones, they told me to start a band up but I never did because I'm tone deaf, that's the reason. But I wanted to be part of it so I started the fanzine off. It was only after seeing *Sniffin' Glue* and a couple of others... Manchester didn't have one so I decided to start my own off. The first one we did was really bad; the photographs didn't turn out, we didn't have any idea how to do it, we just did it. Although it turned out badly we sold 150 copies."

Mike Keogh: "I had a couple magazines called *Shy Talk*."

Fran Taylor: "I bought my first one from Barney while at the Ranch, he told me he was now in a band and I didn't see him for ages. Issue three reviewed new bands including Warsaw, saying they are having trouble finding a drummer, don't have a manager and need all the help they can get to find gigs. Later in the issue is an advert that says "Wanted: Drummer into Clash, Pistols etc... Ready to start gigging, Bernard" and a telephone number. The rest, as they say, is history!"

Even though it was a rudimentary operation there were still costs to be incurred. Access to decent photocopying machines was very limited and usually meant clandestine operations at a friend's place of work. Richard Boon offered to help finance *Shy Talk* by way of a loan, which Steve would pay back through sales of the fanzine. A couple of months later another fanzine appeared in the city. *Ghast Up!* was conceived and written by Mick Middles and Martin Ryan. Despite there now being two fanzines vying for the same readership there was certainly no rivalry between the two of them.

Martin Ryan: "I'd say that Steve became a very good friend of mine over the years. I'd known Mick (Middles), we were at school together, and we went to gigs together, and he suggested that we should start a fanzine. Mick lived in Disley, that's the address given in the fanzine. Now I hadn't seen *Sniffin' Glue* at that time, so I was like what's that then? Mick said, 'we just write it ourselves about bands, punk bands or…' well AC/DC were our first one so… I mean I went to Art college so I could draw and paint a bit and I thought, yeah I could probably lay out a cover and that but how are we going to print it, we'll have to get Letraset won't we, to do the headlines? But Mick was like 'Oh no, you just scribble the headlines!' In the end we did it on a Roneo Duplicator you know, the stencil. The first one, my sister helped because she worked in an office where she had access to all that. We paid to have the cover done professionally, only to have it stencilled you know. We actually bought one after that from the second issue onwards."

As with *Sniffin' Glue*, the lack of relevant local bands meant that keeping to a punk aesthetic was difficult.

Martin Ryan: "We only did one interview in the first issue. The other big feature was AC/DC and I think that the only reason for that was I liked them, I'd seen them at the student's union (which is now The Academy 2), the previous autumn (1976) and I thought that they were pretty good, like I said then, we were into Rock bands, Punk was a new thing. I think AC/DC probably straddled the two genres, whether you'd have described them as Punk, I don't know, but I know they weren't later. To me they played short 3-4 minute numbers, they were unpretentious, straight, good time Rock."

Writing the features was one thing, having photographs to compliment the words was a little more difficult at first. Although gaining access to the best venues in town was surprisingly not only more straightforward, it was practically encouraged.

Martin Ryan: "There was the Circus and The Oaks and I did go into The Ranch once or twice to sell it. So I wrote to the Circus, that was the thing then, you had to write to everybody in them days. Anyway Graham Brookes rang me up and gave me the dates for May I think it was, we asked them if they could give us some future dates and we'd print them in the fanzine. Oh yeah, and while you're on, is it okay if I come down with a camera? It was only an Instamatic. So the Circus gave me access with a camera so I could do an actual feature, alright it won't be as professional but that was the nearest we could get of doing an professional live feature, like a full live review with three crappy photos of the band taken by me on an Instamatic. So the first issue I used my own photos, the second and third Kevin Cummins did them for us. He hadn't started doing the *NME* then."

The next hurdle was making sure that the pictures were fit to use, so there was a nervy week waiting for them to come back from being developed.

Martin Ryan: "I had a Polaroid actually. When we interviewed Buzzcocks I had a Polaroid, we could see them straight away, but the Instamatic was actually my mum and dad's. I took them on a Thursday night so I'd go into work on Friday and nip into Boots in Stockport precinct to drop the film off and then wait to pick it up the next week. Hopefully they weren't double exposed or anything. Mind you we'd have still had to use them."

Kevin Cummins would go on to be Manchester's finest music photographer, his work over the years has covered multiple genres. Some of the most iconic images in musical history have been through his lens. He also helped out with pictures for *Shy Talk* as well. Another contributor for both fanzines was Paul Morley, both he and Cummins went on to work for the *NME* and those early outlets helped to hone their respective crafts.

Wispa: "One of the first bands he (Kevin Cummins) started snapping was Rockslide come The Drones because he was hanging around with us a lot. I used to go out with his sister when I worked at The Grand Hotel, and that's how we got to know him. I think he was at Salford Tech as well studying photography."

Martin Ryan: "He was quite friendly with us and he did contribute to *Ghast Up!* Both Paul Morley and Kevin were really good with us back then, if I'd never known or heard of them ever again and you'd ask me about these lads that we knew back in the day I'd say 'yeah they were great'."

Fran Taylor: "Kevin had a room over, I think it was a newsagent's in Withington, not 100% on that but I always got driven there and back and my geography outside of Salford wasn't too great. I used to spend whole nights, from midnight until 5 in the morning sometimes, in Kevin's studio printing photographs for him. He used to sell packs of 8 x 10's in the back of the *NME*. I'd print off pictures of Marc Bolan, Abba, Roxy

Music, David Bowie, whoever was on tour at the time. It was good fun. Photography in those days was expensive. It cost a fortune to get them developed, otherwise I could have had loads of photos."

Although punk had gained momentum throughout 1977, the bands in Manchester were still very approachable and more than happy to give interviews.

Martin Ryan: "The Drones were quite good mates at the time. The thing with Slaughter was Howard was quite a nice lad, I met him at The Oaks and he gave me his phone number. We'd done Buzzcocks and The Drones so we thought we should really feature Slaughter And The Dogs because whether you like them or not they were the three premier Manchester bands at the time. So Howard was prepared to do it, but I was trying to chat to Wayne Barrett at Rafters and he was a complete tosser, just giving us one word answers being dead cocky, and Mike Rossi was fairly shy I think. Howard was a nice lad, he would always chat to us about what they were doing, about how they'd been in the studio with Nick Tauber who produced the early Thin Lizzy albums; Howard was a big Thin Lizzy fan."

With the Slaughter interview not happening, the next best thing was to review their single 'Cranked Up Really High'. Except that the critique didn't go down too well with everyone.

Martin Ryan: "After we'd done the second issue and we'd done a review of the new single, Ray Rossi came up to me and said, 'Did you write the review of the single?' And I said 'Yeah, why?' He said, 'It's not very good is it?' I thought that it was quite a good review really, I just mentioned that the production was pretty bad which was Martin Hannett but… he was alright about it but he said that we should have given them a full page because they're a Manchester band."

The problem with the Punk scene in Manchester being such a close knit group meant that the chances of bumping into someone with a bone to pick were extremely high.

Martin Ryan: "The Drones played a midweek gig at The Circus, and I think that was the first night that The Circus had turned Punk for the night, you know; the music, the DJ and everything. I met Paul Morley there and Pete Shelley was there, and he recognised me from when we interviewed them. He had a go at me for some of the things in the interview, One of the questions was, 'What were Subway Sect like?', and they said 'Oh we didn't like them', so Shelley was saying 'You're upsetting all my friends there'. Mick said 'Yeah but you did say you didn't like Subway Sect.' and he was like, 'No I didn't', but he was alright with us you know. But that was our first sort of networking night because as I said Paul Morley was there and I overheard him as he was talking to Steve Shy. He'd seen someone holding a copy of *Ghast Up!* it was the first time that we were selling it at a gig, and he asked Steve, 'Is he from *Ghast Up!* over there?' and Steve said 'Yeah', so he put out his hand out… in them days you didn't tend to shake hands, you'd normally slap someone on the shoulder or whatever, but he was very formal.

"That night at The Electric Circus he said 'Can I write something for you?' He wrote a piece for *Ghast Up!* about Paris and The Atmospheres which he just sent to us for no reason. I thought it was about a made up band, I didn't know there was a real band, I only found out years later about these names he said; Bryn and Pete. It sounded like it was a spoof of Buzzcocks really, 'Pete the baby-faced guitarist', but they did release a single in 80's!"

Paul Morley produced his own very brief fanzine, *Out There (Prose For Dancing To),* which ultimately helped him get a job at the *NME* when he allegedly sent a copy down to their offices with the caveat, 'I can do better than you'. Fair enough. Bob Dylan adorned the front cover of *Out There...* and listed Patti Smith, The Stranglers, and Ted Nugent as featured articles. He also put out *Girl Trouble* which was more of a vehicle to promote The Negatives, the mish-mash semi-fictional band he occasionally fronted with a malleable line-up. To confirm and enhance the group's mythical status, he even went as far as to advertise their 'ghost' song titles and record releases while proclaiming that the band "brought fiction back into music".

There were other publications out there including one specifically dedicated to Slaughter and the Dogs called *Manchester Rains*. Originally the brainchild of Rob Gretton, who at the time was running the Slaughter fan club, it was a celebration of all things 'Dog'. Gretton asked his friend Steve McGarry to help him put it together.

Steve McGarry: "Rob and I had been mates since school and spent a lot of time together. He was running Slaughter's fan club at the time and generally helping out on the PR side, as well as promoting shows at The Oaks in Chorlton. I used to do all his art. It was Rob that got me to do the original Slaughter logo (the Alsatian) and that was used on badges and stickers. He wanted to do a fanzine so he came to me with the copy and the photos and I put it all together. I was working in the studio at Great Universal Stores at the time. I went freelance in July of 1977 so that was the last proper job I ever had and I used the office typewriter, nicked a bit of Letraset and then handwrote all the rest."

Along with a 'Dogfacts' article there were individual light-hearted band member biographies; Favourite Single, New Wave band, previous employment etc, including a question on income; '£9 dole money'. It wasn't taking itself too seriously and it only lasted for one copy.

Steve McGarry: "When the fanzine came out it was reviewed by a couple of music papers. Julie Burchill reviewed it in the *NME* and slagged it off, saying it was "too professional" and "slick" - which was funny because it was just my scribbled handwriting and a bit of text done on an old typewriter. Proper DIY punk! Looking at the credits, other than the fact that I misspelled Cummins on the photo credit, it looks like we thanked: Leslie (Rob's partner); Ray (that would be Slaughter manager Ray Rossi - Mick Rossi's brother); Slim: (not sure who that is);Vini: (that was Vini Faal, flyposterer and manager of The Nosebleeds); Uncle Tosh: (that's Tosh Ryan, owner of the fly-posting business and the guy who launched Rabid Records); Adge and Birko (that was my brother Adge and Steve Birkhead, who both worked at GUS and must have helped with camera prints and paste-up). No computers in those days!"

Stanley Vegas: "They did an interview with me, but I didn't really want to do it; it was like 'Ooh the No.1 fan' shit. It made me sound like some sort of fucking Bay City Rollers type fan. Then he wanted to take a photo but I said 'no you're not taking a photo'. He was a nice guy Rob."

There were other one-off publications.

Martin Ryan: "Jeff Noone did a fanzine, he did one issue called *Noisy People* which had lyrics in it. It had 'Repetition' by The Fall, and it also had 'Novelty' by Warsaw."

Pete Shelley also tried his hand with *Plaything*, basically just the thoughtful meanderings of what was in his head at that time.

The initial reason why fanzines were produced was to inform and promote what was at the time a small, underground scene. Towards the middle of 1977 Punk had gone completely mainstream and was being reported by all the main music papers, so the need for a primitive, photocopied version of the same events was more or less redundant. The local bands, whether that was in Manchester, London or wherever, had mostly been signed up by major labels and any advertising budget or interviews were going to be conducted through the *NME*, *Sounds* or *Melody Maker*. They wanted the street credibility, featuring the ever-growing list of bands springing up all over the UK and in turn those groups and their labels wanted the maximum exposure for themselves. It was therefore no coincidence that both *Shy Talk* and *Ghast Up!* lasted for three issues. *Shy Talk's* last issue was published in May and *Ghast Up!* put out their last issue in July 1977 respectively.

Martin Ryan: "We only did three. The first one was finished on Good Friday 1977. I remember because we were off work and my sister bought the stuff round. We took delivery of the cover which we'd had done which was as well as it could be done on a stencil machine. So on Good Friday we were just round our house stapling them together, and then spent the Easter weekend going around Virgin and places to get them to take them.

Steve Shy: "I didn't do anything. I wrote a shitty fanzine, did three issues, where I don't think I wrote anything more than a four letter word. I was absolutely shite; it was because I had people like Kevin Cummins doing the photographs for me, I had Paul Morley writing for me. I used to get letters from Morrissey saying 'when are you going to do American stuff?' I actually did a number four and never released it. The reason being, I was just about to get it printed and I went in Virgin Records, which was on Lever Street in town at the time. I said *Shy Talk's* out next week, how many do you want? And this guy said 'can you give us 1200 for now'. I thought, you fucking what!? They were sending them down to Rough Trade and stuff like that, and I only wanted to do 200, you know? I was photocopying them at my ex's workplace... it put me off then so I just stopped doing it."

Such was the brevity and paper quality of fanzines, any which are still out there in decent condition are extremely collectible and command eye watering sums of money.

Turning rebellion into money indeed.

15. rainy city retreats

"Manchester's got everything. Except a beach."

Ian Brown

Manchester has never been short of entertainment venues, from dancehalls to discos, clubs, pubs and picture houses. Despite their undeniable historical musical influence and importance, there was more to the city than Pips and The Electric Circus. An array of establishments from the opulent to the frugal littered the city, and some were in their last throes of service and function when the Punks reclaimed them for a short while and breathed some fresh air into their foetid lungs.

BELLE VUE

Throughout its illustrious history Belle Vue has been home to a zoo, a public garden, an amusement park, a circus, as well as hosting sporting events such as wrestling and boxing bouts and is still the home to its revamped Speedway team, Belle Vue Aces. In its heyday it attracted millions of visitors from all around the world and was known rather grandiosely as 'The Showground of the World'. In the 1970's it would have been difficult to imagine just how prestigious a place it once was with its 'Firework Lake' which was used for displays all year around, complete with a 4,000 seated viewing stand; it was the Alton Towers of it's day, only with more style and impeccable taste.

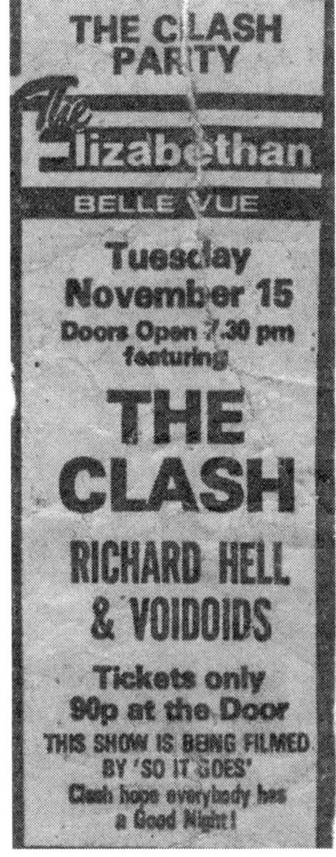

Ever since it first opened its doors, dancing was a major part of its function, with a magnificent ballroom that led onto an outside terrace. Christmas gala nights and carnivals added to the magical atmosphere, but in 1958 a fire devastated the ballroom, along with the viewing stand, and the outside terrace. A rebuilding project culminated in the Elizabethan Ballroom opening in 1960, continuing the dancing theme, but this time it was the turn of the teenagers. Jimmy Savile hosted the Top Ten Club nights there in the 60's, then in the 1970's it was disco all the way in the Zoo-B-Doo Disco.

Fred Carr: "I used to go to the Belle Vue discos. I saw David Essex down there when they were making the film, 'That'll Be The Day?"

The Kings Hall hosted some major league bands in the early part of the 1970's including The Rolling Stones, Led Zeppelin, The Who, Deep Purple, and The Osmonds. As the decade wore on the place began to resemble the rest of the city; run down and untidy, with dwindling crowds. The zoo eventually closed down and the amusement park was left to rot blending in with the grim, colourless surroundings of Gorton.

The place was just about hanging on by the mid seventies, primarily due to its music events attracting a young crowd but it wasn't without it's dangers.

Sarah Mee: "Manchester circa 1975; I was 15 years old and had to put a lot of make-up on to get into the clubs of the day and then still try to get the child's fare on the bus! At this time Belle Vue was the place to be for the Bowie fans of the day, pre-punk. Belle Vue was in a rough area and had a decrepit zoo and a fairground. The fairground blasted out 1950's music and seemed to be mostly run by young Teddy Boys. They took a huge dislike to the Bowie boys and were perplexed by the dress code of the Bowie girls. Getting in and out of Belle Vue was dangerous and we had to stick together in a group to have a sense of safety. I remember once that my friend and I got carried away and after the club had closed we decided to go on the Waltzers at the fairground. The Bowie area at Belle Vue was in a tiny part at the back of the ballroom with its large glittering disco ball. Once we were safely inside, it felt like our place of uniqueness and sanctuary for like-minded people. We either dressed in suits or Trilbies for the Bowie style. Roxy Music was also a band and a style that we followed, and their dress style was far more glamorous.

The DIY dressing up ethic was being practiced long before punk hit the north. Torn shirts and ripped trousers was one thing, but looking good with minimal cost took more imagination and ingenuity.

Sarah Mee: "We had tight satin skirts, fishnet tights, with Pill Box style hats with lace around them. The hats were made out of Corn Flake boxes with the satin and trim stuck onto it. It was lucky for us that they were that style because one night someone threw a bottle at us and it shattered and the glass stuck in the net part of the hat. I guess being young we were more fearless, so we just took our heels off and ran for it."

Brian Johnson: "A club on Wednesday nights called Zoo-B-Doo Disco at Belle-Vue that had a huge dance floor and lots of seating. That was excellent for us dancers and posers. No other rooms to walk through, just Bowie and Roxy people. Belle Vue didn't have an atmosphere of its own - just us! For some reason we really enjoyed it. It was like a break from the main stream of Pips. We were able to try out new looks and new things more easily. For me, I could be myself all the time, as opposed to America at the time, and I learned who I really was in those days."

Mickey Tait: "Belle Vue was good on a Wednesday night. It was open from about 8 o'clock until midnight. There were quite a few Bowie fans there, but we mixed. Later on it was Bowie and Punk. You used to be able to take your own records with you; The Saint's 'I'm Stranded', Radiators From Space; The Boys, stuff like that. I only lived down the road as well. I used to go to any gig I could go to, and I never had any money so I used to sneak in. I remember Mick Rossi outside Belle Vue, he was with a mate and I was with a mate, Peter Frampton was playing there, it would have been '76. I remember him pulling up in his limo and Mick Rossi turned his back to him and saying to him 'look at that Peter, we're going to be big one day', and his jacket had Slaughter and the Dogs written on the back of it. Then he said 'are you going to get us in?' to Peter Frampton and he took the four of us in."

As Punk started to infiltrate the city during 1977, Belle Vue hosted some of the best gigs, and because of its size, the biggest bands.

Stanley Vegas: "Because I was 'in' with Slaughter and the Dogs I'd get to see other bands, because they would support or be supported by, a lot of the other bands. For instance the big gig at Belle Vue with Slaughter, X Ray Spex, Johnny Moped and all that, I promoted that with Ray Rossi, who was Mike Rossi's brother. He was also their manager at the time. Ray ripped me off! [*laughs*] I think if you talk to anyone about Ray, you'll get similar stories [*laughs*]. What happened was, I put a cassette in the mixing desk because I wanted to record the gig for my own benefit, it never crossed my mind to use it for re-sale or anything like that. Anyway Ray Rossi had it away before I could get it back, and that became the official bootleg of the gig a few years later."

Alan Keogh: "Belle Vue was pretty good, and I saw The Slits there."

Belle Vue's Elizabethan Suite was one of the venues chosen for the filmed concert footage for the second series of So It Goes.

Carol O'Donnell: "I used to go to the Elizabethan at Belle Vue because they put on free gigs for So It Goes. Middleton Civic Hall was another venue."

Daniel O'Sullivan: "Me and Mickey (Tait) used to go to Belle Vue, was it the Elizabethan Suite?"

June Buchan: "I did the filming for So It Goes at the Siouxsie and the Banshees gig at Belle Vue and I was covered in gob! I was on the stage with the cameraman and there was gob on the camera so we kept that in. But I just remember thinking how disgusting it was."

Kevin Stanfield: "I used to go to Belle Vue. I remember when The Clash played there, they kicked the fucking doors down! I saw X Ray Spex there, Siouxsie and the Banshees, quite a few played there."

Gail Egan: "The Clash gig at The Elizabethan (recorded for So It Goes); they do 'Garageland'...they do three songs and you can see Mick Hucknall at the front."

Mike Keogh: "We were at the Elizabethan in Belle Vue. The Clash were on, and I think that The Slits were supporting. Anyway there was this girl who we used to drink with, and we're all at the front of the stage, and this other girl tried to get onto the stage. This bouncer just went up to her and kicked her in the face... kicked all her teeth in. So we dragged her outside because she was covered in blood, and we were wanting to hang this bouncer up by his bollocks. So we were outside the front door I looked round and the man himself Tony Wilson was there. He took her in his car to the hospital, which I thought was amazing. Anyway he came back later on in the night, and somehow we got into the after gig party. I think we got in through Mick Jones who'd seen the girl getting beaten up and that we'd helped her, so we got let in afterwards. He came over talking to us, and I didn't really know who he was as such, I knew he was in the band of course but that night was my first introduction to The Clash. He said that he hoped that she was alright and that they were going to get the bouncer who did it, the sack. Whether they did or not I don't know. I never found out what happened to the girl either."

Terry Slater: "I was there at that gig with Mike, The Clash were about half way through their set, and there was this half caste girl at the side of the stage, and this knob head bouncer. Mick Jones, he saw it and she was bleeding like mad, and when we took her outside Tony Wilson came over and said, 'I saw that, is she okay?' I just said that she needed to go to hospital and he took her. He had a woman with him, I don't know who it was. I stayed with this girl and she stayed with me while he went and got the car. I went back in and Mick Jones said to me 'Stay there' at the end of the set. He came down and we went to see the management about this bouncer, and I think he ended up getting the sack anyway."

That simple act of kindness by Wilson was anathema to his public, television persona.

Joanne Slater: "He wasn't as arrogant as people thought he was."

Andy T.: "I remember not having enough money at The Mayflower one night, I think it was the 'Stuff The Superstars' gig. I went up to Tony Wilson and I said to him, "You couldn't lend us some money for the bus", I think it was about 50p or something for two of us. I ended up selling him some Distractions badges to get us home!"

Some of Manchester's most prominent punk band members would be in attendance some nights.

Mike Keogh: "Pete Shelley was in the Elizabethan in Belle Vue as he did quite regularly, I mean this was before they'd really took off. Howard had just left and there was a short period where nothing much was happening. He was with Gail Egan, and they were sat in one of the booth areas, so I went over for a chat. They were just having a giggle, so I said 'What's the crack?' Gail had this Coke ring that he'd fashioned into a ring for her, and I said 'What's all that about?' She said 'We've got engaged' so I took a picture of them and sent it to Gail a good few years ago now."

Gail Egan: "The first time I saw Pete Shelley was at the Electric Circus on the anarchy tour, he had bleached blonde hair. I told Paul Morley that I quite fancied him, so later on when we were in The Ranch he told him. We ended up going out for a little bit. We had a so called 'mocked up' engagement where he gave me a little stainless steel ring. Of course it wasn't real but you know, it was just..."

Terry Slater: "There was the Belle Vue nights, plus we used to go and watch gigs at the Band On The Wall as well, there was always something going on"

BAND ON THE WALL, SWAN STREET, MANCHESTER.

The origins of the Band On The Wall go back to 1803. It was originally the George And Dragon public house. The area around Swan Street was a squalid, dangerous place inhabited by Scuttler gangs and pickpockets. Manchester was growing rapidly, with many businesses, factories and mills around the Ancoats area, the bustling Smithfield Market was developed and eventually expanded to a four acre site, finishing its boundary at the back of the pub. Irish and Italian immigrants made up a large percentage of the population, and it would be the entrepreneurial Irish brothers, Bernard and John McKenna, who bought and developed the pub over the next few decades. They also owned other businesses and went on to build The Wellington pub on Rochdale Road, now known as The Marble Arch. Fast forward over 100 years and the pub was struggling following the relocation of Smithfield Market, and eventually closed its doors in 1974.

A year later local musician Steve Morris, a lover of Jazz, and the son of an illegal bookmaker, took over the lease on the building to fulfil his dream of opening a Jazz club. After refurbishment, including a new stage replacing the raised platform that the previous resident band had played on, inspiring the new name 'Band On The Wall', it re-opened for business on 12th September 1975. Jazz was to remain the musical staple diet of the club initially, but in 1977 the Monday Rock Club night was introduced and promoted by the *New Manchester Review*. The night was designed to showcase local bands as well as broadening the venue's musical diversity. The *NMR*'s first live event was on 8th November 1976 to celebrate its first birthday, and the headline act was Buzzcocks, supported by Tom McMasters, whose band included Martin Hannett on bass guitar. This gig was the catalyst that opened Morris's mind to putting on other genres of music. Morris realised that it didn't have to be about navel gazing, endless complicated guitar solos from gifted musicians, so consequently he actively encouraged artists of varying degrees of competence to get up on stage and do something. Soon there were performances from a diverse range of acts; Country Rock, poetry readings (John Cooper Clarke received his first paid gig here- £5) and the future Poet Laureate, Carol Ann Duffy, there was even an all women clog band!

Fran Taylor: "Another place was Band On The Wall, which had been a Jazz venue for Donkey's years. It became an important place because of the Manchester Musicians Collective who would schedule regular things there, and the *New Manchester Review* who would also schedule gigs there. They were our equivalent of *Time Out* at the time, a bit more arty maybe but pretty much a listings magazine."

In 1977 the Manchester Musicians Collective was formed, with a commitment to encouraging and promoting musicians and bands, and giving them a voice. They received a grant towards the rehearsal room hire and transport, and soon bands were going to them for assistance. Although the people behind it probably didn't fulfil any punk credentials aesthetically, the idea was that anyone could access help and be given gigs regardless of their ability or type of act. Ian Curtis embraced the idea, '*The Collective was a really good thing for Joy Division. It gave us somewhere to play, we met other musicians, talked, swapped ideas. Also it gave us a chance to experiment in front of an audience. We were allowed to take risks – the Collective isn't about groups that need to draw an audience.*'

After outgrowing their original premises on King Street, where The Fall played their first ever gig, they chose Band On The Wall as the new venue to put their showcases on. Sunday was the only night available which clashed with The Electric Circus's punk nights.

Between 1975 and 1979 over 200 different acts had played at the Band On The Wall, and around 1500 gigs had been put on, but the writing was on the wall, no pun intended, for the venue. The *New Manchester Review* went bust, which jeopardised the Monday night gigs, and then the Musicians Collective moved their shows to Rafters, which was a bigger venue. But not before a piece of Manchester folklore was born.

John Maher: "On May 2nd 1977 Buzzcocks played two sets at Band On The Wall. Howard Devoto joined us for the last song. He dropped the mic and walked off. Jon The Postman clambered on stage, grabbed the mic and launched into his first ever public performance of 'Louie Louie'."

Throughout the'80's and '90's Band On The Wall became synonymous with Blues, Reggae and World music, while mainstream or alternative bands/artists overlooked the place on their touring schedules. Band On The Wall is now owned and run by registered charity 'Inner City Music' and is a not for profit venue. Its future looks bright.

THE OAKS, BARLOW MOOR ROAD, CHORLTON, MANCHESTER.

Of all the places that would go on to host early Punk gigs in the city, The Oaks went under the radar. It hosted some important and iconic performances during its very brief tenure. Out on a limb geographically what it lacked in quantity of gigs, it more than made up with quality.

Fran Taylor: "Then along comes The Oaks in Chorlton. It was out on the South Manchester/Wythenshawe end of the crowd, who were involved with Slaughter And The Dogs, Rabid Records, The Panik, and it was basically Rob Gretton, Tosh Ryan and people like that. It's a very important venue in terms of punk because it was *the* first place to be booking solidly punk bands every week. It was literally a pub, a big pub but out of the back there was a raised dais thing with a railing around it, almost like a dance floor type of thing as I remember, but you could cram a band onto there. Somebody, probably Jon The Postman again, suggests going down The Oaks to see whoever and so we go down, and the thing that I remember most about it was for some reason you were able to 'skin up' in the bar and smoke a joint and nobody would bother you.

"The Oaks was just a pub and it was just watching, no dancing. The first gig that we went to at The Oaks I think was in March, and the last one was May 1977. I think Wayne County was the very last one, and the weird thing was that Wayne County used to spend an inordinate amount of time in Manchester, as did Johnny Thunders and the Heartbreakers. There was a guy in Manchester whose name I cannot recall who became a Wayne clone, he always used to wear this big bobble hat just like Wayne. The Oaks only ran for about eight to ten weeks. I'm not sure how they got 'em but they were nearly all London bands who played there. The Vibrators; that was possibly the first time they played in Manchester, The Slits; again that might have been the first time up here, not sure if it pre-dated The Clash gig. Johnny Thunders and the Heartbreakers, Siouxsie and the Banshees, a very early line up before Morris and Mackay joined. I'll have to check my diary."

Dawn Bradbury: "It was just a pub, as you walked in through the door the stage was on your left and the bar was straight ahead."

Denise Shaw: "The Oaks in Chorlton. I saw a few bands there. The Damned played there, The Adverts, nearly everybody played there. It was just a bit enclosed because it was like, carpeted and a stage so there wasn't that much room."

Daniel O'Sullivan: "I saw The Damned at The Oaks and Siouxsie and the Banshees."

Gail Egan: "I remember seeing Johnny Thunders at The Oaks in Chorlton. It was just a pub, and it had the smallest dance floor."

John Maher: "No stage. I whacked 2 x 6 inch nails through the aluminium dance floor to stop the bass drum skating around. In previous years Peter Stringfellow DJ'd there. George Best used to nip in for a swift half".

Martin Ryan: "The Oaks used to be like a Soul Disco type of place in the early '70's. They started putting punk gigs on in 1977, Slaughter and the Dogs opened it and it was Rob (Gretton) and Vini Farl. Vini put the bands on at The Oaks. The first band I saw there were The Heartbreakers, which was a groundbreaking gig for me in March '77. The thing about The Heartbreakers at The Oaks was that it was so different to me. I mean obviously I knew that two of them had been in the New York Dolls, but I hadn't seen or heard The Heartbreakers before. They were this really tight band playing a strong, almost bubble-gummy rock music, when what I was used to was watching bands just doing a few originals which were pretty flat, and loads of covers like Eric Clapton or whatever. Competent but… obviously the 'real' bands you'd see them at the Free Trade Hall. It was the first time I was seeing a real band, playing original songs - but in a pub!

"That was the fullest I ever saw The Oaks. It was a bit edgy as well. You always hear about the early days of Rock and the early days of Who gigs that they were always a bit edgy. Obviously, previous gigs at The Phoenix, they were a serious audience, if they didn't like a band they would just politely clap. I found out after that these big gangly youths, a bit like Sid Vicious with the leather jackets on, I think they were The Heartbreaker's entourage, the roadies and that. They seemed to be checking everybody out, but then again I suppose that was what they were there to do."

Once again a concerted effort was required to go to a gig there.

Stanley Vegas: "It was a bit far… it was a bit awkward to get to from Gorton. You'd have to go into town and then out again, so it was a bit of a pain in the arse, so I didn't really bother with that."

Andy T.: "All there is down there in South Manchester was the cemetery; Southern Cemetery. The Oaks was the pub where everybody went to for the wake. I had an Auntie that lived in Withington and I used to stay at her house after going to a couple of gigs, because getting back was a bit too far, even on the motorbike."

Southern Cemetery is where Tony Wilson is buried.

Mark Windsor: "The Oaks was a really awkward place to get to from Audenshaw so I only went two or three times. I saw Siouxsie and the Banshees there and there were about six people in there. I also saw The Adverts play there and this bloke just walked up and punched TV Smith in the face!"

Fred Carr: "We saw Buzzcocks quite a lot, they played Chorlton quite a lot at The Oaks. I was walking through Chorlton one day and this van pulls up and this girl asked me the way to The Oaks. So I jumped in the van and showed them where it was, and they came round to the flat afterwards, not mine. Paddy ended up going back down to London with them!" Those girls were The Slits.

Stanley Vegas: "I went to The Oaks to see Slaughter. I can remember Kevin Cummins taking some photos. It might have been the first time that Wayne Barrett wore his cape. There was a big staircase as I recall in The Oaks and he took some photos of him coming down the staircase with his cape on. He took some pictures of me, because I had a pretty cool Slaughter and the Dogs jacket that I'd done myself. But I'd never seen them."

Andy T.: "I can only remember a handful of gigs there. Rob Gretton did some promoting there as well as Ray Rossi, Mick's older brother. Both Rob and Ray were connected with Tosh Ryan, who did Rabid Records and the Music Force thing they had before, with all the posters everywhere. Slaughter played there a couple of times, and when they went down to London to play The Roxy, they got to know Don Letts, he was managing The Slits at the time, so The Slits and the Banshees were the first to come up or it may have been The Heartbreakers. But it was because of The Drones and Slaughter going down to play at The Roxy which in turn got people coming up, because they realised that something was going on up here."

The Oaks went the same way eventually of nearly all of the Punk haunts of 1976 and 1977 when it was closed in the 1990's to make way for the Christie Fields development.

MANCHESTER MUSICIANS' COLLECTIVE 101

name. . . . .
address . . . .
. . . .

keeping control

THE SQUAT, DEVAS STREET.

The red brick municipal style building that would eventually become known as The Squat used to be the old Manchester University College of Music, a beautiful building with a concert hall in the centre, which had removable seating, and then rehearsal rooms all around it. In 1973, the college relocated to a new site on Booth Street and was given the new name of Royal Northern College Of Music. The site was earmarked for demolition and was going to be turned into a car park, but the Student Union stepped in and a number of the students 'occupied' the place as a protest against the lack of student accommodation. There was a hard core of about 15 who thought that the space could also be utilised for other events, and that knocking it down was too drastic a measure. Another idea was to use it as a loosely based community centre, providing gigs, usually on Friday nights, in cooperation with the local organisation Music Force, who would supply the bands. They succeeded in giving it a stay of execution, and a limited redecoration was undertaken, with the University footing the bill for making sure the building had adequate fire proofing. The concert hall could be booked for whatever particular artistic genre that wanted to appear there. But it never really took off, and the original perpetrators of the occupation soon lost interest and over the following years not a lot went on in The Squat. Until it inadvertently became another one of the off-kilter venues for the emerging bands in the city.

Andy T.: "It might have had something to do with the Albertos, who were quite active in the early seventies, way before Punk. They were all a little bit older than the rest of us. It didn't do much, and I can't remember if it even had a bar, I think it was just tins of beer and a raffle ticket. You swapped the raffle ticket for a tin of beer."

Fran Taylor: "The Squat in Devas Street, which in 1977 did a few gigs, usually a combination of The Fall, The Worst, The Negatives and Jon The Postman, who had now officially become a band. They were usually put on by the Students Union.

Andy T.: "That was where I first saw Warsaw, and also the first time I saw The Fall. It was a weird University building that people had stopped using. Some students got this little club together in this little bit of it. It was on one of the streets at the bottom of Oxford Road."

Warsaw played there twice in June '77; on the 6th where they were bottom of the bill to Harpoon Gags, Bicycle Thieves, and Split Beans, and again on the 25th. Rock Against Racism also hosted gigs at The Squat.

Gail Egan: "We used to go to The Squat. I remember seeing Warsaw and having the privilege of meeting Ian Curtis.

There were also the rehearsal room spaces, left over from its college days, so at a time when finding decent, affordable rehearsal places were at a premium, this was a welcome attraction.

Stanley Vegas: "V2 used to rehearse in The Squat, before we went to TJM. I'm not sure how it came about. I think it was something to do with Jon The Postman, it might have been a mate of his. We used to be able to eat in the student canteen and get cheap grub and what have you. I remember seeing The Drones down there, and I remember seeing Skrewdriver there before they became what they became."

C.P. Lee: "To me, it was an absolutely magical point in Manchester's alternative history, because so much came from it. The creativity that was generated in that place was wonderful, and as much as you can say that the Sex Pistols at the Free Trade Hall changed a generation, it could be argued that a lot was changed by The Squat, by allowing the people who wanted to change their generation and also by giving them a space to do it in."

On the 3rd of February 1982 it was eventually knocked down and ironically, and inevitably, it became a car park.

APOLLO THEATRE, STOCKPORT ROAD, ARDWICK GREEN, MANCHESTER.

The Apollo opened on 29th August 1938 in the Art Deco style as a cinema and variety theatre. There was also a cafe and a ballroom, in 1962 it changed its name to ABC Ardwick. It wasn't until January 1977 that it became solely a music venue, just in time to benefit from the growing popularity of the Punk/New Wave scene. It's situation on the outskirts of the city centre meant a good 25 minute walk from Piccadilly train station, and a dash back to get the train home sometimes meant missing the encore. The theatre was the next step up for the first wave of Punk bands who had outgrown the small clubs and University halls of Manchester. The Punk movement was gathering momentum and bands such as The Clash, The Damned and The Jam were starting to make the step up to play to thousands instead of hundreds of punters. Although in The Damned's case, initially it was as the support act.

Ian Fawkes: "In February '77 we went to see The Damned supporting T. Rex at the Apollo. Bolan was on the slide then and this was our second proper punk gig months after the Pistols. There was hardly anyone there, perhaps a couple of hundred people in the place, and when The Damned came on they were so loud that I couldn't tell what the first song was initially and I'd already bought the first album 'Damned Damned Damned' so I knew all the songs. This time we went to the front and there were probably just two or three other people with us. I remember my mate Chris shouting at Rat Scabies and Rat got up from his drum kit and pointed his sticks at him which made his night!

"At the chaotic end of their set Vanian put his microphone into the monitor creating hellish squealing feedback, Scabies dismantled his drums and Sensible, who was playing bass at this time, was dressed in a nurse's uniform and kept lifting it up and of course he had nothing on underneath, meanwhile behind us there's about 200 Marc Bolan fans wondering what the fucking hell is going on!! After The Damned had finished we just turned round and walked out, and as we walked out past everyone I can remember feeling defiant whilst the crowd were calling for Bolan. We'd seen who we came to see and walked out, which looking back was a slight regret because we never got to see Bolan because we were making our protest, you know? We were Damned fans, and we'd seen them now so let's fuck off"

Chris Lambert: "We saw T Rex's last ever gig, well we'd gone to see The Damned. After we'd seen them we went upstairs and had a drink with Captain Sensible and Rat Scabies and they were teasing the Punks. We didn't see Bolan either, we legged it off to The Electric Circus where we thought there was a Punk band on and it was actually a prog band."

Mark Windsor: "I went to see The Damned supporting T. Rex at the Apollo. A couple of things I remember; We were at the bar and Captain Sensible and Rat Scabies came into the bar, where the audience were! The other thing was, at the end of the set they jumped off stage and ran off through the crowd. It broke all the rules. I suppose it made Bolan look tired and old - he was 29!"

To put that into context, Joe Strummer was 24 years old at the time. Ironically Bolan was enjoying an upturn in his career as he embraced the Punk movement and the new breed of young bands coming through, giving them television exposure on his own programme 'Marc'. The programme was first shown on 24th August 1977, and was produced in Manchester by Granada TV. It was shown in the 'after school slot', before the early evening news. The first band on that first show were The Jam, playing 'All Around The World' live in the studio. Other bands that appeared throughout the six episodes were Generation X, Radio Stars, Boomtown Rats, Eddie and the Hot Rods, along with a jam with David Bowie. Marc Bolan would be dead by the time of the last episode on 28th September.

Some of the early gigs at the Apollo could get quite violent, although it wasn't always the crowd that were the root cause.

Ian Fawkes: "You had unregulated bouncers in those days and it was at The Jam gig at The Apollo that I got smacked by one. They were telling everyone to sit down, but fuck that! I was there to enjoy myself and instead of sitting down I stood up and from there I got up on my seat dancing. I felt a tap on my shoulder so I turned round to see this fist coming towards me knocking me to the floor. They were wankers looking for a fight and if there wasn't one to be had, they'd just start one"

Gail Egan: "We went to see The Clash at the Apollo and Kevin and Paul were in the orchestra pit. The audience decided to rip all the seats out, you know the ones with the wooden backs? They were throwing them and it was really bad, so Kevin Cummins grabbed me under my arms, I was only dead little, and literally catapulted me into the orchestra pit. That was mental that gig, absolutely mental."

If it was a little fractious inside the venue, outside could be complete chaos. Getting there was often a frightening experience, and the walk back to the station could sometimes be just as daunting.

Ian Fawkes: "We went up to the Apollo to see The Clash and when we got nearer to the venue we saw that there were police vans outside but I never found out why. We also went to see The Jam there and we were walking through the subway and a gang of skinheads came running towards us. We thought 'oh shit we're gonna get battered here' but they carried on past us, so I presumed that they were either running away from an incident or running towards their next victim. Anyway there used to be a pub on the right hand side called The George, I think it's long gone now. As we were walking past there was another gang of lads running across the road towards us, and one of them had a machete in his hand. For some reason as they got nearer I blurted out 'the Skins are down there mate!' and I don't know if that's who they were chasing but they just carried on down the road After that Jam gig there were running battles outside just like a football match. I don't know if it was between Mods and Punks, or Skins and Punks, I've no idea but it was scary and we were with our girlfriends so we decided to walk the long way back to Piccadilly Station avoiding the subway. As the train departed from Piccadilly back to the comfort of Chapel I was still wary that some of these gangs could possibly have followed us and got on the train to get to us."

Despite the potential for hassle, the venue was a major stopping place on many people's world and UK tours for the next decade and beyond.

Joanne Slater: "Oh God yeah the Apollo – when I think of the people we saw there. We went to see Iggy Pop with David Bowie."

Bowie appeared at the Apollo on March 3rd 1977 as Iggy Pop's keyboard player on 'The Idiot' Tour, with support from The Vibrators.

These days it hosts gigs from a wide variety of musical genres as well as comedians, and has also gone through many corporate name changes and is now a Grade II listed building, so it should be around for many years to come.

RAFTERS, MANCHESTER.

Rafters was situated in the basement of Fagin's nightclub in the St. James's Buildings on Oxford Street in the city centre. Fagin's had been trading since 1970 and Rafters opened its doors a few years later and would go on to play a major part in the history of Punk in the city.

Fran Taylor: "Another place where they did a few gigs, not many of my type of gigs and a bit later on, was 'Fagins', which was directly above. Rafters was basically the cellar of Fagin's, and that was a proper chicken in a basket type of place and was also another place where you could go and get a late drink. This was another thing - people like me couldn't get into clubs."

Steve McGarry: "I can remember wandering upstairs many times into Fagin's. Dougie James and the Soul Train played there a lot - I can recall seeing Tony Wilson get up on stage with Dougie one night - and you'd sometimes find Sad Cafe in there having a drink."

RAFTERS
Oxford Street, Manchester
Advance Tickets at VIRGIN RECORDS FAGINS RECEPTION and PANDOMONEUM RECORDS, Wilmslow Road
Wednesday, 15th March
BOB HALL
Thursday, 16th March
GENERATION X plus Support
Saturday, 18th March
THE PLEASERS plus the Heat
A prize for the Girl with the Miniest Skirt
Monday, 20th March
(From France)
LITTLE BOB STORY
A really Brilliant Rock and Roll Show
plus Doo Wop Saints
Tuesday, 21st March
(Ex Deep Purple)
David Coverdales White Snake
plus Virginia Wolf
Wednesday, 22nd March
Terry Butters and Steve Carr
Two Man Band
plus No Mystery
Thursday, 23rd March
SUBURBAN STUDS plus the Elite
Saturday, 25rd March
THE SAINTS plus the Snyde
NO MEMBERSHIP REQUIRED — COME AS YOU ARE

Fran Taylor: "Rafters came along a little bit later in the year (1977) and they started doing a few Punk gigs, and I think that had something to do with Rob Gretton as well. Rob was a football hooligan, I believe he was well known for it apparently, had a bit of a reputation as being a bit of a hard lad. I knew lots of lads who were like that, who were on the scene. They were largely working for bands because you had to be a bit tasty to work for a band then at times."

Daniel O'Sullivan: "I was a DJ at Rafters, I was quite lucky really.

I met a guy, Dougie James...he was a soul singer in a band called Soul Train. He was promoting at Rafters, I think that was '76. He was a very easy-going guy and me and my friend Pete Mulkay got a job humping gear in and out for the bands, it was perfect because you got to see the bands for free. Then I started deejaying with Rob Gretton, in fact his record collection was really crap and mine was great. Later on I DJ'd at the Russell Club in Hulme with Alan Wise. Fagin's next door was a much bigger venue and would have Soul bands on. We were downstairs one day and Dougie says, 'Can you score some coke for the band?' So I asked who they were and he said, 'it's the Commodores'. Anyway Lionel Ritchie comes down with his big fur coat, Dougie was a bit like that as well. So me and Pete thought, fuck we'll pretend we can find some gear although we didn't have a clue actually. So we found ourselves in this bizarre situation where we escorted, I think it was two of them, Lionel Ritchie and one of the other musicians around town. We took them to Virgin Records, we took them to the Market Centre, and all our mates are like, who's that then? Lionel Ritchie was like, 'Are you gonna score us some gear?' We said yeah, yeah we're just trying to find some for you! Basically we were just dragging them around town to meet our mates! [*Laughs*]

Steve McGarry: "Rob Gretton was the house DJ, so he was working there and I'd be hanging out two or three times a week. That's where Rob first saw Warsaw, if I recall correctly, before the name change to Joy Division. When he started deejaying at Rafters, I was the venue's poster designer, so we'd see each other in there on a regular basis. I'd use Day-Glo paper for the upcoming gigs probably three to five feet in length. The lettering was all hand drawn in black with various shades of red and green, in a kind of graffiti style. Dougie James was the promoter, and each week he'd give me a list of names of the upcoming bands and I'd do a separate poster for each one. I remember that Rob played a lot of Blue Beat in among the Punk and New Wave. In my mind's eye, I can still see Gary Holton and the rest of the Heavy Metal Kids bouncing around the bar at Rafter's as Rob played Dillinger's 'Cocaine In My Brain'. To this day, if I hear Junior Murvin's "Police and Thieves," I'm back in Rafters with Rob. Mine was a lager, his was a Pernod and black."

Wispa: "Rafters was a major draw for bands, a lot of big bands as well, Elvis Costello played there, I know The Clash played there, as did The Drones. It was Alan Wise and Rob Gretton mainly."

Alan Wise's importance to the Manchester music scene can't be overlooked. A theology student at Manchester University, Wise met

Dougie James one night at Rafters and ended up becoming his roadie/ manager. Although his musical tastes were geared towards Blues and Jazz, he embraced the scene that was happening in Manchester, particularly the fact that it had no outside influence from London record companies or promoters. His real legacy came later with The Russell/Factory Club, which he ran, along with Alan Erasmus. Wise, Erasmus, and Tony Wilson started Shop Floor Entertainments company and traded as The Factory, this was before the record label of the same name. Wise would also act as promoter for the venue and around the country along with managing a number of groups.

Daniel O'Sullivan: "The first time I met Alan Wise was in 1976 when he was a skinny, geeky, kind of awkward guy. He had been at Oxford University, flunked his course and ended up in Manchester and Dougie employed him to put posters up. Alan would take us out to go and poster around Oxford Road for Tosh Ryan. So I'd do a bit of deejaying, roadie for bands, and occasionally run errands for the bands. I remember sometimes the band would turn up and Dougie would say to me, 'entertain them for the day'. We had a membership of Soame's Casino around the corner and I remember taking The Adverts in there... Gaye Advert with all the leather gear on, and all these Chinese guys were playing Roulette wondering, what the fucks this, you know? The Flamin' Groovies were doing a tour in the UK and they said, 'do you want to come to Leeds with us?' Normally we'd sleep in the van but they were very good to us and I think we stayed in a hotel. My greatest memory of the Flamin' Groovies was their manager. After the gig this really suave looking character came in and I mean they all wore suits didn't they, shades on and all the rest of it they looked really out of place and he opened this suitcase... we got the gear out in rapid time you know! A band called The Killjoys played at Rafters, which became Dexy's Midnight Runners, and Kevin Rowland asked us if we wanted to go on tour with them. So we got into the back of their minibus and off we fucking went for three or four days. It was just the perk of working in a club I suppose."

As with every other venue in town, trouble wouldn't be too far away.

Daniel O'Sullivan: "Rafters, generally speaking, was a pleasant place to go, but it had its moments. We put Sham 69 on once, it was quite funny really, I've asked people about this, but I know it happened because I was there. Sham 69 decided to bring a support band with them called The Dentists, and they were from Liverpool, and they turned out to be right bunch of Nazis and after about two or three songs it was clear that they were racist fuckers, a bit like Skrewdriver who hid behind the Punk thing. Somebody threw a bottle at the drummer which caught him on the ear. Next thing you know this big crew come from behind the stage, who were obviously with the band, with bloody sticks. The whole place was fucking trashed within about 20 minutes, it was the most incredible thing and then you had this bizarre situation where Dougie James, Mr. Soul Boy, is on the stage trying to quieten everybody down and several police officers had arrived by then, the police sergeant saying 'the gigs over, shut the power off' and Jimmy Pursey is like, 'come on kids!' It was one of the most surreal moments of my life. I found Rob Gretton hiding behind the DJ box absolutely shitting himself."

Steve McGarry: "The Sham 69 gig, that was one where it all kicked off, I remember. A band of skins steamed into the club during the set and there were pint pots and bottles flying all over the place. Pretty ugly."

Una Baines: "I remember going to see Johnny Thunders, who I absolutely adored, at Rafters. All the punks were spitting at him and I was horrified, how insulting to a great artist you know?"

Carol O'Donnell: "Francis Cookson used to manage The Spitfire Boys at the time. Paul (Rutherford) was in them, and Holly was in Big In Japan with Jayne Casey. The Spitfire Boys used to play at Rafters quite often, and I actually got up on stage one night with them in 1977. They used to do a cover of 'Gloria' by Patti Smith and I was a massive Patti Smith fan."

Mark Windsor: "We used to do really well at Rafters because Dougie James asked us to step in twice for Sham 69 when they didn't turn up. You'd get a call at 9 o'clock at night from him, 'Can you help us out please Mark?'"

Una Baines: "I went to Rafters one night and Paul Cook and Steve Jones were there, and I was pissed, and I was writing this dream down on the back of beer mats telling them, 'You've got to give this to John!' basically I had this dream about John Lydon; We were walking through a beautiful forest and we were holding hands walking down the path, and I was saying to him, 'Look at that' and everything was Green and lush and beautiful. But he said 'No, look at that', and everything was dying and decaying. A bit like life and death I guess, it was a very powerful dream. Then right at the end of it was a deer that had been killed with its head cut off, and then I woke up. I told Mark and Martin (Bramah) and everyone about this dream, and a few weeks later on we read in the *NME* that they were making some kind of a film, 'Who Killed Bambi?'. I thought that it was really spooky. I was very embarrassed afterwards and of course Mark was having a good old sneer."

12 months later and the venue was still playing host to the occasional special nights. On Monday 3rd July 1978 The Clash played an impromptu gig at Rafters. They had played at the Apollo the night before as part of the 'Clash On Parole' tour. New York's Suicide were support at both gigs. The band had been for a walk around town record shopping before going back to the Piccadilly Hotel, where there was an altercation between Jones and Strummer. Joe was unhappy after being told that getting fans into the gig for free would be difficult.

Alan Keogh: "I was at work one day and Johnny Green and Mick Jones came into the shop and it was either the night before or the night after they played the Apollo, not too sure but anyway. Johnny said that the band were playing Rafters that night to an invited audience. So I saw The Clash with about 50 other people."

Fran Taylor: "One of the other places that we used to go to was at Cavendish House at the Poly. One band that played there was Skrewdriver, who were from Blackpool, and it was their very first gig and I remember talking to them backstage afterwards. They were supporting a French band that we used to go and see called Little Bob Story, who had this short arsed singer who was a real maniac. I'm not too sure when Rafters bit the dust because it became 'Jilly's Rock World'.

Rafters closed in 1983, and was re-opened as Jilly's Rock World' soon after.

16. ain't bin to no music school.

"When it all started, record companies - and there were many of them, and this was a good thing - were run by people who loved records, people like Ahmet Ertegun, who ran Atlantic Records, who were record collectors. They got in it because they loved music."

David Crosby

Music Force was set up in 1972 initially by Victor Brox and drummer Bruce Mitchell, as a kind of musical co-operative, giving bands places to play, which offered a more realistic, affordable alternative to the well-known venues of the city, and without having to go through one of the big agencies from London who were controlling the market - 'The Slug' as Brox called them. His argument was 'why should a Manchester band have to move to London?' Taken from the *Manchester Independent Newspaper*, written and edited by University of Manchester students in November 1972, Brox describes 'the Slugs' thus, "*If you look at the people who control the music industry - the record companies, agencies, managements, - you're looking at a collection of chartered accountants and businessmen. They're only interested on finding a formula for making money. That's nothing to do with music.*" That statement could have been made last week. He went on to state his intention of setting up a Manchester record label, concentrating on recording local artists. Along with helping to get venues and equipment, Music Force even provided an AA style service that went out to recover bands who had broken down on their way to venues.

Soon another local musician joined the scene. Tosh Ryan had been involved in the Manchester music scene since he was 14 years old, playing with the likes of John Mayall and Victor Brox, before he became involved in Music Force.

Chris Hewitt: "Music Force was founded by Victor Brox, Norman Beaker, Tosh Ryan and Bruce Mitchell, that was the original committee. It was a musician's co-operative, which was a bit of a con really because it was basically Greasy Bear and Victor Brox Blues Train looking for more gigs, and looking to borrow equipment off other bands. So they'd say 'we're a musician's co-operative, you can join, we can give you some gigs in Manchester, if you can give us some gigs in Bolton, and you can borrow our small amount of gear if we can borrow your large amount of gear'. That's how it started. Martin Hannett came along as a bit of a sound man, and Tosh didn't like him. Tosh was a Mod, going right back to the pill days and he used to hang around with Gareth Evans, who ended up managing The Stone Roses. So they were more into the Jazz and pills sort of scene, Tosh was always a snappy dresser."

It was Hannett's shoes which caused most offence to Ryan.

Chris Hewitt: "Tosh once told me, 'Martin came in the room with these shoes which looked liked big clumps of foam rubber on the end of his feet, so I just didn't like the guy. He wore scruffy clothes, he was a hippy, with dirty shoes, and I just didn't like him, so I voted against having him in'. He was outvoted by Bruce, Victor and Norman so Martin was co-opted in, and then eventually they became best friends and pretty much took over Music Force. Bruce went off, I think, with the Albertos".

Music Force carried on for a while until a new business venture was set up, promoting gigs and new releases of some of the biggest acts across the country. That was fly-posting, which in the 70's was a lucrative but dangerous business.

Chris Hewitt: "With the money from the fly-posting they bought a co-op type shop which was the HQ for the fly-posting empire and Rabid which was on Cotton Lane, Withington. I think one of the problems was that nearly all the money was cash so they didn't know how much they could put through the books. So I think that might be why they did the records; to spend some of the money. Apart from London, they took over the whole country fly-posting. We used to have to take pictures of everything to prove to the record company that we'd put them up. Then the Farl brothers got involved and that's when Tosh got out, because there were threats, turf wars and people shooting guns and threats to break each other's legs and stuff."

The streets of Manchester would be plastered with wall to wall posters, blanketing whole stretches of the city.

Ken Park: "We'd be in town on the Saturday, buying records and stuff and you'd see the posters on the walls. In Manchester there was a kind of poster war, you know. People could make a lot of money. It was crucial to get your poster up."

Chris Hewitt: "Bruce had started the fly-posting through Music Force, then Martin and Tosh pretty much took it over. They were also looking after support bands for the Free Trade Hall and the Universities. Then they brought in Lawrence Beedle when they started Rabid and he became a third partner in Rabid because Music Force mutated into Rabid really.'

The record label that Victor Brox had hinted at in 1972 was about to come into fruition, directly inspired by the Spiral Scratch release, so now with the capital to get it off the ground, Ryan and Hannett started to look for local musicians to promote.

Based at 20 Cotton Lane, Withington, Rabid Records was another influential and important cog in the Manchester Punk wheel. Spiral Scratch may have been the first independent release on New Hormones but Rabid Records was the first independent label in Manchester to compile a roster of markedly different local acts: John Cooper Clarke, Jilted John, Ed Banger and the Nosebleeds, as well as releasing the first material from Slaughter and the Dogs.

Interviewed in the *M62* magazine by Colin McMillan, Ryan explained the theory behind Rabid:

> *"Well the Buzzcocks EP whetted our appetites and we thought there's got to be something in the area that we can find which would be representative of the working class rock 'n' roll end of things. There was Rabid Records and Absurd Records, we issued about 20 singles, the intention being not to look to make money. The idea was that if we could put out records that the big five record companies wouldn't touch, it was a kick in the eye for them. In that respect it was to a certain extent anti-capitalist, we had a fairly democratic profit sharing method in the company. We weren't that interested in being a part of the music scene, we were more interested in destroying it I think."*

Slaughter and the Dog's 'Cranked Up Really High' was the primary release on the new label, with the recording costs being aided and abetted by a £1000 helping hand from Slaughter fan and friend, Rob Gretton. Martin Hannett had seen the band at The Mountain Ash pub in Wythenshawe and he was the common thread between Spiral Scratch and Rabid; after cutting his 'production' teeth on Spiral Scratch, he was responsible for taking the role as the producer for the complete output of Rabid.

The part that Music Force, the fly-posting, and Rabid Records played in promoting Manchester's continually changing and forward thinking musical output can't be overstated. Collectively they set the tone for Punk, and indeed Factory Records, in their anti-establishment rhetoric and bloody minded stance in challenging the grip that London had on the music scene, and promoting Manchester and the north-west but there was now a growing number of influential people willing to help those around them and take things to the next level.

Fran Taylor: "The only people you've got promoting are the independents; so Richard Boon's doing the odd one here and there, there's a guy called TJ Davidson who's doing a few promotions plus he's got the rehearsal rooms that people start to use in Little Peter Street. Then there's the Rabid guys; Tosh Ryan, Rob Gretton, but *New Manchester Review* actually started promoting gigs at a lot of venues. They actually promoted the first Magazine gig in late '77 and they did a lot at Rafters. Martin Hannett was linked in with the Tosh Ryan side of things at the time, out in Wilmslow and Wythenshawe. These were things moving around in the background that you weren't really aware of at the time, I mean you didn't care who was promoting the concerts as long as the concerts were being put on."

Chris Hewitt: "Without Rabid, without the fly-posting, there would have been no Factory Records. The AMS delay that was used on Joy Division and Durrutti Column was bought with John Cooper Clarke's royalties, so it wasn't something that Factory invented, and said 'Oh yeah we'll get Martin (Hannett) to get this delay and we'll use it on all the drum sounds and create the Joy Division sound'. It was bought by Rabid, and it was bought with fly-posting money and from Clarkey's CBS record deal advance."

RABID RECORDS SINGLE DISCOGRAPHY:

TOSH 101 - Slaughter And The Dogs - Cranked Up Really High/The Bitch
TOSH 102 - The Nosebleeds - Ain't Bin To No Music School/Fascist Pigs
TOSH 103 - John Cooper Clarke - Innocents E.P.
TOSH 104 - Gyro - Central Detention Centre/Purple And Red
TOSH 105 - Jilted John - Jilted John/Going Steady
TOSH 106 - Ed Banger - Kinnel Tommy/Baby Was A Baby
TOSH 107 - Gordon The Moron - De Do Dough, Don't De Dough (Unreleased)
TOSH 108 - Unreleased
TOSH 109 - Chris Sievey - Basier/Last
TOSH 110 - Tim Green - Who Can Tell You/Keep Me With You
TOSH 111 - Gordon The Moron - Fit For Nothing
TOSH 112 - Unreleased
TOSH 113 - The Out - Who Is Innocent?/Laura's Just A Statue

Albums

HAT23 - Slaughter And The Dogs - Live Slaughter Rabid Dogs
NOZE 1 - John Cooper Clarke - Ou Est La Maison De Fromage
LAST 1 - Various Artists - The Crap Stops Here

17. in my area

"I worked in Rare Records on John Dalton Street. I worked in the basement and the job I got was Ian Curtis's before me."

Alan Keogh

In the prehistoric world of the mid 1970's, gaining access to what was going on entertainment wise relied on the printed word in the local newspapers or the national music press. Way before the age of mobile phones, communication would usually mean a trip to the nearest public telephone box, or if it didn't have a lock on it, as was the case in many households, you'd use the home telephone. That's if you had one.

Carol O'Donnell: "We never had a phone, growing up, never had one."

Dawn Bradbury: "Your weekends used to start with the *NME* and *Sounds* on a Friday morning. Then I'd ring Denise at work at 2 o'clock in the afternoon religiously every Friday from a public phone box. On a Saturday afternoon you'd go into Manchester, go into the Underground Market and buy whatever you were gonna buy. You'd meet up with a few mates around Piccadilly, Steve Shy would be there if City weren't playing at home because he was a steward at Maine Road. You would bump into people and start gabbin' and that was your Saturday afternoon. Then back home, bit of tea, shower, get changed, go back out. By that time we'd both have had a look to see who was on, and circled where we wanted to go to, for instance we'd be like, right... Dr. Feelgood are on at Eric's tonight, Ramones are on at The Electric Circus on Saturday, you know? Such and such were on somewhere else on the Sunday and you'd planned your weekend, job sorted. What amazes me it that we all managed to meet up and move en masse using public telephone boxes. Or sometimes it would be word of mouth, which meant that you'd have to be so well planned and organised. Plus once you went somewhere you'd see the listings for the next few weeks."

Denise Shaw: "Even before I met Dawn I'd go down to Manchester, knowing that wherever I went, somebody would be about. As the scene grew it would eventually be possible to go out every night of the week and see a quality band, sometimes there would be two or three on the same bill. We all used to meet up and you always knew that if you went out somewhere, one or another of the group would be there. So I never thought that I was going out on my own. That's stayed with me, it wouldn't bother me now if I went to a gig on my own."

Alan Keogh: "You used to find out about things. I went to see Slaughter and the Dogs and Joy Division at Bowdon Youth Club. My mate Martin Henning phoned me up and told me about it but you used to find out about things. Working in a record shop, you'd find out. In those days it was only word of mouth you know?"

There were certain places that would constitute a meeting place, a gathering that consisted of the like minded along with the more sinister element of society.

Daniel O'Sullivan: "I remember the Virgin store on Newton Street. That was a kind of meeting place."

Mickey Carr: "We had a hang about place in town, Virgin Records. It's where the Punks used to hang about then. It was on Newton Street at the bottom near Piccadilly - it was great with hippies serving behind the counter. It was just somewhere to hang around, go on little missions and fuck about you know? I don't think that we had a good effect on sales or made it very attractive for people to go in but you don't care when you're young where you hang about, we were always up to stuff. If it was your own shop, we wouldn't have tolerated it because we were horrible really, and there were some horrible ones among us who weren't even dressed as punks, but they were our mates you know? Some really serious criminal types. I remember Tony Wilson coming in there a few times. It was a bit hostile for him really because he was someone off the T.V. Kids trying to nick his wallet and that carry on."

Deb Zee: "We were always in Manchester, we used to sit in Virgin Records and you'd find out what was going on yeah."

Gail Egan: "It had booths and you were able to sit and listen with headphones on. I remember buying X Ray Spex 'Oh Bondage Up Yours!'. You'd go in and ask 'Has it been released yet?' You know, waiting for it to come in, it was first come, first served on coloured vinyl, picture covers, that was the exciting bit."

Richard Branson's venture into the music business with Virgin had a tangential nod to Hippiedom about it, because he wasn't your archetypal looking businessman, with his Catweazle-like long hair and straggly beard. The name arose from Virgin office staffer Tessa Watts, who suggested that they were 'virgins in business'. Although Branson is usually associated with Virgin it was business partners Simon Draper and Nik

Powell who basically ran the enterprise for him. After successfully selling records through his mail order company, Branson decided to take on the established record labels with a complete step by step guide to making an album. He acquired The Manor recording studio in Oxfordshire to make the music, formed the record label on which to put the music out, and opened large independent record shops all over the country to sell the records he was going to make. He'd hit pay dirt with Tubular Bells, part of the first four albums on the Virgin record label simultaneously released on the 25th May 1973. The others were The Faust Tapes, which sold for 49p and introduced Krautrock into the homes of 100,000 people within its first month; Gong's The Flying Teapot, which built on the success of Camembert Electrique; and the Manor Live, a jam album by 'Camelo Pardarlis' with characters such as Lol Coxhill, Elkie Brooks and Boz Burrell. Tubular Bells rolled on and on. The record stores would expand and, for many, that was their interface with the Virgin brand.

Andy T.: "Virgin was great. It opened in '74 I think, and you could get all sorts in there including second hand stuff as well. It was always a good place to meet people because people just used to hang around there. The Underground Market was a good place to meet people as well."

Daniel O'Sullivan: "The other shop I seemed to remember very well were the market sellers, underneath in the Underground Market on Market Street. There was one there - Yvonne. Her and her husband ran this record store, Collector's Records, they had one in Blackpool as well. So we kind of got friendly with them and she tolerated us you know? People hanging around not buying records you know? [*Laughs*]

As well as big chains like Virgin and HMV, there were also the smaller, independently-owned record shops in the city.

Alan Keogh: "I worked in Rare Records on John Dalton Street. I worked in the basement and the job I got was Ian Curtis's job, he worked there before me."

As well as the Manchester gigs, trips out of town to support two of the main home grown bands were organised. Travelling any long distance was an arduous undertaking back then. Most cars were low powered and not built for comfort, especially at the lower end of the economic scale, and anyway most of the crowd were either too young or too cash strapped to own a car. Luckily Ian and Allan from The Worst had access to slightly more practical vehicles, so vans were hired or borrowed, with road worthiness and passenger safety being an optional extra. Venturing into other territories usually meant attracting the unwanted attention of the ubiquitous local knuckle draggers, suspicious of anyone from 'out of town'.

Denise Shaw: "The Manchester bands were just The Drones and Buzzcocks really, and we used to go everywhere with them initially. At the beginning I used to go to a lot of the gigs with them and we'd all pile into the vans and it was just that set 20 of us, and if we weren't going with the band we'd get a van and just, you know, follow them round. We used to go to quite a lot of gigs because some of them were close enough that we could drive to them. There was one particular place, God knows where it were, we were dancing, me and Dawn in this club, and this bloke came up and said something to her. Dawn may be only little but she can't half… so she said something back and carried on dancing, and I could feel the tension building in the club so I said, 'Dawn, we're going'. Now there was only Woody, bassist out of The Worst, who was with us. So it was just me, Dawn and Woody, in my Hillman Imp I might add, and the next thing I can remember is us legging it out of the door with 20 to 30 blokes chasing after us wanting to kick the shit out of us. Woody was panicking more than anybody because they'd have gone for him first, being a bloke, and so we all got into the car and of course it wouldn't fucking start would it"?

Dawn Bradbury: "The more it wouldn't start the more that Denise is shaking, trying to get the key to turn, and Woody's in the back seat shouting 'FOR FUCKS SAKE GET IT TO WORK!".

Denise Shaw: "It was just like The Sweeney, and just as they thumped on the back of the car, it started".

Sometimes though, nights out could get a little more frightening.

Denise Shaw: "I went up to Stockton one time and went in this pub, and it was like they'd never heard of Punk, it was like going back 50 years. So I'm driving out of this club with the two guys that I'd gone up to meet, who were friends, just going up the road, and this car came up at the side of me with this iron bar and scraped it all the way down the side of my car, and smashed both my windows in. So I pulled over because it was obvious that they were going to follow us. I went down this small side road, turned all the lights out, my mates dived out of the car and got these bricks and started to brick this car as it was coming down the road towards us. It was just unbelievable."

Dawn Bradbury: "There was some unbelievable stuff… there was aggravation wherever we went."

Denise Shaw: "We'd gone to the Polytechnic in Leeds when it all kicked off with Buzzcocks, and for some reason the students took an instant dislike to the band. It was like there was 50 years between Yorkshire and Lancashire, and they started throwing things so Garth jumped off the stage and started wading into one of them. Of course that was it then, it was a free-for-all, and all I can remember is Richard Boon pushing me and saying, 'Denise, get in the dressing room now'. We sat there for an hour waiting for them to clear the place. Again all I could think about was my car!" There is an audio recording of that night including Garth's violent altercation with the audience worth checking out on You Tube.

S.P.O.T.S. - LAFAYETTE CLUB, WOLVERHAMPTON

One such excursion to Wolverhampton was particularly memorable. Sex Pistols had been banned from playing in a lot of the provincial towns in England and Wales, so to get around this the band employed pseudonyms so that those in the know would twig what was happening but the venues remained clueless until it was too late. With an army of Punks descending on whichever town they happened to be playing in, it was easier to let the gig go ahead rather than cancel it and have a disgruntled audience to deal with.

Denise Shaw: "We all met up at the Electric Circus and somebody had organised a coach to take us to Wolverhampton to see the S.P.O.T.S. (Sex Pistols On Tour Secretly). So we got on this bloody coach and as we were getting on, the drivers going 'no booze, no smoking' and this that and the other, he's stood there with this really stern face you know? I had this massive canvas bag full of beer which ended up around my ankles so he wouldn't spot it in his mirror, making the journey down quite uncomfortable, but we got down there with no further problems. When we arrived there was a queue around the building because word had spread that it was the Pistols who were playing. We got off the coach and Malcolm McLaren was at the door and happened to see Pete and said 'Ah! Manchester…the whole of this bus is on the guest list!' so we all walked in, in front of everybody else, which didn't go down too well.

"The Sex Pistols started playing and we were sat on some stairs to the left of the stage so that Dawn could see the band. Not that we saw much because the NF had got in. So as soon as Sid Vicious said something on stage they all started throwing cans and we just thought, Jesus! This is all going to kick off. Next thing we knew, smoke is billowing out from the stage. They'd thrown a smoke bomb onto the stage. So there's all this smoke, there's a fire, you could hear the bloody fire engines, but we were that drunk we just carried on gabbin' to each other; I said to Dawn, 'Do you think we should go?', Dawn replied, 'I'm not going, I'm not losing my spot! I'm not losing my good spot just in case they come back on'. So, gig over, we came out and the coach was waiting for us and we all got on and straight away they started to stone the coach which meant that the driver was by now going totally ballistic. He got out of there as fast as he could and we're driving back home, and of course after a while people are going to need the toilet. So one of the lads was saying to the driver, 'you've got to stop the coach because people need the toilet', but the driver said that there was no way he was stopping. To which the lad replied 'look! If you don't want piss all over your bloody coach, you'd better pull over!' So anyway he pulled in at a service station. We went to the toilet and got back on the coach and we were waiting for certain people to get back on when these two coppers got on. The driver had got off and phoned the police. So these coppers are walking down the aisle of the coach taking everybody's names and he gets to me and I make up a name and then they came to Gus out of The Drones who was opposite me. One was a young copper and he was the one asking for names whilst the older one stood behind him. So he gets to Gus and says; 'Name?' 'Gus Gangrene'. So this copper's writing it down repeating it to himself 'G.U.S. G.A.N.... do you know how you spell that?' So that was it, we all started laughing and he still didn't clock it, he had no idea what we were laughing at.

"Anyway eventually, they got off the coach, because they couldn't do us for anything, Pete Shelley and I think it was Eric Random hadn't got back on the coach yet because they'd had something to eat. So we were saying to the bus driver, you can't set off yet because there are two more to come back. No, he shut the doors and set off leaving Pete and Eric behind. They had to hitch it back home. Also, he was supposed to drop us off at the Electric Circus but he carried on driving past it with us all shouting at him to stop, but he just drove on and eventually stopped right in the middle of Piccadilly. When we'd stopped there must have been about 50 coppers, with dogs and Black Marias waiting for us. There were only 32 of us so we were a bit outnumbered! Ian and Allan were at the back of the bus, so after seeing all of this they were like 'Bastard!' and pissed all over his back seat".

Odgie: "That does sound absolutely like me I'm afraid, but I can't remember it. That's the sort of thing that I would do and instigate it as well. We were probably at the back with the Evo-Stik."

Fran Taylor: "The coach driver wouldn't take us back out to

Collyhurst afterwards. There was dogs and everything waiting for us when we got back to Piccadilly, and the police were saying 'You've got to get off this coach, he's not taking you anywhere."

Dawn Bradbury: We had to walk from Piccadilly to the Electric Circus with the police escorting us, and it's a fair walk between them you know, 35-40 minutes. Then of course this alerted the Perry boys who were like, what's going on? So the police ended up protecting us from them. The coppers were fine after we'd started walking they realised that we weren't a threat and we asked them why? And to be fair they didn't really know, it was a complete and utter waste of police resources. Just because we looked different, we were trouble. Well, you know, different doesn't always mean trouble. By the time we got back up to the Circus they were laughing and joking with us 'goodnight', 'enjoy yourselves' and all the rest of it, not a problem."

Alan Keogh: "I went down to Wolverhampton to the infamous SPOTS tour. That was an interesting journey down. On the coach down you had Steve Shy, Buzzcocks, The Drones, Magazine - Howard Devoto is quite a serious guy and I ended up sitting next to him at one point on the coach. We had a pickup at the Electric Circus in Collyhurst, we all met at the Circus, everyone who was going. So we get on this coach, and it was basically anyone who was anyone was on it, but it was still fucking half empty because that's how small that crowd was, you know? There weren't many people involved in the scene. I was going with Woody from The Worst and they were sat behind me and Howard Devoto on the coach. They were leaning over the seat going to Howard 'deeelovely, deeelightful, deeelicious, Deeevoto!' Just taking the piss. He's not even entertaining it. So we get down there, The Lafayette and we got off the coach and go into the club early doors, the band came on and immediately there was already a load of violence in the air from football - Wolverhampton Wanderers. We'd been challenged three or four times already what with me and Woody being Mancs...'Where you from? What time is it?' asking questions to hear your accent. You couldn't actually see the band, there was that many fucking bouncers, it was like a wall of bouncers. So Johnny Rotten is stood on an amp so you could see him, it was ridiculous, the atmosphere was so heavy. We were still getting people coming up to us, we were like, sighing you know? Fucking hell. Rotten himself, when he came on, addressed the crowd, 'Good evening Wolverhampton. And all you lot from Manchester, what the fuck are you doing here?' So he'd already advertised that there were Mancunians in the audience. When we went outside, the coach pulled up and there were two lines of police to get us on the coach. If I'd have been there with the football lot we'd have fought 'em, you know? Fuck off."

Richard Boon: "It was pretty horrible, there were about 40 beefy guys across the front of the stage, and an awful lot of stupid fighting..."

Carol O'Donnell: "We went to see the Pistols at Doncaster as S.P.O.T.S."

Deb Zee: "We got a coach from Portland Street Bus station. It was just a normal coach that was going that way, so we paid whatever it was and just got on it. The Pistols were playing there and I think Ari Up was there, we knew they were playing so we just got the coach. There would have been me, Carol, Gav, Steph and Jodie. I'm sure Jodie was there from Manicured Noise. There was a big queue to get in but I don't remember any hassle."

ERIC'S

Opened in 1976 by Roger Eagle, Pete Fulwell, and Ken Testi, Eric's was another significant venue in the growth of Punk throughout the UK. It was another place for the new breed to play and at just 35 miles west at the other end of the M62, it provided another venue to go to.

Denise Shaw: "The first time I went to Eric's I had a Hillman Imp, and the car always got me there, but it always fuckin' broke down on the way back or wouldn't start, every bloody single time! So I went to Eric's and I'd never been to Liverpool before so I had no idea of where I was going, and I can remember going around and around this roundabout thinking where the fuck do I go? Next minute this copper on a bike is flashing me so I'm like 'oh fuckin' hell, here we go'. So he pulls me over and he says, 'I've just been watching you and you've been around that roundabout four times, what's the problem?' So I told him, 'I'm trying to find Eric's club do you know where it is? I think it's where the old Cavern used to be'. He said, 'Follow me love', and honestly he took me down one way streets the wrong way, and he took me right to the bloody door, and I actually got a hug and a kiss off him. I've actually got a photograph of that copper somewhere, so you know, you do get good and bad in everything don't you?"

Fran Taylor: "We used to quite often trip over to Liverpool as long as we could get transport and Denise used to go quite a lot because she had a motor. We went over there one night in Gus's van to see Buzzcocks at Eric's. On the way back we got pulled over by the police and amazingly Gus passed the breathalyser, it was about 5 o'clock in the morning on the outskirts of Manchester."

Denise Shaw: "I got my window smashed one night at Eric's club once. I'd parked it right outside, there was a tiny little area where you could get two or three cars in. Again it was Woody... Woody and Suzanne. We were going to drive from there to Blackpool and spend the day there, but the side window had been smashed so..."

Andy T.: "We used to go to Eric's because they'd quite often have the bands on the same tour, so they might play Eric's on the Friday or Saturday and then at the Circus on the Sunday. So if you could afford it, you could go to both."

Carol O'Donnell: "I used to go to Liverpool nearly every other week to see Paul (Rutherford) and I never used to see any trouble."

Deb Zee: "I went quite a bit because I used to go and meet Holly (Johnson) out of... well he was in Big In Japan, Paul Rutherford was in The Spitfire Boys. We used to hang about with them and I saw loads of bands there. We went to a great party maybe a year or so later on with Holly in some disused Police station and Pete Burns was playing behind these cell bars, that was when he was in Nightmares In Wax. It was really brilliant I loved it but I was only a teenager."

Denise Shaw: "Dawn started on Palmolive in Eric's toilet one night! It ended up with all of The Slits in the bloody toilet."

Dawn Bradbury: "I can't remember what it was about; she'd have looked at me or said something you know - bloody Londoners. About two weeks later we'd gone to Huddersfield or Halifax, somewhere beginning with 'h', to see Johnny Thunders and there was a queue all the way round the building outside, schoolkids mostly, and I heard one of them say, 'It's The Slits!', because we were dressed like them, you know? One minute I'm fighting with her and the next week I am her! Tonight Denise, we'll be The Slits! [*laughs*] plus we got in for free which was the whole purpose; go to see a band, and not pay, which we very rarely did. That night a lad called Dave was with us and he could talk his way in anywhere, and he told the bouncer that he had the drugs for Johnny Thunders, and that's how we got in. Dave wasn't a punk and he didn't have any drugs, you just say whatever you have to just to get in. Mind you we spent the entire night avoiding the bouncers, who clocked that we'd got in for free and that we weren't who we said we were."

Andy T.: "I remember Roger Eagle said once that the Pistols were supposed to play in Liverpool on the Anarchy tour, and someone told him, 'You've got to put these on, they need a gig', but Roger said 'No I can't, I've been leaned on. If I put them on they'll close me down'".

They actually played there only once, on 15th October 1976.

18. that there london.

"I only ever went to The Roxy twice, it was such a long way plus there was so much going on around here that you didn't need to go anywhere else, it was just for a change of scene really."

Denise Shaw

Even though there were clubs sprouting up all the time throughout 1977 which were closer to Manchester; The Outlook Club in Doncaster; The Windmill Club in Rotherham; 76 Club in Burton Upon Trent, as well as places in Derby, Scarborough, Birmingham and Middlesbrough, London was still seen as the main hub of Punk. On Saturday 2nd April the Manchester crowd with their collective, inquisitive nature of what it might be like down in the capital city, led to an away day at The Roxy. As with many of the memories of the people who went on those trips there are conflicting reports, and what follows is an amalgamation of two trips to The Smoke.

Fran Taylor: "Like I say things move on and suddenly you're a recognised face in this club (The Ranch) and people were saying hello to you and you're chatting to a few people. It got round to sort of March/April '77 and they turned round and said that they were going to see Buzzcocks playing in London and did I want to come? They were getting a van and meeting outside The Ranch at 9 the next morning and if I was there for that time then I was in. Me and Jon The Postman said 'yeah alright we'll go'. So I met up with Jon in Stevenson's Square and he turns up and he's got this package. So I said to him 'What's that Jon?' and he says 'Oh me mam's made me some sandwiches because we're going out for the day' [*laughs*]. So we rock up and there's this Transit van parked outside The Ranch. There's the lads who are driving it, Allan and Ian from The Worst, who open the back doors of the van and its crammed with kids, some of who I know and some that I don't know. Anyway Jon takes one look at this and says 'Fuck off. I'm not getting in that all the way to London'. I said 'Well I am' and so in I went. In the back of that van there was the core of what I would say was Manchester punk scene at the time. There was Steve Shy, Paul Morley, Allan and Ian and their mate Vinny, who was there at the start and a bit of a nutter and in and out of the nick quite a bit. There were about 16 people in this transit van, no seats, so we're all sat on the floor. There were two sisters who used to come with us, one of them was only 14 in '76 and her older sister couldn't have been more than two years older. They both used to wear Green combat all in ones with high heels, and they had very close cropped hair."

Denise Shaw: "I remember one night going down to The Ranch and Ian, who had a little Escort van, was parked up outside and he said, 'I fancy going down to London who wants to come?' Well there must have been about 15 of us, so it was one of them, 'right we've all got to get in then.' All I can remember is that the roof was soaking with condensation because there were that many of us in the back of this bloody Escort van. He'd decided that he was going to avoid the motorway so there we are going down this country lane when next minute, blue flashing lights, then the Police pulled him over. We were thinking shit we're going to end up back at Manchester. Well, it was like watching something from Benny Hill… I wish somebody would have taped it because these two coppers are stood there, right and they said 'whoever's in the back come out now'. One got out, then two got out and so on, and these coppers were like 'what the fuck!'. 15 of us piled out, we were dripping, I remember my makeup was all down my face and my hair was flat to my head, but it was one of those memorable nights because that was the weekend where they took the photographs that are in the 1977 London punk book, and also the New Wave album, we were there at the best time."

There is also a difference of opinion on the size of the van (which is why perhaps these are the recollections of two different trips) some remember it being a Transit and others a smaller sized Escort van. The number of people would suggest a Transit but…

Odgie: "Oh the little Escort van [*laughs*]! Yeah there were 12 or 13 of us in it. It was supposed to be a fucking Transit but it ended up being an Escort. We'd gone to see X Ray Spex and Wire if memory serves. We were stopped because there'd been a bank robbery in Cheshire somewhere; we were somewhere near Jodrell Bank when we got stopped. The police were checking all the cars and they opened the back doors and it was like the Keystone Cops; there's people just coming out and coming out. There were the girls in their stockings and suspenders and ripped shirts and the coppers were just, 'You're not bank robbers get on your way, there's far too much paperwork here'. Thinking about it now, they actually let 12 or so people get back in an Escort van. Nowadays it'd have been 'Right you lot are walking home'. I'd never really thought about that until now"

Health and safety issues aside, the crew made it down to London and set about visiting all the places they'd read about in the press.

Fran Taylor: "We went to Seditionaries on the Kings Road, it had just changed its name from Sex. I've never had some many suspicious eyes burning into my back. They watched us like fucking hawks, it was only a tiny little place and three or four of us piled in there but I did not feel welcome at all. Even though the girls were well Punked up and Allan and Ian fitted right in; Allan used to wear this 'rapist' mask, if you see early Punk films and you see a guy hopping around in a stripey blazer wearing a black leather mask on with 'rapist' written over the forehead, that's going to be Allan. We had a look in Boy, and we were hanging around outside there and this guy starts clicking the pictures and he's got a nice camera, so Morley goes up to him and puts his hand up, 'No pictures, no pictures, because you're press - money, pay money', and he gave us a fiver with which we bought a bottle of Scotch. We went down to Covent Garden and nobody would serve us, we wanted to get something to eat but people just wouldn't let us in. Denise was full on, Allan was all covered in leather with condoms and safety pins hanging out all over the place, old condom packets pinned to his jacket and what have you; outrageous. There was Ian and Paul Doyle who were just as outrageous, Paul was a mixed race guy with bright blonde hair wearing a plastic bag. Eventually we found somewhere to eat in this Italian place. As we were leaving I looked around and Paul was having a piss under the table onto the floor. I was like 'for fucks sake' you know? In the middle of the only restaurant that was good enough to serve us. But Paul was only about 16 at the time and was a very badly brought up young man.

"So we went over to The Roxy, walked in the door and the first person we see at the top of the stairs was Sid. We got to where to pay and we explained that we'd come all the way from Manchester and we were on the guest list. He says 'There's no guest list here mate', but Boony (Richard Boon) got us in for 50p each in the end. So we're at this gig at The Roxy. It didn't mean nothing to me, it was on a par with Manchester; it was a 'dive' bar; Downstairs into a cellar, not very big, with a stage at one end. That night was fabulous, the bands just kept coming on one after another. Wire were on, they were fabulous, X-Ray Spex were on, they were alright, a bit panto for my liking. Johnny Moped was on, who were more of a blues band than a punk band, but nobody cared you know? There were no distinctions, there wasn't the snobbery.

People didn't say 'I'm not going to see Eddie and the Hot Rods because faces don't go and see them', you just went to see whatever there was, it didn't matter. So that was our outing to The Roxy, which ended up with Pete Shelley jumping in the back of the van to come back with us to Manchester. Pete was always like, one for the crowd and all that business, or maybe he just didn't fancy being with Garth in the car all the way back, because Garth had a bit of a reputation of being an awkward bastard. I've got a note in my diary that the whole day cost us £2.50. The two sisters that came to The Roxy with us in the van were Angela and Carmen."

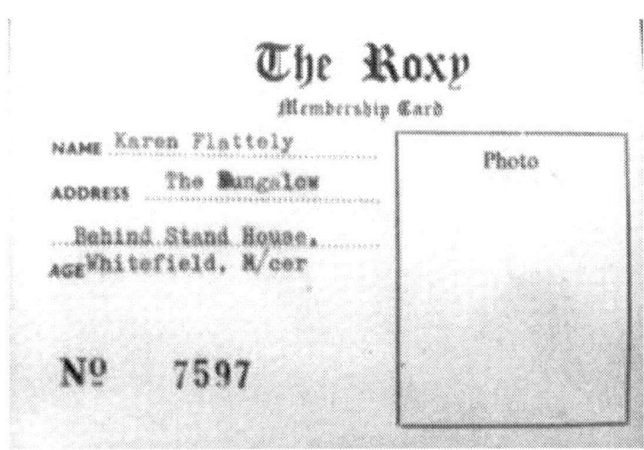

The Roxy
Membership Card

NAME Karen Flattely
ADDRESS The Bungalow
Behind Stand House,
AGE Whitefield, M/cer

Photo

Nº 7597

That night was recorded and some of the bands who played went on to feature on the album 'Live At The Roxy WC2'. Unfortunately not everybody got to go down to the capital that day.

Alan Keogh: "The night at The Roxy, when all the Manc kids went down, the interesting thing about that night is there are some famous photographs from that night, Denise, Paul, Ian, Alan, Adge is on them and Ian Dalglish is on them. They weren't part of the core but they were on those photos, so they were there. The only reason I didn't go was that I had the' flu. So I didn't go. Ian Dalglish came round to me house and was like, 'we've got the van, we're going in the van'. So I'm not there, I'm not on 'em."

There are quite a few photos from the subsequent books documenting The Roxy and Punk in London, plus The Punk Rock Movie also features some of the Manchester punks. Also, the Manchester bands were beginning to add their names to the The Roxy's gig posters. Slaughter and the Dogs and The Drones had played in London since the turn of the year, and both had first played The Roxy, on the 19th and 27th January respectively. They would collectively go on to grace the stage numerous times throughout 1977.

Martin Ryan: "I saw The Drones at The Roxy, it was the only time I went down there. Steve Shy went down with the band and Paul Morley was managing them then as well. It was just after Andy Czezowski had moved on and there was a new manager, and they were pretty flatly received. But it was quite posey I think the London scene, I mean obviously the prices down there… a lot of the lads up here were out of work at the time, like Fran and Steve. It was very expensive down there and the punks seemed to have all the proper bondage gear, it wasn't hand made like it was in Manchester. I remember we got off the train and there was this Punk lad and his girlfriend, and I just felt so straight when I saw them. I can't remember what I had on, probably just a t-shirt, straight jeans and a jacket, nothing outrageous you know."

Stanley Vegas: "I remember going down to The Roxy with Slaughter, and there was a band called The Beastly Cads were supporting them (12th February 1977). I know for a fact that Marco Pirroni was in them but I've got a feeling that it might have been The Rich Kids you know, but I didn't know who the fuck they were, but I got talking to Marco Pirroni. He did a deal with Mike Rossi; Rossi used to have a Marshall guitar stack, but he had a Les Paul copy. Marco Pirroni on the other hand had a real Les Paul, so he did a deal with him, he said, 'You can use my amp, if I can use your guitar'. Marco said okay and he went on first, used Mike's stack system, and fucked off! [*laughs*] So Mike never got to use the real Les Paul."

Carol O'Donnell: "Paul Morley was writing for the *NME* and Kevin Cummins was doing the photos. Kevin would take us to London, you know, to see Buzzcocks when there wasn't enough room in the car or the van. He was going working so he'd take me along with him."

There were other venues in the capital city that filled the gap as The Roxy's star was beginning to wane.

Martin Ryan: "I saw The Heartbreakers again at The Vortex. The Heartbreakers gate-crashed that one; Buzzcocks, The Fall and John Cooper Clarke, 4th July 1977, that's why The Heartbreakers ended up getting on the bill because it was American Independence Day. Plus they reckoned at the time that they were going to be deported, but I don't think they ever were. Kevin Cummins drove us down in a mini-bus. John Cooper Clarke was in the van with us. He absolutely died at The Vortex, that was the first time they'd seen him in London so the audience were like, 'What's he doing, reading bloody poetry.' He didn't mind the punk crowds though, he'd done all the working men's clubs so he could handle a bit of backlash"

Gail Egan: "Me and Paul Morley managed to scrape enough money to get the train fare, which I think was about £13.50 return, and like I said I was on £11 a week then, so I made a load of egg butties and we went down. The Slits were playing, The Clash were playing, and Buzzcocks were playing, it was The Rainbow Theatre. All I could afford was 10 Benson and Hedges, and because Paul was writing the review, we had nothing to write on, so I'd written the setlist on the back of this cigarette packet."

Fran Taylor: "At that time I was living with Pete Shelley, Francis (Cookson) and Carol (O'Donnell) in Gorton. Me and Eric (Random) decided that we were going to go and see The Slits at the White Hart in Acton. It was mooted as being *the* venue after The Roxy closed; Sid was there, John was there, Nancy Spungen, Mick Jones was there because Viv was going out with him on and off. Surprisingly there were other people like Clive Langer from Deaf School, who was being touted as being the producer of The Slits album. We had nowhere to stay and Palmolive was living in a squat on Elgin Avenue, so we ended up staying there. We all went to the supermarket and they told us to go in and look suspicious, which we did, we met them outside and they'd stolen dinner! Palmolive was a superb shoplifter. We were in Derby on the tour and we'd gone to an Indian restaurant which had an open wine rack in the room. All of a sudden Ari and Viv started a mock fight in there, rolling about and stuff. When we got outside Tessa and Palmolive had about 8 bottles of wine between them!"

Odgie: "I remember we were down in London, we must have played somewhere and we went to an after bar. I think it was Billy Idol, the blonde haired singer from Generation X, anyway, he comes in giving it the big 'I am' and tried to push in at the bar and the guy we were with noticed him and just turned around and said, 'And you can fuck off or I'll fucking hammer you' you know? He was just looking after his northern guests!"

Fran Taylor: "We'd organise trips by coach, there was a girl called Lindsay and she had the idea of going down to Croydon, Buzzcocks were playing there and the numbers of people that wanted to go were increasing so we said why don't we book a 'charra'. So she organised that and we went down; a 'charra' full of Mancunians."

As well as going to see the bands, there were connections to the capital which were developing into lifestyle choices.

Mickey Carr: "My brother Fred, he was a hairdresser, he was still a rough kid off the estate, very good looking you know, tall. He got into Punk but he never changed the way he looked. His girlfriend Wendy was an art student who'd gone to Liverpool first I think, and then she went to Chelsea Art College. He used to go and stay there and we started to stay down there as well. They were staying in squats and places. We used to hitch-hike a lot to London, either in a group going to football matches, in the middle of the night at Knutsford service station. We also used to stay at some of these squats in London, and a few people from the Manchester Punk scene established roots down there."

Fred Carr: "We used to hitch it down to London quite a bit. One of us would stand at the side of the road and when the car pulled up the other two would appear! Wendy was working down there and she was staying in student accommodation but we had nowhere to live so we were just crashing on people's floors. To be honest we were just looking for action. Wendy knew all the main people and I'd get to meet them. Adam Ant, Siouxsie was always there and drummer Kenny Morris was at the college."

Alan Keogh: "I actually went on a couple of trips down to London with this art college stuff, going down on the train. So we're on the train and dressed pretty outrageously, and this girl walked up, and I was only 17 at this time, and I did a double take, triple take; it was my ex-girlfriend from school. She was very straight, and she's looking at me like, what the…? She was fine, but her mates were looking at us, Punk rockers… dangerous! You know?"

Mickey Carr: "There were also a couple of girls, I think they were from South Manchester, they looked fantastic, they always did during the Bowie time, they were two sisters. They had the big heavy make-up, and the white/blond spikey hair. They went to London as well, so we used to go back and forward with my little crew football wise 'City's Punks'. We used to go down the Kings Road, that's where we headed for. Not so much to hang about with the Punks but to steal from the shops, primarily Malcolm McLaren and Vivienne Westwood's shop. We'd sell it, whatever, maybe wear the odd bit, but that was the mission. On the way there we were nicking from the machines at service stations, we'd no money."

The reasons for travelling down to the capital extended beyond just going to watch the bands, some were lucky enough to get to know them, as the accessibility factor between fan and group was still quite strong.

Juliette J. Williams: "Through the conversations we used to have with The Clash after gigs, they started to put us on the guest list wherever they played. It most certainly wasn't about being a groupie, it was about wanting mates, who were guys, who were in bands, so that they could teach you how to play. Joe gave me his address and phone number and he said 'If you're ever in London, drop in and say hi'. So when I finally got a job, me and our drummer Julie saved up and got the train to London. We'd promised ourselves that we *would* go down the Kings Road and *would* go in these shops. Joe at that point was living on Albany Street, which was just off Great Portland Street, so we walked from Euston station and we found Albany Street and ended up at number 31. Luckily for us he was in that day, so we were talking and I mentioned that I loved the shirts that they wore, with the stencilled lettering, and he said 'we have them made by a girl called Alex and she actually lives in the front bedroom of the house'. The house was a four or five storey building backing onto Regents Park, and the guy that owned the house was Sebastian Conran, who was the eldest son of Terence Conran. Anyway Joe invited us in to see Alex and we saw The Clash's threads, and I was like 'Oh I want a pair of those Grey bondage trousers and a White shirt and a Black shirt with their logo on', and he just said 'Take them'. So I had a pair of Black and a pair of Grey bondage trousers which I wore with 'monkey boots', and 4 shirts, so we didn't need to go down the Kings Road. There was nothing seedy in it and there was nothing expected in return.

Deb Zee: "I was in London and me and my friend Jane had gone to see someone at The Venue. I met this guy called John MacDonald and he gave us somewhere to stay and we stayed at his for a couple of nights. It was through him that we ended up staying with Youth from Killing Joke; he was living in a room in a hotel on Belgrave Square, I've still got his address somewhere. When PIL played Belle Vue I just turned up at the door and said, 'Is Jock here?' and it was John Lydon's brother Jimmy who just let me in. John Lydon was fine, he just sat with this red furry coat over his head. They played that gig and me and my friend Lesley were just stood at the back of the stage dancing. You look back and it's just mental, we got on their coach and everything. I've had a few scary moments. The Teddy Boys in London, that really scared me because when I heard them smash a bottle on the wall, I was thinking 'this isn't good, they're going to smash our faces open'. So we trotted over the road to this posh house and he let us in and then he gave us some money to get a taxi. I went back years later, knocked on the door and just gave him the money back. I don't even know if it was him, he may have moved on, but he took it anyway!"

Martin Ryan: "We were lucky because Mick (Middles) had a car."

Juliette J. Williams: "People like Una, Denise, and Steve Shy are all three or four years older than me. Denise had a car and she had a job, because when they did the Brass Tacks thing it showed her going to work with her mum. Francis Taylor, I think he had a car as well and they all used to take off to London and go to The Roxy and Seditionaries or Sex, whichever it was then. I didn't have a hope in hell of going down the Kings Road, because I didn't even have a job and I had no money."

London may have had the majority of the limelight but the rest of the country was catching up, and in Manchester, the summer of youth discontent was about to be documented for posterity.

19. brass tacks

AUGUST 3RD 1977

Featuring: *Brian Trueman, Pastor John Cooper, Eric Robson, The Vibrators, Denise Lloyd (Shaw), The Drones, Allan Deaves, Paul Doyle, Steve Burke (Shy), Ian Hodges, Pete Shelley, London Councillor Bernard Brook Partridge, Birmingham Councillor Edward Hanson, Glasgow Baillie John Young, Newcastle Councillor Arthur Stabler, Mike Wood, Vivien Lipschitz, John Peel, Virgin Record's Simon Draper,* London Evening News's *John Blake.*

Despite the fact that the Punk scene had grown considerably from its embryonic state just over 12 months previously, the BBC produced a documentary/debate programme, filmed in Manchester, which mirrored the sensationalist coverage given to it by the national newspapers. In his introduction, presenter Brian Trueman described Punk's rise in popularity as 'a bigger threat to our way of life than Russian communism or hyper-inflation', he then went on to invite the viewers to phone in to express their opinion on whether Punk was a threat to society, and if they thought that anything should be done about it. It's unbelievable now that the fear and dread of a musical genre was deemed threatening enough to warrant its own television debate. Although looking back 40 years on, it seems a little tame and is trying too hard to be reactionary. Then again, those same fears had been highlighted with Presley and The Rolling Stones in the 50's and 60's respectively.

The studio was split into the usual 'for' and 'against' camps. Representing the 'for' camp were; Denise Shaw, Ian Hodges and Allan Deaves from The Worst, Paul Doyle, Steve Burke (Shy), and Pete Shelley, aided and abetted by John Peel, who was situated on a different, 'independent' table. On the 'against' team were; Pastor John Cooper, along with various councillors from all over the U.K. with names straight out of Upper Class Twit Of The Year, who contributed from their respective local BBC studios. Also in the studio, and sat with Peel, were Simon Draper from Virgin Records, and John Blake representing *London Evening News.*

As well as the studio guests there was a filmed section of footage from The Electric Circus featuring The Vibrators live onstage in front of an enthusiastic large crowd of punks and straights. This is interspersed with comments from various band members including a fresh-faced Pete Shelley, clearly exasperated by the ludicrous suggestions being put forward. At one point he interjects the conversation, *"there's people branding us vile and obscene. Do I look vile and obscene?"*. Outside the venue there are contributions from some of the audience including Denise Lloyd (Shaw), having to explain why she goes to The Electric Circus. "*Because it's the best place where they put punk rock bands on, and it's got a great atmosphere. That's about it.*"

Denise was chosen as the punk focal point of the programme, recording her home life, the relationship with her mother, as well as her job in the offices at Courtaulds. She wasn't the stereotypical punk from the poor estates, on the dole and on the scrapheap; she lived a relatively comfortable life on the outskirts of the city. The film shows her mum helping to make Denise's clothes despite the fact that she's not very happy with her wearing them, and at one point declaring that she was sometimes ashamed of the way she looked, although this was said with a glint in her eye. It must have been hard for her to understand, like so many parents, why her daughter had taken to such a dramatic change in appearance, but she knew that Denise wasn't a bad person. She also expressed her fears for Denise's safety because of the stories of Punks being beaten up and tells of how one night Denise had to catch the wrong bus to escape the unwanted attention of someone. "*I'm scared that she might come home one night with her face slashed*".

Although Denise's mother was filmed, her father wanted no part of it.

Denise Shaw: "The only people who accepted me were Dawn's mum and dad. Right from the minute they saw me. I was the only one who dressed as a punk at the time. My mum and dad hated it, especially my dad, he hated the way I looked. So much so that when they came to film the Brass Tacks programme he went and hid in the shed at the top of the garden. He didn't want to be involved in it, and the only time he came out was to ask me. 'I hope that the BBC are paying for all that bloody electric they're using!'

The inclusion of Allan Deaves shown at work and at home also countered the myth that punks were just foul-mouthed, illiterate yobs. Allan was the 'guitarist' in The Worst and another anomaly to the identikit punk as portrayed in the media. Married with a small son, Leon, and working in his father's business repairing motorcycles, Alan's views are more overtly political, primarily in promoting the right for free speech.

Alan Deaves: "It's been said throughout time; if you don't understand it, kill it. You see a spider crawling across the floor, you don't understand what that spider's doing so you stand on it and crush it. That's what people are doing with punk."

Another band featured playing live at The Electric Circus was The Drones. The song which was featured was 'Lookalikes'. In the audience is Paul Doyle, with his striking bleached hair highlighting the fact that he is the only non-white person in the room. There was a short film of him walking the streets of Manchester and shots from inside his flat, which he shared with his cat. Paul was 16 at the time and a refugee who came up to Manchester from London, a bit of an outsider, although everyone I've spoken to about him has nothing but love for the guy.

Janine Hewitt: "I remember Paul Doyle well, he was a quiet, unassuming bloke, and a bit of a loner. He always looked like an old fashioned tramp in a dirty looking, old ripped leather jacket along with threadbare trousers."

Gail Egan: "I remember me and Paul Doyle being chased through Manchester by a load of Skinheads, really scary. He was a lovely guy, really nice, but he got a lot of attention… because the National Front were quite prominent then."

Martin Ryan: "I remember Paul Doyle. He used to hitch down to London. He was in The Roxy when we went to see The Drones."

In the film he narrates over the video footage, giving an insight into his everyday existence and outlook on his life. "*The last job I had, I got a little bit of stick you know because I had my hair ginger, and for a half caste lad to have his hair ginger is a bit funny. They gave me some strange looks. I'm on the dole now, I want to enjoy myself.*" A good looking young man, the sparkle in his eye contrasts acutely to his mundane existence on the dole and living in his sparsely furnished flat, on one meal a day with his pet cat for company. "*When you live in a flat you find you don't eat so much as if you're living at home, because you're used to three meals a day and snacks in between. Eventually you inform the body not to eat that much, one meal a day will do you… One thing you learn living on your own is that you've got to have friends, you know, because if you sit here on your own, you're going to crack up, or take an overdose or do something stupid. You've just got to be on the move all the time. Simple as that.*"

Along with live footage from The Electric Circus, there were scenes outside the venue consisting of Vox pop style comments of the punters and some of the curious non-punk younger kids.

Janine Hewitt: "I just happened to be involved with Brass Tacks documentary by chance. I was going to an event at the Electric Circus - it was The Drones that night, they are on the film. I was standing outside waiting to go in when a couple of blokes with cameras said that they were making a documentary about Punk and did I have anything to say that they could use. Actually I was too camera shy, said a couple of things that didn't get used and later ended up behind someone having a real rant about how the youth of the day were unemployed and forgotten by the Government"

That rant was conducted by Ian from The Worst, right at the start of the programme. One of the managers at The Electric Circus, Allan Robinson, was also interviewed and he took the opportunity to voice his concerns on camera as to the negative hype given to the Punk bands and their audience, "*As a manager I've never had any trouble from Punk bands at all. You see, people phone and say they've heard this and they've heard that, but they haven't come down and seen it and that's what I tell everybody. You've got to come and see what is happening.*" Members of the audience are interviewed as well including Lynn Mee, "*It's different, it's a laugh, it's not boring and straight. People can be themselves.*"

Also featured is Steve Burke (Shy) talking about his fanzine *Shy Talk*, his contribution to the scene, putting it eloquently into context, "*I see it as fun. It's new, exciting music. You've had rock and roll with the Teddy Boys, Mods, Skinheads and everything, this is just a new form.*"

The programme's negative connotations were seen by some as a positive portrayal of the city, and how relevant and culturally important Manchester was at that time.

Andy T.: "It was a Drones and Vibrators gig, I was in the audience. I thought that it was quite a fun thing at the time because it was Manchester, it gives us a bit of kudos because everything was London centric."

Back in the studio, the selection of guests from both sides argued their respective viewpoints. The councillors were justifying their objections to putting on gigs in their respective local areas, which included concerns of rioting and general misdemeanours by the Punk gig goers. Pastor John Cooper was one of the protesters in Caerphilly when the Sex Pistols were scheduled to perform there, singing hymns and preaching a sermon outside the venue in the cold, whilst the band looked on from inside in the warmth. He talked about Punk parents, Punk clergymen, and Punk sportsmen, as a general decaying of society. In some respects he was proved right, as the dumbing down of Punk into mainstream society over the years gave us footballers with multi-coloured hairstyles, and the lessening of the generation gap between parents and their offspring; The prospect of my mother or father attending a gig with me back then was anathema to both them and myself.

John Peel was asked if he thought that, "*Punk rock was anymore than a pop music fad?*" Peel started by comparing the excuse of violence in Punk to the tribal mentality of the religious bigotry of the Old Firm derby. "*Before I answer the question could I ask the man up in Glasgow if he is planning to arrange for the banning of the Celtic v Rangers football matches this season as they certainly endanger public order?*" Uninspired and clearly angered by the response he receives, Peel loses his generally serene disposition. Then, getting back to the question of punk, Peel eulogises about his life changing experiences of hearing Rock and Roll in the 50's, and that those feelings are just being replicated for this generation. He also mentions Punk's '*important but naive political messages*'.

Trueman then brings up the old argument about the hypocritical juxtaposition of the Punk ethos being anti-commercial, whilst some of the groups are tied to major labels who are exploiting them. Simon Draper from Virgin Records: "*There's been a welcome return to small record companies putting out singles at low cost but I think all the groups want to be successful, they want their records to be heard by lots of people and I do think it's about the music…they want to be successful on their own terms.*"

The language used by the presenters and the councillors was as if they were describing Punk as a disease. The press headlines were discussed, concerning the fights with Teddy Boys etc. which were made worse by inaccurate and sensationalist reporting.

Despite the protestations there was overwhelming support against the banning of Punk gigs from analysis taken from the public ringing in to the programme.

Dawn Bradbury: "That Brass Tacks documentary… my dad was in work the next day and they were all talking to him about it. 'Oh my God did you see that last night?' and my dad was just, 'yeah, yeah' dead quiet my dad. 'What did you think of all that?' you know spouting off about it, and my dad just went, 'Eh! Steady on now. Denise is my daughter's best friend, and she'll be at our house this weekend. You have got no idea about what these kids are like. They are all good kids.'"

But not everybody conveyed such goodwill and well balanced opinions.

Denise Shaw: "I got a real backlash at work. I was worried because they'd filmed my mum and dad's house, and people were ringing the switchboard at work saying 'Why do you employ scum like that?'

Dawn Bradbury: "They were demanding that she should be

sacked… for wearing Black eyeliner!"

Denise Shaw: "I thought, if this is happening then my mum and dad's house is going to get attacked you know? It never did thank God, but it could have done."

Right at the end as the opinions of the viewers were being assessed, there was a poignant caller to the programme.

Odgie: "I was a bit wary of doing it to be honest… I'm not really a public person. I'm really quite anti-social. They filmed Allan in the daytime bit, and for whatever reason I was persuaded to go and do the studio bit. My mum rung in; 'I just want to say that my lad's alright'. Bless her."

The programme ends bizarrely, fading out to the end credits halfway through a discussion about religion between Pete Shelley and Pastor John Cooper. It's available to watch on You Tube and is a quite charming slice of social and musical history.

20. transmission

"There was an appreciation of creativity, you needed to support young talent, and you needed to support the region, and that was really important to Granada."

Geoff Moore. Producer, So It Goes.

SO IT GOES. SERIES 2. OCTOBER 9TH-11TH DECEMBER 1977.

The first series of So It Goes had hinted at what was to come. It had given the Sex Pistols their television debut on the last show which had alerted a wider audience to the band. But Granada had a history of ground-breaking music documentaries going back to the original rock and roll era.

Geoff Moore: "Granada's music history before 'So It Goes…' let's not forget people like Johnny Hamp, he was head of entertainment for years and he bought us Little Richard and Jerry Lee Lewis in the early '60's. Then in the late '60's you got the serious mob who did 'Stones In The Park' - Leslie Woodhead; 'The Doors Are Open' - John Shepherd; 'Johnny Cash at San Quentin'. These were just great major documentaries featuring bands that were important, so Granada had a history of that already; they were all made at Granada. I remember thinking that it was pretty cool to be working for a company that had made all that stuff; Granada was pretty damn cool.

"The culture of the '70's is hard for people to understand now, in the media it was much freer and there was more scope to do what you wanted in television. I mean Granada Reports had bands playing them out every night, but you can't get that now. There was an appreciation of creativity, you needed to support young talent, and you needed to support the region, and that was really important to Granada. Granada was the best ITV company at supporting its region. Other companies down south just didn't have that connection with the people. You've got to remember that the environment that Granada flourished in was kind of a non-commercial environment; it didn't have competition, it only had the BBC to worry about so it was free to experiment. Back in 1976/77 there were only three TV channels; BBC1, BBC2, and ITV, now you can get as much music as you want. It was a breakthrough time."

Although it took 12 months for series 2 to be shown, it was a quick decision for it to be commissioned.

Peter Walker: "They got the go-ahead to do a second series of So It Goes quite early on."

That second series was aired from October to December 1977, but the majority of the filming had been done months earlier. Another addition to the programme was producer Geoff Moore.

Geoff Moore: "I came from World In Action at Granada. I joined in 1969 and left after 18 months to become a rock and roll star; I was a professional bass guitarist for three or four years, and it was great fun but I never got the breakthrough I wanted, and I ended up playing cabaret. Anything from The Carpenters to My Way. It paid the rent but it didn't add up to much so I decided to go back to World In Action in 1974. I didn't really know anything about So It Goes series one because with World In Action you were always away or in London. I was in Japan in May working on World In Action and by the end of the month I was working on So It Goes. It was known that I'd had a music career and was interested in music so they thought that maybe I was the right guy to do this.

"I have to say that Punk was never my scene, I mean we were too old for it even then. I was 31. But we were just TV people told to work on this programme. Now of course it was Tony Wilson's brainchild and we had a good working relationship. We just hit it off right away, we were absolutely fine about everything… I knew what he was about. It wasn't my taste, but journalistically he was spot on. You couldn't really define Wilson. He loved doing Punk, he loved doing World In Action, which he did for a very short while. He was very open to the types of TV that he was called upon to do. He was a great champion of the north, he was always saying, 'Let's get things done up here'. He needs to take most of the credit for So It Goes."

Andy T.: "I thought he (Tony Wilson) did really well for Manchester, he always wanted things to stay in Manchester and not go anywhere else. Now with the BBC being relocated to Salford, he was right."

Geoff Moore: "I suppose that the first series of So It Goes helped to kick-start the scene possibly? Punk was seen by the powers that be as a bunch of silly kids looning about, and it was wasn't worth taking much notice of, they were proved wrong over time, but they were conservative times. The other thing was all that stuff was seen as a London thing, it didn't belong up here. You had to be pretty brave to be a punk in Manchester in the mid '70's."

At that time the Punk banner was very broad, which tended to include bands more akin to pub rock, which isn't that far away: small venues, energetic, raw, short sharp uncomplicated songs.

Martin Ryan: "Eddie and The Hot Rods were probably the first band I linked to Punk when I saw them on So It Goes. They were doing 'Wooly Bully' with Andy Mackay on Sax. I did quite like them, I mean I know people said 'Oh no, they're not punk, they're just a teenage Dr. Feelgood' but to me it was about the Punk scene, it was about playing in the small venues. These bands were coming through, and we were catching them when they were still playing the pubs and the small clubs."

Although it was a regional programme, So It Goes did venture further afield via the independent television networks.

Geoff Moore: "It wasn't a full network show, it was shown in most of the country but not at the same time. The difference between series one and series two was that series two was more about the music, series one was more about the culture, it was a bit too 'groovy'. I just wanted to show the right acts."

The 'right acts' could occasionally throw up some mild confrontation and required an intervention from Wilson.

Geoff Moore: "The Clash is an interesting point; I wanted to put on Graham Parker and The Rumour because I thought they were better. But Tony was like, 'no, no, you must put The Clash on, this is *the* opportunity to put them on, you've really got to change your mind Geoff'. So he battered me down and I said 'okay I'll put them on' and we did, and he was right of course. They were sensational at Belle Vue they really were, and that night was a memorable night. All the concerts were shot on film, there was no taped outside broadcast, just 'film nights'. It was just a film crew, with a van and a four-man crew, including a camera assistant, who would help the cameraman through the crowds and make sure that the cables aren't trampled on. It was a chaotic thing… The sound was rough and ready on So It Goes because we recorded it in the conventional documentary way. They weren't hip, young dudes recording this stuff, these were time served Granada people like me. It was like 'Oh God, do we have to go there, it's horrible' but they recorded it live as best they could, all the instruments would be miked up and then fed into a mixer. There was no post production or overdubs, all credit to Harry Brookes, the sound-man.

Not only were theses bands being visually documented on their doorsteps, but there were rules and regulations concerning the filmed nights that for once were in the punter's favour.

Geoff Moore: "The gigs were all free, we weren't allowed to charge because we were filming it. I think we made a selection from the set lists rather than shoot the whole gig, I mean the thing about So It Goes was that it just went through acts; we'd pick a band like Penetration and they'd get two songs plus we'd feature tracks from bands we liked such as Television, Talking Heads, Jonathan Richmond. I thought Steel Pulse were fantastic, XTC the same you know? Mink Deville too... I was really proud of the line up of all the bands we had on. But a band like Buzzcocks, for me with my taste... I was too old for it. I liked their music but Buzzcocks were just making a nice noise, it was quaint, cute. I had more free records than you could count, all the A and R men were coming up to my office with free records, because there were so few outlets for music, just Top Of The Pops. Then along comes this other show, so we'd get all the major companies. I remember John Otway and Wild Willy Barrett were in the studio and a few others, but the studio stuff with Tony were just used as links to the films."

Andy T.: "They used to give out tickets, and they used to have them on the counter at Virgin Records. That was the old Virgin Records with the sticky carpet and little booths."

The groups which were featured spanned the broad church that was early punk.

Geoff Moore: "I'll read through some of the film nights: Eric's in Liverpool - Elvis Costello, Nick Lowe, Dave Edmonds, The Movies; Electric Circus – (I think this must have been done over two nights) The Jam, Buzzcocks, The Clash, Penetration, Jon The Postman; Belle Vue, Elizabethan Ballroom - Siouxsie and the Banshees, The Pirates, Magazine, John Cooper Clarke, and Steel Pulse. I think that's right about Steel Pulse. Middleton Civic Hall - XTC, Tom Robinson, Mink DeVille. That was a good night. Rafters - Albertos Y Los Trios Paranoias. Apollo Theatre - We went to the Apollo to film Iggy Pop. I mean Iggy Pop doing 'The Passenger' was just fantastic wasn't it? What a performance, I was in awe."

June Buchan: "I didn't actually work on the second series, but a lot of the clips I remember being involved in the filming of them. I wanted to do the Iggy Pop recording but I was in hospital, and I felt really pissed off."

Gail Egan: "You can actually see me at the very front of that

Penetration gig. When she sings 'Don't Dictate', there's a fight; there's a guy, who I didn't know, next to me, and he's shaking up a bottle of beer and the next thing he starts squirting it everywhere. Pauline tries to pull it off him, but she can't get it off him so Danny (O'Sullivan) and a few of them from The Ranch all started on him. You can see my head going down!"

Tony Wilson may have argued, cajoled and stamped his feet to get the bands he wanted on, but a lot of the credit must go to the people who would eventually acquiesce to his demands.

Geoff Moore: "Tony Wilson was just the presenter, he wasn't the producer. He didn't have the power to put these acts on, he could argue his case, and he did, but we worked together. I think Chris Pye deserves credit for going down that direction because Wilson was a renegade, wasn't he? He was a maverick. Granada didn't trust him enough to put him in charge of a programme, with budgets and people and all that. He was an anarchist, a delightful man and a great professional. He went a bit silly when it came to Punk; he was overawed by these bands, but he was right journalistically. He had no time for musicians, but then again nobody had any time for anyone back then, they just got together and did it. You see, I was a musician, and Wilson was never a musician. He was a hustler, a journalist, talented, but he knew nothing about music. I reacted differently to stuff, so for me to get Iggy Pop… I was so chuffed. We'd done the deal, we'd arranged to film it in Manchester, and I even had some flowers delivered to his hotel room. 'Hi Iggy, this is Geoff from Granada, so pleased you're here and look forward to seeing you'. Ha ha! But I was dead chuffed, yeah. He was a one off wasn't he, Wilson? He loved bands like Buzzcocks and Joy Division."

The last show was transmitted on December 11th 1977 and featured Jon The Postman at The Electric Circus, Steel Pulse performing 'Macka Spliff' and 'Ku Klux Klan' recorded at The Elizabethan Suite, Belle Vue. Recorded at the same venue were The Clash playing 'Capitol Radio' and as the final end credits rolled they ripped through an incendiary version of 'Janie Jones'. The performances that were recorded in Manchester throughout the two series of So It Goes, account for the vast majority of archive footage of the first year of punk. It is widely available on You Tube, including a collection put together and narrated by John Cooper Clarke, it's a valuable time capsule of a pivotal point in music history.

When So It Goes was denied a third series, another programme which Wilson presented and Peter Walker directed was What's On, which was another arts based programme that would be aired on a Thursday night. As Tony Wilson later explained, "*I was doing that for a local programme, it was my job in the culture. I backed off for a couple of months, I was so depressed by the response to So It Goes. People didn't like it because it was too fast, it was irreverent, it wasn't The Old Grey Whistle Test, which was dull and dead and became fashionable because we were the opposite, which people hated.*"

John Maher: "Buzzcocks performed 'Boredom' live on Granada teatime TV on What's On. Fellow guests included Albert Finney, Margaret Lockwood (with her fingers in her ears), and a man with an eagle."

Geoff Moore: "I had Joy Division on another programme, What's On, much later in 1979, I produced What's On for a year. That wasn't their first time, the first was '78 when they did Granada Reports. All these bands were miserable and difficult ,you know? A real pain in the arse. And they didn't appreciate what Wilson was doing for them, some of them, but he got off on the fact that they were miserable gits and ungrateful, it made him laugh. I thought he was better at serious stuff than light stuff. Just keep him away from posing as Mr. Cool, and he was a natural presenter. He loved television; working on it, appearing on it, he loved Granada. Plowright was great, and he let Wilson have his head. But it wasn't Plowright's thing and he got fed up with So It Goes when it caused him trouble. There was the Iggy Pop incident; he was doing an in-between spiel to the audience: 'I met a girl in fucking Denmark…' or something like that. Of course it had to be taken out, and we would argue to keep it in, that was the trouble. He just said 'I don't want to have these discussions anymore'.

"Plus there was the Albertos incident. I had to dub out 'fuck' from their concerts. All of the way through this of course, the BBC had 'Whistle Test'. We weren't 'entertainment' people, that was the other thing. If you looked at what the London companies like Thames were churning out - variety programmes such as Sunday Night At The Palladium, Seaside Specials, variety shows – where would you put So It Goes? It wasn't any of that, it was just something different. I think Granada lost interest, they didn't see the point of it. They were wrong to drop it.

"On December 13th 1977 at the Placemate 7 club there was a joint Christmas party for World In Action and So It Goes. It was a great night and it was a great club too, and I was in my element. We had our own band; Myself, Chris Pye, Peter Carr (director of So It Goes series 2), Jules Burns, Tony Wilson, and Jonathan Silver, who was a manager at Granada."

Wilson would go on to cement his place into Manchester's musical history in the following months.

June Buchan: "I introduced Alan Erasmus to Tony Wilson. Alan lived in the same house as me in West Didsbury, there were a number of flats in a big house. Alan and Tony got on really well and Alan had a flat on Palatine Road, which is where they started Factory. I used to help them put the record sleeves together. Now there's a Blue plaque outside."

21. what a way to end it all

"You are the music while the music lasts."

T.S. Eliot

Meanwhile back at The Ranch, as the Punk scene in Manchester was gaining momentum, the national tabloid's sensationalist reporting was continuing it's vilification of the movement, which meant that The Ranch started to attract some unsavoury characters. Where once it was a safe(ish) haven for anyone with any individualist tendencies, the original clientele were regularly having to deal with 'straights' and football thugs looking for trouble. Punk-bating and general mischief making was becoming more prevalent.

Terry Slater: "It started to change, as things often do."

Fran Taylor: "People would try and get into The Ranch to beat people up. Whether that was because of the gay aspect or the Punk aspect I'm not sure. I don't think the Punk aspect was big enough to be honest. I used to know kids who would go into town to 'rogue' gays, mainly to rob them more than anything else. They knew that they could tempt them into a quiet area and then beat them up and take their money."

Stephen Perrin: "Of course, it didn't take long for the secret to get out and for a certain kind of straight male to turn up."

Wispa: "There was a lot of straights in there, yeah. They were usually pissed or whatever, you could smell them a mile off, you know? They obviously weren't into the scene, and they'd go onto the dance floor and barge into people on purpose, just to get a reaction."

Mickey Carr: "Gradually, more and more people starting coming and it became as much, if not more of a Punk place. They were then followed by what you might think were undesirable types, just general thugs, but were into the music."

Gail Egan: "I can remember as they were introducing more and more of the Punk music into The Ranch, and the hardcore Ranchies weren't impressed, you could see because it was bringing another element in there,"

Mickey Tait: "The Ranch was wild. Loads of scraps in there in the punk era. In the 70's there were a lot of lunatics wasn't there? On a Saturday night you'd get the football fans in coming in but there was a pretty hard core group of punks in there as well."

Deb Zee: "They used to have a Blue light going when there was a fight."

Daniel O'Sullivan: "When we used to go to The Ranch there was crew of Rockabilly/Teddy Boys who would frequent the Midland Hotel in Didsbury, it's now called The Metropole and they'd come down to The Ranch and we'd have fights with them. Eventually I got to know them and became quite good friends with them. There was a certain amount of hostility and there were regular fights in there, so no I'd say it was quite heavy. Until your face fitted, perhaps it took two or three visits in you know? There was a lot of trouble."

The level of violence is one of the most contradictory topics in people's recollections of The Ranch Bar.

Stanley Vegas: "I don't think there was much trouble, but you got a lot of conflict. It could feel quite uncomfortable in there some nights, but I don't remember seeing any mass brawls in there, it was just more like a post code sort of thing. 'Where are you lot from?' and all that. We weren't a gang of punks anymore, I don't think, towards the end of The Ranch."

Sometimes the undesirable element would overstep the mark to a sinister level.

Odgie: "I got glassed in The Ranch Bar. Some 'townies' got in one night and they were picking on people and one of them started a fight with someone I knew, who was a Punk. So I beamed in, so naïve really because there's always a crew behind them waiting outside or whatever. So I pulled this guy over and said 'there's no need for that, come on' and I got sucker punched at the side of the head with a glass. They were normally pretty good but these guys had got in, and Foo Foo wasn't adverse to getting someone by the scruff of the neck and turfing them out."

Stanley Vegas: "I got stabbed in The Ranch one night. It was a stealth attack... I dunno, about six or seven United fans had got in and they were just generally looking for trouble, you know? Anyway I think a couple of Punks squared up to them and a fight erupted, then I got a pain in my back, and the next thing I knew there was blood pissing out and I realised I'd been stabbed. It wasn't anything...it was more of a slash."

Stephen Perrin: "The first night Mike and I went there I split up a knife fight by walking into the middle of the two protagonists and saying 'You don't really want to do this, lads, do you?' I admit that I probably wouldn't have done this had I been completely sober but somehow in there anything seemed possible. Again, the sense of shared solidarity was probably partly due to the fact that we all knew that there was a good chance of getting attacked on the bus on the way home for looking the way we did so it was pointless fighting among ourselves."

Terry Slater: "I was working behind the bar one night and Joanne, my wife, came up to the bar and said that this guy kept putting his hand up her skirt. He had a National Front badge on, quite tall, so I went up to him and I said, 'Excuse me mate, have you got a girlfriend?' And he said 'Yeah'. So I said 'How would you like it if I put my hand up your girlfriend's skirt like you're doing to her, because that's my girlfriend'. Well anyway he went into a rage and he jumped on the bar, and Alf, one of the bouncers came over and picked up a bottle and twatted him around the head. Then it all kicked off, and I mean kicked off. Behind the bar was a massive mirror – it never got smashed – I'll never know how it never got smashed because we were ducking behind the bar dodging bottles and stuff. Frank was on stage next door and he came in with his skirt on and punched these lads out, I mean he could handle himself could Frank. Anyway it all died down... and where was Joanne? Asleep in a corner!"

The Ranch Bar had also started to serve as a hangout for those early punk bands who were playing a gig in town.

Mickey Carr: "Visiting bands used to go in there as well. Adam and the Ants, members of the Banshees, there was a London connection, plus Buzzcocks."

Terry Slater: "I saw a lot of new bands come in."

Alan Keogh: "The Fall were great at The Ranch, it was fantastic."

Mickey Tait: "All the musicians were there you know; The Drones, Slaughter and the Dogs, Buzzcocks, they were all knocking about. The Distractions were always about, they were all in The Ranch. The Reducers, they were really good; Bury's finest."

Wispa: "Eventually it became so popular, that most of the bands used to go there, it was like the band's local after gig haunt you know. It was a sort of musician's hangout. We all used to go in there on a Friday or Saturday night if we didn't have a gig. It was only a small club. It's a funny story actually, how we got involved with The Ranch. When we were Rockslide, we played next door at Foo Foos, we got a week's work, a week's gigs with him, supporting him you know? We'd play a bit of Shang A Lang, that sort of thing. We always used to have to hang about the club to get paid, so we had to wait until he'd gone on so we wouldn't get paid until about 3 in the morning. So we got to see the lay of the club, the people that went in there and everything. The club next door was The Ranch Bar which was Frank Lamaar's club as well, and that was a Roxy/Bowie club, but it was slowly changing and once Punk came in the likes of The Drones got their first gigs there."

Fran Taylor: "The Ranch wasn't really a venue, it was a club, but bands did play there. Buzzcocks played there, The Drones played there, and The Distractions in '77 used to play a residency there, or it seemed like a residency, they seemed to be there every Thursday night. But it was too small."

Stephen Perrin: "I'm not sure which band played at the Ranch first but it might have been Buzzcocks when Howard was still with them. There was no stage, you just set up in the corner. Foo Foo' Lammar owned the place and the rumour was that he had given it to his brother to run, in order to keep him out of trouble, but I've never had that verified. Frank was a neighbour of our friend Noel Keane so we sent him round to plead our case. He said that we could have a one off spot and if the club made a profit on the bar we could play again. Our friends came and drank so much that we played there three times and could probably have had a weekly residency if we had wanted."

Alan Keogh: "I played at The Ranch, which was wild, with Ian Dalglish on guitar - I think it was someone called 'Dog' on drums, who was from Gorton. We may have had Eric Random on bass but I'm not sure, maybe not. I just made vocal noise. I would have been about 15, but nobody will remember it because a) we were shit and b) we didn't know anyone."

Once again, there were contrasting recollections.

Denise Shaw: "You see, I don't remember any of the bands coming into The Ranch."

As more and more bands from around the country travelled to play for the first time in Manchester, there was a connection between the groups and their relatively small audience.

Carol O'Donnell: "People were more accessible. Before Punk, Pop stars were just Pop stars and stayed away from us. But in those days the people in the bands, they were just part of the crowd. I used to have loads of people coming back to my house. My dad was ill and then he died, but while he was ill he was staying at my brothers so I had a 3 bedroom house at 17. We had everyone back at our house; X Ray Spex, The Worst of course, in fact they came back a bit too often! (*laughs*). After my dad died the council kicked me out of the house because obviously a 17 year-old in a three bedroom house... so they stuck me in a 1 bedroom flat in Hulme."

Deb Zee: "I remember being there and Holly Johnson came round and Paul Rutherford. Paul was in The Spitfire Boys."

Carol O'Donnell: "We were close me and Paul, close in the sense that we'd always sit together and we'd hold hands walking down the street, that sort of thing. I mean he was gay, but I didn't know that at the time."

Fran Taylor: "My home had become a bit of a crash pad as everyone knew my Dad was away. When Jon Savage asked me if I could put a friend of his up from London who'd come to see a gig, I said of course. That, dear reader, is how New York punk diva, Patti Palladin wound up spending the night on a Salford Council Estate! I wish I had a video of her leaving next day; dressed head to toe in leather with cowboy boots with spurs, the local kids ran after her pretending they were cowboys riding horses and shooting pretend pistols."

Gail Egan: "Mike Peters, who went on to form The Alarm, used to come over to Manchester, he lived in Prestatyn I think and him and his friend got friendly with one of my mates Pat, and Mike stayed at my house one night because it was a long drive back to Prestatyn. He was a nice guy"

Fred Carr: "We went to a party on Dickenson Road one night and there was a guy living there who designed Buzzcocks first single sleeve (Malcolm Garrett) and there was another guy there, a small Scottish guy who was a guitarist. He became guitarist for PIL a lot later and he was also guitarist for Magazine I think (John McGeogh). We were quite pally with them and one night at a party Pete Shelley was there and he was playing his guitar in the kitchen, people were asking him to play stuff, mostly Bowie."

It wasn't always camaraderie and togetherness though, and occasionally there would be flare ups including musicians and The Ranch clientele, as well as more violent clashes with the football fans and people only out for confrontation.

Mickey Carr: "There was an incident with a member of Slaughter and the Dogs, their lead singer. He was at the bar, I never said anything to him, they were a bit older than us, he might have said something to my girlfriend but it turned into a situation. He stood on a chair and he sort of dived down towards me, as if he was going to throttle me. So I just hung one on him and then this fight started, then we got separated and they were waiting for me outside, a gang of them from Wythenshawe.

The kids I was with were from the estate, so we went out and biffed 'em. They were quite surprised, we all took our belts off. It came back to haunt me because one day I met my girlfriend in town, she worked at Woolworths. So we met up one dinnertime and we were just sat down eating our pies, when all of a sudden we were surrounded, so we had to get on our toes you know? But I don't remember it going any further than that. It wasn't carried on or anything."

Denise Shaw: "Gavin (Owen), he's an editor now for *Playboy* in Miami, I think... he was one of our gang but he was younger and would come to the occasional gigs. Apparently I was coming out of The Ranch one night and he was getting beaten up in the bus station in Piccadilly. I'm told now that they were Perry Boys, but we didn't have a name for them, they were just idiots to us. Anyway he put it in a mini documentary that he made that I went wading in with these six lads kicking shit out of him, and all he could remember was this six foot Amazonian diving in with her handbag and kicking out. He said that I could have actually saved his life but I don't even remember it because there was loads of things like that you know?"

Unfortunately it seemed that there was a new breed of punks who seemed content to live up to the cartoon image dreamt up by the tabloids.

Fran Taylor: "There were people on the punk side who just wanted the violence. I met a couple of guys down The Ranch one time and they were going to some Rock Against Racism thing, so I was like 'You better watch it there, these Fascists can be a bit tasty'. They replied 'That's what we're fucking going for, to rip the heads off a couple of Fascists!' And this was a guy in make-up with feathers hanging out of his ear."

The pace of change in music and fashion was developing extremely quickly which meant that eventually people moved on, either away from the city or into another scene which had its own clubs and meeting places. Nothing stays the same and things have to progress but The Ranch was, for a short time, the epicentre of the transition from the Bowie/Roxy era to Punk. But added into the equation was the fact that the place was on the radar of the local constabulary, who wouldn't be happy until it was closed down.

Wispa: "I never used to go out until 10 o'clock because we used to rehearse. So I'd go home, get changed, washed and go out. So anyway one night I'd got the bus into town and arrived at The Ranch about half ten and I'd just got my drink and the place got raided for drugs, so the cops come in heavy handed, and they've got me up against the bar and I've nothing on me. So they're like 'Name?'; 'What do you do for a living?' all that shit. So I told them, 'Musician', 'Musician eh? Well you can come and play at the Policeman's Ball!' I should have kept my mouth shut, but that was it, straight down to Bootle Street – drunk and disorderly; I hadn't even had a fuckin' drink! That's what it was like back then."

Steve Nuttall: "The Ranch Bar was eventually closed down. I was there when it got raided for drugs, but we're not talking crack or heroin, it was just pills: amphetamines, and speed. There were loads of police, and they searched everyone in the place, tipping cigarettes out of their packets onto the wet floor, stuff like that. Then we all had to go outside and line up against the building and be searched again, some were taken to Bootle Street police station. Not long after that someone died outside during a fight and it was closed down."

The fight was not connected to The Ranch or anyone in there, and it certainly shouldn't detract from the fantastic memories of the people who went there for the music and peace of mind, but as with The Electric Circus, the police didn't need much of an excuse to make things very difficult for the place.

Mickey Carr: "I was one of the last ones to let go of The Ranch. I remember it closed down and I remember being disappointed because it was like your base. I would talk to the guys behind the bar, Mike Blaney I think it was, he told me as it came up to the end, Frank/Foo Foo was looking at expanding his side of the club."

Denise Shaw: "We go out now with friends and people we know, but we'll never have that same relationship with them as what we all had then, never"

Alan Keogh: "When I think about it now The Ranch was the only place because I don't think that Pips is really as significant as there in terms of punk history. It was still rooted very much in the Bowie/Roxy kind of culture. It was mayhem outside The Ranch sometimes, but inside there was a group of people in there… Pips was a more fashion conscious place whereas The Ranch was more radical, it had more outsiders which I think is where most interesting things come from."

Terry Slater: "I left in 1979. I loved it, you know? I met a lot of people, I was privileged because I met a lot of people who went on to do great things in their life, do you know what I mean? Yeah I really enjoyed it. It was definitely a buzzin' place. You'd get all sorts coming in; old, young, just curious. They'd heard about it and wanted to see it. I ended up working there, behind the bar. The Ranch was firmly on the map in

Manchester from '76 to early '78."

22. the electric circus (reprise).

"Why did the Electric Circus close? It closed because the authorities wanted it closed, not through lack of success."

Fran Taylor

Throughout 1977 anyone who was anyone on the punk scene played at The Circus, although still mainly on Sunday evenings. From as little as 50p you could see The Clash, The Jam, The Adverts, The Saints, Siouxsie and the Banshees, Ramones, Talking Heads, Johnny Thunders, The Fall, John Cooper Clarke, The Stranglers, Rezillos, Ultravox, The Slits, The Boys, The Drones, The Slugs and The Worst. Sometimes, as in the case of Ramones and Talking Heads, they would be on the same bill.

Ian Moss: "Once it started after the Anarchy tour, the Circus was the place to go and see bands."

For many people, too many to fit into this book, nights at The Circus would remain with them forever.

Alan Keogh: "I was at the Circus every week. I'll give you a quick rundown of the people I saw at the Circus: The Pistols, Clash, The Jam, The Damned, Johnny Thunders and the Heartbreakers, Talking Heads, Ramones, Penetration, X Ray Spex, just off the top of my head. It's a long list."

Fran Taylor: "Sunday nights, plus they did a few on Tuesdays, of all nights. I remember seeing Siouxsie and the Banshees there on a midweek, and towards the end it was pretty much all punk. They were still booking middle of the road bands who liked playing there because it was a standing venue and you could dance. Also Motörhead played there and they became part of the early punk ticket."

Chris Hewitt: "Motörhead were touring about the same time as punk was starting. I had to go and pick up Lemmy and the band from Knutsford services because they'd broken down. I'd met Lemmy before, I'd worked with him in London, so I had to pick him up, it was in the middle of winter, because they'd got no fuel, no oil, and no money for food, and they'd only managed to get as far as Knutsford. So I rescued them and did the Electric Circus date and ended up doing the rest of the tour in the north, including Wigan Casino. I used to do the PA and I'd also do the bar run, go to the wholesalers and pick up all the beer for them."

Stanley Vegas: "I was there every Sunday night. I mean, the bands I've not seen at The Electric Circus for a quid aren't worth talking about. Sunday night was the big night. I had a group of mates from Gorton and we used to meet in a pub called 'The Swinging Sporran'. Basically we'd turn up and if you had your bus fare, that was all you had, because one of us would have some money left over from the weekend, and it'd be like 'Right, here's a quid to get in, then we'd do some 'mine-sweeping' and what have you for beers. To be honest I was pissed most of the time so I can't really remember a great deal!."

Andy T.: "There were a few gigs in the early part of '77 but when The Clash brought the White Riot tour to the Circus, that's when it really kicked off. Then it was bands every weekend."

Carol O'Donnell: "The first time I went to the Circus was to see The Clash in 1977; it was the day before we buried my dad. I was 17 and I had the tickets so I wasn't going to miss it. My family hated me for doing it but I remember getting the tickets from Virgin. The Slits were supporting them as well as Subway Sect. That was a great night."

One band that was just starting to make a name for themselves was AC/DC, and they played at the venue on 17th March 1977 to a pretty sparse crowd. Although not punk by any stretch of the imagination, the band were a similar age to the main punk bands and were extremely raw and very loud without the need for 20 minute guitar or drum solos. The gig was favourably reviewed by Martin Ryan for the Manchester fanzine *Ghast Up!* and due to the paucity of punk gigs at the time, it meant that the fanzine had to branch out from time to time.

Gail Egan: "I saw AC/DC there and I think that was one of their first U.K. tours.

As the venue started to increase its audience numbers, it also started to attract other, unwanted attention from the local constabulary, who took umbrage at young people having the audacity to go out and enjoy themselves.

Andy T.: "They were always a bit wary about who was in there because of undercover police, people smoking weed and underage drinking. The police were awful, they were really trying to clamp down on everything. They tended to leave some of the gay clubs alone, but I think that they were taking backhanders for that."

Fran Taylor: "To get a late licence in Manchester you had to provide hot food, right up to closing time. The Circus used to get the police regularly turning up to check that there were actually pies on sale on the hot food counter, even though nobody ever bought the fucking things! So you would go to the most outrageous bar in town and there had to be pies; only in Manchester!

Andy T.: "They used to have these 'warmers' on the bar with pies in, although you wouldn't eat them because they'd probably been there for about 3 weeks!"

The Electric Circus finally closed its doors on October 2nd 1977 after continued hassle from the police and fire authorities. They'd finally got their wish.

Fran Taylor: "It closed because the authorities wanted it closed, not through lack of success. The fire brigade started to take an interest in how many people were in the building and how many people were allowed to be in the building. We knew very well that there were places where ordinary entertainment went on where they'd jam 'em in to the doors and nobody cared. But people in authority didn't want any of this 'New Wave' stuff and they were determined to stamp on it. Obstacles were thrown in the way of the promoters; to whoever was promoting it and wherever they were promoting it. But it was the fire brigade's limit on attendance at The Electric Circus that eventually signed its death warrant, well that and the fact that the coppers kept turning up and raiding it at any given opportunity. There was definitely a clampdown in operation, and they won. The number of people that would have been allowed in there would make it financially impossible to continue. So that was the end of that."

The last weekend of music was recorded for posterity over the 1st and 2nd of October 1977, and was marked by the release of the album 'Short Circuit'. Initially planned as a double album it eventually saw the light of day in 1978 as a limited edition 10" mini album, consisting of 8 tracks and marketed in Blue, Orange and Black vinyl editions. The bands that made it onto the finished article were: The Drones, The Fall, John Cooper Clarke, Buzzcocks, Joy Division, and the only non-Manchester act, Steel Pulse from Birmingham. Some copies included a free EP by local comedian John Dowie.

Fran Taylor: "Not all the bands that played the gigs appeared on the Short Circuit album. I think that The Worst played both nights and I'm not even sure that they were recorded. Then of course they did the brilliant thing of putting on two benefit nights to close the place and then running off with the money. They presented a cheque to the charity it was meant for and it bounced."

There were also rumours that the sound wasn't great and some of the recordings were drowned out by the noise of the crowd.

Stanley Vegas: "We got recorded for the album but the sound was diabolical, we were crap, and the microphones packed up so we made an executive decision that we didn't want to put it on the album"

Fran Taylor: "I believe that they had a mobile studio at the back, so it should have been coming straight off the mics which should mean that there was no problem with that. I mean the stuff that's on it is reasonably well recorded but what made the final cut would have been largely affected by who had deals."

Deb Zee: "Warsaw did the weekend when it closed, they played and so did Magazine and The Negatives because Steve played and Paul Morley and Kevin Cummins. It was brilliant, £1.50 for the weekend."

Alan Keogh: "We tried to get a spot on the last night of the Circus gig, you know, that album, the 10" album. So we tried to get a spot on that. We invented a band to try and get on it... we weren't really in existence as a band or anything. So we went up there and Paul Morley sat there behind a fuckin' desk with two other people. So Ian Dalglish does all the talking, as I didn't have the confidence, desire or whatever. So Dalglish goes up and says 'yeah we want to play at this last night of the Circus' and Paul Morley is sat there, literally with a fucking pen and paper and says 'what are you called then?' Ian Dalglish; 'Asylum'. Morley; 'you sound like a heavy metal band, No!' And that was it."

Carol O'Donnell: "The Negatives did the last night of the Electric Circus, I mean it was just a laugh. Paul (Morley), Kevin (Cummins), Richard (Boon) and was it Marvin or Marlon? They were talking about getting a band together so me and Steph and Jodie were saying to them, 'Yeah we'll be in it' and they said, 'Okay come and sing for us'. We did two gigs, that was it; the last night of the Electric Circus and we also supported Sham 69 at Pips? I can't remember where it was. That was a good night."

Denise Shaw: "I didn't go to the last gig at the Electric Circus, and the last gig I went to was Buzzcocks and The Fall on Friday 18th November '77 at Eric's. The Wednesday before was V2 and Nervous Breakdown at Pips. It was dying out for me by then."

The closure of the Circus also signalled the closure of a chapter of what was arguably one of the most vibrant, exhilarating scenes in Manchester's illustrious musical history. Its brevity was matched only by its legacy. To the people who attended the gigs, whether at the start or at the finish of its tenure, the place holds a special place in their hearts that will stay with them forever.

Wispa: "The main place for me was the Electric Circus. There was an energy there. You couldn't take your eyes off the bands, because you didn't know what was going to happen."

Odgie: "I suppose we saw the Circus as being our own really and so whatever band would be playing, we thought nothing of it because we'd be backstage or whatever. In the middle of somebody's set, I'd just walk on and say to the drummer 'When you've finished, we're going to use your gear and do a bit of a thing' – not pre-arranged before the gig but halfway through their fucking set on stage! You can't believe it now but those were the times, you know? So at the end we'd pile on stage, however many of there was of us, pick up the instruments and do 'Louie Louie' with Jon the Postman at the end of whoever was playing at the Circus, or not if they wouldn't let us you know? Then we wrote them off if they wouldn't let us do it."

Mark Windsor: "Me and Peter Hook would be part of the ones who got up with Jon the Postman to do the traditional rendition of 'Louie Louie'."

There were a couple of mementoes from the venue's most famous performances recorded for posterity.

Fran Taylor: "The first Pistols bootleg and the first Clash bootleg came from Manchester. The Clash one had a picture of Denise on it and the Pistols one had Ian from The Worst playing golf on it. When they came out, the covers opened out, which is why they didn't stay together very well over the years because they were badly glued together by those who shall remain nameless. I bought 50 of them, me and my mates all clubbed together to buy them, there were hundreds of them going around. When we got them, we got a box of albums and a box of covers so we had to put the records and the sleeves together. Kevin Cummins took all the pictures so that tells you how organised it was. Mind you Kevin used to take a lot of the pictures for the pamphlets we were talking about before."

Steve Shy: "People would be paying in at the desk and you could get the Clash bootleg and the Pistols bootleg for £4, it was £2.50 each or £4 for the 2. Denise is on the cover of one, and Ian out of The Worst is on the other."

Another landmark night in Collyhurst left its mark indelibly etched into the memory bank.

Alan Keogh: "I went to see Talking Heads supporting Ramones... it was a great gig. Just before the Ramones finished I decided I needed a piss so I go into the toilet which was at the side of the stage. So I'm in there having a piss and the Ramones finished, I could hear the applause, so they run off the stage, and they think that their running out to their tour bus but they ran into the fucking toilets! So the Ramones are in the toilet and Joey's stood there going, 'okay, I guess this isn't the way out' while I'm having a piss! Then one of their guys wouldn't let them out because of the crowd outside, so there I am locked in the bog with the Ramones."

Gail Egan: "The Ramones and Talking Heads; I've never seen anything like it, Joey cut his lip on the microphone. It was just like, 'What is going on?'"

Andy T.: "I'd gone down to the Liverpool v Man United Cup Final at Wembley on the supporters club coach, and the night after was the Talking Heads and Ramones gig at the Circus, so that was a busy weekend! Sometimes you could go to three gigs in a week, and occasionally you could sneak in because you knew the bouncers."

Not everybody had such good memories about the place. If you lived in reach of the bus routes, you were fine, but for teenagers without cars, it would make for a frustrating evening.

Ian Fawkes: "I can't remember where I found out that The Jam were playing at the Electric Circus but I knew that you could buy tickets from Virgin Records. I asked the girl that I was going out with at the time to buy a few tickets for the gig as she was going to Manchester shopping with her mum. Quite a few of us went down on the train to Piccadilly, and I was used to going to gigs in the city centre. So I got my A-Z out and we traced the map up Oldham Street and across and up in the general direction of the venue. As we were walking through the city centre cars kept passing us, slowing down, full of lads who seemed to be sussing out the strangers in town and it felt quite threatening. When we got to the Circus it didn't get any better. There were blocks of flats and this run down place on the left which turned out to be The Electric Circus, and there was glass all over the road outside. There was a queue outside and once again we were thinking, what the fuck are we doing here, it was a dump and if this was the outside what would the inside be like? Over the road outside the flats there was what I'd call normal people goading us as we were standing in the queue waiting to get in.

"When we did get in we went up a flight of stairs and above was a balcony and there were lads throwing beer or it could have been piss, at us as we walked underneath. We sat at the back and the place filled up, and there was a kind of punk disco with kids pogoing about and we kept ourselves out of the way of all this. Eventually we asked what time The Jam would be on and this lad, I think he was from Huddersfield or Halifax maybe, I'm not sure, but anyway he told us that they would be on at any time between ten o'clock and half past ten usually. Now bearing in mind that this was a Sunday night and our last train left for Buxton at about 10 o'clock, so we had to leave to set off back home without seeing The Jam."

Odgie: "I remember we got The Jam booed off stage because they arrived with suits on coat hangers."

Dawn Bradbury: "It's funny because we used to talk through most of the bands, especially if it was The Jam, they got booed off"

Juliette J. Williams: "I saw The Jam on that very first tour, 'In The City', at the Electric Circus in summer 1977. Even then they were getting castigated in the press, 'They're not punk'. It was all about, 'what is punk?' and all that, but they were excellent. They were so tight and they delivered. The place was jumping."

Daniel O'Sullivan: "The Circus was probably my favourite place, even though it was on the other side of town for me. It had a rougher, more raucous feel to it, and I got the impression that the punks from the north side of the city were much more full-on than the poseurs on the south side! I saw so many bands there. I was a big fan of The Damned so whenever they were there..."

Ken Park: "What I used to like about the punk gigs were that the music that was played beforehand was usually Reggae."

Two of the Circus's early regulars were awarded certain perks of the management. Other punters would complain about the fact that they weren't allowed to stand in their exulted position.

Dawn Bradbury: "That was our spot, and they'd be told, that's Dawn and Denise's place, that's where they sit"

All that's left to remember it by now are a few iconic photographs taken by Kevin Cummins.

Denise Shaw: "I never even thought to take a picture of the actual place because who'd have thought it was going to be pulled down."

As for the immediate future of the Circus; throughout all of the previous 12 months of speed and noise, the 'Electric Circus Rock Disco' had remained a permanent fixture, just to let the kids know that the dinosaurs were still roaming the planet, musically speaking at least. On 3rd October 1977 the disco moved to a new venue, The Merry-Go-Round Club on Broughton Street in Salford.

Stanley Vegas: "When the Electric Circus shut, they tried to do like an 'Electric Circus 2'. All the local kids used to throw bricks at us and everything, even more so than the original Circus, it was really dodgy."

A month later The Circus re-opened and changed its' name to The Venue with the sub title of 'The New Electric Circus', but this was short lived. The fact that The Electric Circus only existed for one year enhances its iconic status, as well as its immense important contribution to Punk and will always be fondly remembered by those people who witnessed some fantastic nights, drenched in sweat, beer, blood, and spittle; It never got the chance to go stale or outstay it's welcome.

Fran Taylor: "The Electric Circus came back as The Venue, but only for a very short time, and then it became the New Electric Circus for a very short time, then it was knocked down."

Stanley Vegas: "The Mayflower took over after that, which was in Gorton, which was great for us. It was an old Reggae club and we used to go there, I can't remember if it was on a Thursday or Friday, and there was two old Jamaican DJs...they used to play a lot of old Ska stuff. One of the DJs was called 'Charlie The Phantom' and the other was called 'The Baron Hi-Fi'! You could get a two pint bottle of cider for a quid. They'd be playing the Reggae really loud and there were probably, I don't know, 30 or 40 people in at most and all the old Jamaican guys would be sitting round playing dominoes, and you could hear them slamming the dominoes down over the music you know?"

Along with The Mayflower in Gorton, a new club would open up in the Hulme area of Manchester with a similar ethos to The Electric Circus; The Factory. Initially it was a special club night, but grew into another significant venue which took over the baton from the Circus and continued to make sure that Manchester was at the epicentre of what would follow punk.

23. time's up.

"It was such a good time for me. It's only years later when you start thinking about it, you know it was pretty cool actually… to be 17 and amongst it all."

Daniel O'Sullivan

Punk was really taking off and had started to spread out to the satellite towns and cities of the UK towards the end of 1977. Bands were appearing more regularly on television, particularly Top Of The Pops, with singles infiltrating the charts. The major record companies, who ten months earlier had been reticent to take a chance on this new musical revolution, had snapped up all the major players and were in the process of clamouring for groups further down the talent table. Anybody with a safety pin and snotty attitude were getting signed regardless, the A&R people were desperate not to miss out on the next Sex Pistols, Clash or Buzzcocks, so the quality filter began to clog up with mediocrity and genuine bandwagon jumpers. Every corner of the country had their own punk band, even if the venues were still trying to catch up.

Andy T.: "There wasn't really a venue in Rochdale, only the Champness Hall, and it was a Methodist place so it didn't have a bar. They had the 'Stiff' tour there in October '77 with Elvis, Larry Wallis, Dave Edmunds and Ian Dury and that was brilliant. I remember being there in the daytime and I was in a pub called The Fusilliers, which was opposite the Hall. I got talking and playing pool with Wreckless Eric, I heard his stuff on John Peel, and I really liked his lyrics. It was about 2 o'clock in the afternoon and the band had set up and they'd come over to the pub, then gone back over, but Eric had stayed all afternoon, so he's basically sliding down the wall by the time I left. I went home and had some tea and came back down for the gig, and this guy came on, I think it was Cosmo Vinyl, and announced that Wreckless Eric wouldn't be playing tonight because he'd come down with an illness. I was thinking, 'shit I hope it wasn't my fault!' He just kept drinking and drinking while we were playing pool. I really wanted to see him because he had Ian Durham on drums, Dury's girlfriend on bass, plus David Payne from The Blockheads on sax. The only recording of that band is a Peel session."

Ken Park: "When the Pistols announced the tour of the provincial towns and cities you kind of almost knew that they'd be immediately banned by the councils. We bought tickets for the Rochdale gig at Champness Hall 22nd December 1977. The irony of the Rochdale tickets is that if you took your ticket back you'd get the £1.75 refunded. Those tickets now would be worth a fortune because they never played."

Even at that late stage of the Pistols lifespan, the newspapers and councils were still in scaremonger mode. That particular gig in Rochdale was reported in the *Rochdale Observer.* At first the band were seen as a coup for the town, one councillor said, "*This is a very big scoop for us. Everybody wants them, but they are coming to us because we've a reputation for running successful and trouble free concerts.*" Then the Methodists got involved and threatened court action if the gig went ahead because the building's lease agreement stated that anything that was deemed 'offensive, noisy, or immoral' was not allowed. They eventually got their wish. An anonymously written letter was published in the paper two days after the gig was supposed to have been played."

'I am astonished that 2 (young?) men who write so expressively ('Sex Pistols; Hysterical elders don't understand'- Observer 21st December) should be devotees of this vile brand of noise -hardly music. These 'musicians' take macabre delight in stressing all that is vulgar and debasing in the character of some of today's young people. The screams that accompany these orgiastic performances by the Sex Pistols and their like seem to express agony and despair rather than adulation and pleasure. Worse to my mind is the lack of intellectual stimulation inherent in this type of 'entertainment'- a sad augury for the future of our younger citizens. If they can be satisfied with such rubbishy, undisciplined elements now, how will they view the more serious problems of life in their later years? Some elders may react hysterically, but not because they do not understand - rather it is because they understand so well how quickly indiscipline can lead to anarchy'

AN ELDER

So after a frustrating and turbulent year, the Pistols finally got to play what would be their last gig in the UK on Christmas Day, just over the Pennines in Huddersfield.

Mark Windsor: "I got a phone call on Christmas Day off David Bentley, The Drone's manager, and eventually our manager, asking me if I wanted to go and see the Sex Pistols. I was like 'but it's nightmarish weather and Morecambe and Wise are on and….' but I got a lift, which on Christmas Day is a feat in itself, and we got there really late. It was rammed outside and Dave had already gone in with the tickets so, and this sounds really pathetic now, I thought I'll knock on the door to see if the bouncer will go and find him. I'd gone in my stage gear because we were playing there the week after so I thought I'd punt our gig about. So I knocked on the door and this bouncer went, 'Come in'. Which was mental, and I certainly wasn't expecting that. I think they thought that I was a vicar and something to do with the earlier kids show! So if I'd gone in my normal clothes I wouldn't have got in (*laughs*). They sounded intimidating, but by the time I saw them in Huddersfield they were the friendliest bands I'd met but by then I'd seen loads of Punk bands, all the ones that became famous and the others that didn't, and most of them were just shouting at you and I was sick of it you know? Stop patronising me you cunts!

"Rotten came on and he was telling jokes and the music was brilliant and they were just arseing about in between songs, having a laugh; there was a really warm-hearted vibe going on in there. I'd got out of the RAF and a few months later The Clash were saying 'I hate the army and I hate the RAF'. They hated it, as did I. They were reflecting me, back at me, very accurately you know? So were the Pistols, but in a piss taking way, especially when I saw them on Christmas Day. Johnny Rotten was so clever, for me he was like my generation's Eric Morecombe! They were mocking themselves and mocking us, but letting us in on the joke."

Although the writing was on the wall for the Sex Pistols, the pace of change for the rest of the original Punk bands was beginning to increase. In the following twelve months, Buzzcocks would release their debut album, The Clash went classic Rock, The Jam recorded 'All Mod Cons' and 'New Wave' was the new buzzword. The initial excitement and adrenaline rush of Punk music and its attitude, was beginning to become diluted and safe. Once the media circus had gone into overdrive towards the end of 1977 the scene that had once been exclusive and exciting was beginning to lose the appeal that had made it so special. A whole host of new groups were being labelled as Punk, including The Boomtown Rats and The Police, not that that was their fault, but the media just love to compartmentalise things. For those who'd experienced the whirlwind of the previous twelve months of musical and cultural change in Manchester and around the country, things would never be the same again. The burning intensity that only youth can harness was beginning to cool, the flames extinguished from the tide of people who were catching up. The dirty little secret was out.

Mark Windsor: "When it all meshed into the Bowie scene at The Ranch and Pips, and then the gigs started at The Oaks, Rafters and the Circus, it was like... dead witty, it was funny, it wasn't nasty, it was in its own little world."

Janine Hewitt: "I thought that Punk music was astounding and original, the raw quality, the lack of finesse in that they couldn't sing or play their instruments. The energy just filled the room with its fast pace, sheer loudness and heavy thumping beat. The audience would jump around and jostled each other at the front. The lyrics spoke to me as the bands were singing about council estates, unemployment, boredom, anger. The chart music of that time had nothing to do with my life in Manchester. For me at that time, music wasn't about big bands making loads of money, spending hours in the studio honing their craft. That may seem idealistic looking back now because the Punk mantra of 'selling out' applied to quite a few bands who made money out of the Punk scene. I actually feel a little bit conned because of that."

But just as those young kids from around the city had moved from Pop to Bowie, then Roxy to Lou Reed, and Modern Lovers to Buzzcocks, it was time to take the next logical progressive step forwards.

Mickey Carr: "It was a core of about 8 to 9 months I reckon, by this time you'd start to branch out."

Chris Lambert: "That early punk scene will always be there, it's not just reminiscence, it's the attitude that it gave you. I've got this theory that when you had adverts in the back of the *NME* with drawings of punk clothes that people are selling, when it becomes a catalogue, it was time to move on. In my opinion it was 18 months, 2 years maximum, as a valid statement. It got diluted... New Wave... just diluted. Thank God for bands like Magazine and Public Image for moving things on."

Gail Egan: "It paved the way for so much that never would have happened. I just felt that it had run its course, that was my opinion, and it became very commercialised. My view was that that wasn't what it was all about, it was about anybody could get up there and play guitar. It became manufactured and that's what we were supposed to be getting away from with Punk. In my opinion Magazine never got the credit they deserved."

For some, it was more straightforward.

Denise Shaw: "I was bored with it. So I went out with a Teddy Boy and got into the rock'n'roll scene. This guy, called Rambo, came over to me one day and said that he wanted to stop all the fighting between the punks and the Teddy Boys, and he asked me if I'd be prepared to come down to The Oaks in Didsbury, which was a well-known Teddy Boy place... you never went anywhere near there... and he would protect me if I came down. So, like a fool I did! I still dressed punk, and so I walked in and it was just… silence. Rambo said 'she's with me' but that didn't stop the girls… the guys were fine, the girls were the worst. But I can hold my own, I've never shown any fear from anybody, whether it's a 6ft plus Australian who I clouted once in The Ranch, or whoever. I went through the thing of ten of them following me into the toilet trying to kick off with me, you know. I just went, 'one at a time, which one of you is first?' They changed their tone then and we started talking and they were asking me why I was there. I went again and Dawn started coming as well.

Dawn Bradbury: "Yeah I got dragged in as usual! But we enjoyed it for about a year and then got bored again, like you do."

Odgie: "I wouldn't say I got bored with it but we'd done it for long enough. It wasn't as much fun and the scene had moved on and there wasn't that… it became New Wave and sanitised and packaged."

One of the most stark differences between the present day, and the world of over forty years ago, is in the paucity of photographs. In this modern age where *everything* is scrutinised by cameras, even down to the food on your plate, the faded Polaroid pictures that have survived, beautifully document the rights of passage experiences. Most people however were just living out their youth without any thought of collecting mementos for future reference.

Andy T.: "I never had a camera, so I never took any photos. To us who were there, me and my mates, it was just an explosion of music, it didn't matter who'd come from before, or who'd jumped onto it, it was about the now, it was about the moment. Consequently I never wrote anything down or saved any posters because it was just 'happening'."

Dawn Bradbury: "If I'd have known then what I know now, I'd have taken more photos, ripped more posters off walls and saved more stuff, you know. When you're in the moment you don't really realise that you're in the moment, it's only after with hindsight that it was something special. We were trying to explain to somebody a while ago, it was the experience, the feeling, you know? When you think back about what happened, I can't remember dates, times and all that, it's just like little flashbacks. You just get these little pictures… it might be a smell, it might be a record, it could be anything, and you just remember little pockets that happened throughout it all. Bearing in mind that most of the time we were pissed, absolutely bladdered, 'cause that's what you did. You went out, you got drunk, watched a band, get more drunk, hopefully you remembered getting home."

Fran Taylor: "There's so little footage around from that time."

Stanley Vegas: "The thing is, you didn't carry a camera around with you in them days, so photos are pretty rare. Even if you did have a camera, you'd probably take the photos and then not develop them."

Brian Johnson: "It was funny. For me, I knew something special was happening. I knew these people and these clubs were special. And I knew I was meant to be part of it. My Bowie dream had been taken to the max! That's why I always had my camera with me. It was one of those old skinny Kodak cameras. Easy to keep in my pocket!"

Denise Shaw: "The photos I took were on a little Brownie camera and I haven't got the negatives. In fact I gave half of my pictures away. I did start a diary in '77 though, simply because... and I never ever do a diary... I've only ever done one, in 1977 but only up until October. I didn't do one in '76 because I used to take pictures, and then I started thinking, I can't remember which bands I'd seen so I started one. I wrote in the back all the bands I'd seen from January until August when we got into the Teddy Boy thing. I had over 200 bands written down and I look at it now and some of them I think, who the hell were they? But I'd seen them... in eight months."

Steve Shy: "I took my pick of the bands I liked. I hate to say it but... I didn't like X Ray Spex for some reason, but I loved The Slits, I loved The Prefects, Penetration, Wire. The way I look at it, I was the wrong person who happened to be in the right place at the right time."

Fran Taylor: "I saw somewhere around 177 bands in 1977, many of them more than once. There was no solid venue all the way through, and that was part of the reason why it just kept morphing."

Mike Keogh: "There's not very many pictures which I can understand because most Punks I don't think had enough money to have a good night out full stop, so having a camera, that was the height of luxury. Money was tight joking apart, I used to go out with maybe a quid in my pocket on a Friday night, and still have a few pennies of change in my pocket when I got home."

Alan Keogh: "Everyone was skint. We also, don't get me in any trouble here, we also stole stuff from Seditionaries. I had both the Destroy muslin shirt and the cowboy t-shirt, the one with their dicks hanging out, but I didn't pay for them someone else gave them to me. Ha! Ha!"

Stanley Vegas: "Although we didn't have any money we seemed to be out all the time. They had a Punk disco at Belle Vue on a Wednesday, and there was always something going on on a Thursday. That was quite a big night wasn't it? Then Friday and Saturday night at Pips, and on

Sunday it was The Electric Circus. There was always something going on. We always drank whatever was the strongest thing that would get you pissed. It didn't matter what it tasted like."

The contrast in the Punk ethos between the north and the south of the country was quite stark in some quarters.

Alan Keogh: "There was a bit of an arty side to the Punk scene which probably hasn't been exposed enough in the way it should be in terms of snobbery and pretentiousness. There was definitely a class issue, but it was a class issue related to art, people like Jamie Reid, Malcolm McLaren you know? I will always seek knowledge and information, and no matter how much resistance I meet, I'll still try to seek it. That's where power is you know? I'm a working class kid from Glasgow and Levenshulme. There would be this feeling of like, you're not really part of this... just the middle class and rich kids."

Mickey Carr: "The other side of that was the art students. I used to get onto guest lists because they were right in the thick of the Punk thing. They were like groupies in a way to bands like The Slits. They always seemed to be with them when they came up to Manchester, two guys from the Banshees came to me Mam's council house in Harperhay. A few people did."

As well as the class issue, the question of age was a conundrum for some.

Fran Taylor: "I considered myself then at 19... I used to think to myself, am I too old for this crowd? At the time my thoughts were; this movement as it stands, i.e. Punk, can't ever be massive for a very, very basic reason; Working class kids don't go out looking dirty. Middle class/art school kids go out looking dirty. Working class kids are dirty all fucking day, why would they go out looking dirty? They go out dressed up, they save their money up to look good, that's why in my opinion, 2-Tone and the Mod/Ska movement that came later was a bigger movement at the time than Punk was. You don't want to look like Sid Vicious when you've looked like Sid Vicious all day; you want to look like Paul Weller."

One of the major issues that Punk would address was racism. The National Front were spreading their vitriolic message around the country, targeting the weak-minded who thought that Black and Asian people were here to take their jobs; the jobs they weren't prepared to do in the first place.

Ian Moss: "We all knew how institutionalised racism was, and sexism. All of a sudden, where I might not have liked this, all of a sudden this means because I've taken this on in my head, when people start talking that way, I'm confronting them. And it doesn't make you popular, you know? Some of these people were my bosses, and I'm dressing them down. So for me it wasn't a happy time, it was 6 months into 1977 and I'm being treated for depression, and I'm not surprised because my head was exploding. So it wasn't hedonism for me, and that's what I'm saying, if I'd lightened up, if I'd been a bit more like Denise etcetera, it might have been better. But I wasn't; that wasn't my reality, that wasn't my world."

Una Baines: "The Anti Nazi League was quite a strong thing at the time, and there were the Rock Against Racism gigs, and that brought a lot of people together. There'd normally be three bands on, for instance The Fall, The Worst and John Cooper Clarke, and we'd be so democratic that we'd change who was going to headline."

Ken Park: "Punk was always in my head. I never had spiky hair or anything like that. There was also a political alignment, not just clothes and a musical alignment. The interesting thing about us reviving the band is that the political issues back then are still relevant now. You'd go on a CND march and there'd be 250,000 people there. Rock Against Racism, the Right To Work marches."

Janine Hewitt: "The Socialists organised a coach trip to London where myself and a friend marched and collected money. There was a Punk night at the students union on Oxford Road for Rock Against Racism. A friend of mine was beaten up by some National Front members for wearing a Rock Against Racism badge, we had just come out of the gig when about eight men came around the corner and he was punched to the ground. They were pointing at his RAR badge as the reason. Political groups did try to get involved and would hand out leaflets at gigs, but people mostly ignored them. Rock Against Racism did a concert in Manchester near Platt Fields with Buzzcocks."

Deb Zee: "There was the Rock Against Racism gigs. I don't know how this happened but we were at Strangeways for a Rock Against Racism march and gig as that's where it was starting from. Anyway for some reason it ended up that me and one of my friends ended up on The Mekon's float! They just asked us if we wanted to come on it. They wouldn't let... it was either Morrissey or Mick Hucknall I can't bloody remember, they wouldn't let them on. We stayed on all the way to Alexandra Park to where the main gig was."

Protest and personal political agendas aside, the overriding feeling from those who first witnessed it was that Punk meant fun, a freedom of expression, a natural progression, and it also opened the doors for what was to follow. They'd always been music lovers, and that's the thing that hits home first, the music. Then the attitude, and then the clothes, and added to that, the camaraderie of meeting like minded people which completes the chain. Wherever you were from, geographically or socially, Punk was the glue that bound everybody together. Kids arrived at Punk for a myriad of reasons and departed from it with a multitude of life skills and attitudes that have stayed with them all the way through their lives.

The last word should be with them.

Deb Zee: "I got into Punk because my brother used to play Roxy Music, but my friends were into David Essex and David Cassidy and The Osmonds, that kind of thing. Before I was a Punk I used to wear two-tone brogues and Ben Sherman, then I was into Bowie and sort of starting doing the Ziggy Stardust look. I met this lad who was into Ziggy and was in a band, and we went to the Electric Circus and I heard New Rose by The Damned which I thought was absolutely amazing and I bought it for 70p. There was a record shop on the way up to Piccadilly station and I bought that and Anarchy In The U.K. on E.M.I. for 70p each from there. It was like… that changed my life yeah. It's in your heart isn't it, and in your mind. I'd just like to be transported back."

Ian Moss: "A lot of my memories about Punk… to me it wasn't about the clothes, or even about the music *per se*, it was more to do with the transference of ideas. It was a feeling, and a sort of code; a way that you could conduct yourself, a way that you could live. I suppose the thing that Punk gave us was, it was empowering. When I was at school there was always a limit put on you, they were just churning out factory fodder. If they thought that your aspirations were a bit too high, they'd try and knock that out of you. So what Punk did was it that it opened all these doors and allowed you to think 'I can do that!' On Patti Smith's first album; 'Open up the sea, the sea of possibilities'. That really resonated with me. When people talk about Manchester I always say, look, it gave us the best writer of our generation in Morley, the photographers who sprung up, as well as John Cooper Clarke."

Stephen Perrin: "What Punk gave me was a sense of possibility. I was a working class kid with a lousy education. The furthest I'd been out of Stockport was on family holidays to Blackpool and Prestatyn and I had only ever met people like me. Within months I was hanging out with Tony Wilson who told me, as he told everybody, that he had been to Cambridge with Germaine Greer. I had no idea who Germaine Greer was and only a vague sense of what/where Cambridge was but I realised that there was a big world out there and I had better start finding out about it. The people around me helped and inspired me. It is because of Punk that I have a PhD. It is because of Punk that I have lived and worked in Italy, Australia and New Zealand. It is because of Punk that I have the close friends I have. It is also because of Punk that I have a broken nose but if you're going to wander around Stockport late at night wearing eye liner what do you expect?"

Andy T.: "The books that have been written (about Manchester) are all sort of built around Factory and Tony Wilson's involvement with The Russell Club. But they completely miss out people like Alan Wise and Tosh Ryan, who were putting gigs on and doing a lot.... I mean Rob (Gretton) gets his fair share of mentions but no one mentions the work he did with Slaughter. He ran the Slaughter fan club and did *Manchester Rains* which is basically all about The Dogs. To me, it was all about the people. It still is."

Denise Shaw: "We never really took that much notice of the bands, it was more for the adrenaline, it was such a rush, you know. It was so fantastic and it's something that stays with you for the rest of your life."

Gail Egan: "That's the way it was back then, we all went out and got hammered, so your perception of things... It was just a lot of ordinary people being in the right place at the right time, that's the way I look at it. I don't like this elitism that some people have about it because I was just lucky, I was on a bus with my friend, with nothing to do, invited to a gig and got carried along with it. It was amazing times, amazing times."

Wispa: "There was a good sense of friendship about the Punks in Manchester, there was a lot of camaraderie and we looked out for each other."

Alan Keogh: "I really do think that the Punk thing was very much about people feeling alienated through difference, who found a place to meet and get together. If there is a 'Mancunian' way, I think it's about energy, a certain energy of going 'fuck you'. It was discussed, it was actually spoken out loud. 'Fuck London, we don't need London, let's just make it happen here'. That was said time and time again. I was going to move down to London when I was 16, the only thing that stopped me moving down was the music scene here. I could see it was happening; Buzzcocks were kicking off, and The Fall and then I thought no, let's not go to London, they can come here if they want. I agree with Tony Wilson on that one."

Terry Slater: "It was about let's have something fresh"

Juliette J. Williams: "It really was about the time and the place."

Joanne Slater: "You could just go wild. I don't think that you needed much to drink. It was the cusp of something that was starting wasn't it? We were just in the right place at the right time."

Daniel O'Sullivan: "It was such a good time for me. It's only years later when you start thinking about it, you know it was pretty cool actually… to be 17 and amongst it all. Mickey Tait and I were great friends and there was a few of us who used to knock around, and generally living the Punk lifestyle; squatting in houses, fighting with Teddy Boys at The Midland Hotel in Didsbury. We thought that we were the hardcore ones, you know what I mean? Living it, breathing it, not weekend jobs, we were full on. So we thought we were better than anybody else. Of course when it died down we didn't know what the fuck to do."

Carol O'Donnell: "You can walk down the street now and look at people, and you don't know what they've done with their lives. People can look at us now and just see old people, completely ignorant of the fact that you might have been young once. In my opinion we were young just at the right time, exactly the right time. I hate Rock and Roll, hate it, even when I was a kid I never found any musical genre that I could actually say, 'Yeah, this is me'. Even since those times I just think that we were lucky to have been born at the right time. I wouldn't have wanted to be anywhere else but Manchester. We had a ball. I'd love to go back, just for a week."

Mickey Tait: "If I look back on really great times in my life, it was before Punk broke I think. The Punk scene was really fantastic, and it was a fantastic energy. Playing the gigs, the music as well was fantastic, but so was pre-punk. There was no Punk royalty, it's all bollocks. Punk was a movement about sounds. I blitzed out at the end of '77, got into other things. I didn't linger around the scene too long because basically I was a music lover. I got into other things, I still listened to Punk but I got into Reggae, Ska, Linton Kwesi Johnson that sort of thing you know?"

Deb Zee: "I went on for a long, long time. Even when I started work as a nurse I'd be told to go home because of my bright blue hair and that, they said that I might scare people that I might give some of the patients a heart attack!"

Fran Taylor: "Viv Albertine sent me a letter, basically saying that they were doing a tour with The Clash at the end of the year and they wanted me to come and roadie for them. I told them that I'd have to check what was happening with Buzzcocks, which actually turned out great because their tour finished two days before The Slits/Clash tour, so I said 'yeah, I'll do it'. They were now being managed by Deaf School's old management and I had to go to London to do an interview! I got the job. I was staying in a hotel in St. John's Wood and they told me that they would pick me up outside the hotel and the first gig was in Edinburgh the next day. They duly arrived at 7 in the evening, I grabbed my bag and off we went. I think it was the 'Sort It Out' tour. Nora was driving the van, their gear was travelling with us, and we used to hang about with them and go back to their hotels and stuff.

"We finished the tour at The Greyhound in Croydon and John Lydon turned up, and he was wearing a top hat which he insisted he'd nicked from Disneyland because it had a 10/6 tag like The Mad Hatter. He poked his head out from behind the curtain at the back of the stage, and of course when people saw him they were shouting for him to do a song, but he declined the offer. That evening Nora invited us all back to hers for an end of tour party and when we got back there she had no beer, wine or anything. Then the doorbell rang and there was Johnny and his mate, both with arms full of beer. So we were having a drink and a spliff and I noticed this guy talking to John, giving him a bit of a hard time, I didn't know who he was and where he'd come from. He kept pestering him and repeating over and over, 'You're supposed to be outrageous, why aren't you being outrageous?' going on and on at him. John was being very patient with this wanker but in the end he just turned to him and psffstt! He put his fag out on this guys' forehead and said, 'Is that fucking outrageous enough for you?'"

Odgie: "There was an element of... you thought you might be able to change something. There was the Beatnik movement and the Hippie/ Peace movement stretching back to when people had more leisure time and life wasn't so fucking shit that you'd work until you died; there was a bit more psychology and philosophy was starting, there was all this stuff going on; an elevation of consciousness if you like. I suppose at the time that we did think it was a movement that was going to change something because it was very political and anarchic. Things were shit and we wanted them to be better. In some respect it was probably the last protest movement really."

Alan Keogh: "It was such an opening for me. I mean nowadays in my life, I taught theatre for over 20 years, directed shows, I've performed music and I've performed poetry and all sorts of things. I would say all that I've done since was down to that time. Because it opened me up artistically and I'm not just talking about Punk rock. I think that is an attitude, it's not about a style of music at all."

Gail Egan: "I ended up being a bank manager for 15 years, everyone that knew me thinks that was the most hilarious thing ever but I was a very controversial one because I refused to conform and fought that system for 15 years, how I managed to do that I'll never know. Somebody would come in and they'd need an overdraft but the computer would say no, and I was like 'Why? Why can't they have one?' I'd get on the phone and be so persuasive and in the end it would be, 'Oh God it's her again'. Punk just created some sort of attitude, it's hard to explain."

Dawn Bradbury: "But it's like I've said before, you don't realise at the time what you're actually involved in. You were a teenager, it's your thing, it's what you do, but you don't actually realise the impact that it's going to have, in the music industry, the fashion industry, you know?"

Denise Shaw: "I find it weird that there was 30 years of nothing and now over the past few years it's just blown up all over again"

Dawn Bradbury: "It was 500 days. I calculated it, yeah, 500 days from start to finish. It was like a train whistling through - you either got on it or you didn't. If you didn't, then tough. If you did; you had the time of your life."

source material

Andrew Davies guardian.co.uk August 2011.

bandonthewall.org

personalpages.manchester.ac.uk

Social Housing in Post-war Manchester: Change and Continuity.

Manchester and Salford Better Housing Council, Report of a survey undertaken in part of St. Michael's and Collegiate Wards of the city of Manchester, the Red Bank Survey Group, 1931.

Manchester University Settlement, 'Ancoats: A Study of a Clearance Area,' Report of a Survey made in 1937- 1938, Manchester, 1945.

Manchester University Settlement, 'Ancoats: A Study of a Clearance Area,' Report of a Survey made in 1937-1938, Manchester, 1945.

Manchester and District Regional Survey Society No. 12, 'Some Social Aspects of Pre-War Tenements and of Post-War Flats,' Manchester University Settlement 1932.

manchesterhistory.net

Buzzcocks - The Complete History. - Tony McGartland.

BBC Television- Brass Tacks.

The England's Dreaming Tapes - Jon Savage.

Sniffin' Glue;The Essential Punk Accessory- Mark Perry,Terry Rawlings.

Brad Pitt's Dog: Essays on Fame, Death, Punk - Johan Kugelberg.

Unknown Pleasures - Peter Hook.

I Swear I was There - David Nolan

salfordstar.com

'77;The Year Of Punk & New Wave - Henrik Bech Paulson.

thefall.org

punk77.co.uk

Manchester Music District Archive.

Chris Hewitt Archive.

www.factorybenelux.com

boredteenagers.co.uk

Mancunian Newspaper

punkygibbon.co.uk

killyourpetpuppy.co.uk

M62 Magazine - Robin McMillan

Manchester Independent Newspaper, written and edited by University of Manchester students. With thanks to James Peters at the University of Manchester Archives and Ben Ward at The University of Manchester Students' Union.

Time's Up 40th anniversary box set.

johncrumpton.co.uk

loudersound.com

index

Printed in Poland
by Amazon Fulfillment
Poland Sp. z o.o., Wrocław

52451761R00186